The Mother of Washington

And Her Times

The Mother of Washington

And Her Times

BY

MRS. ROGER A. PRYOR

" That one who breaks the way with tears
Many shall follow with a song "

New York
THE MACMILLAN COMPANY
LONDON: MACMILLAN & CO., Ltd.

1903

Norwood Press
J. S. Cushing & Co. — Berwick & Smith Co.
Norwood, Mass., U.S.A.

SUPPOSED PORTRAIT OF MARY WASHINGTON.

To the Hon. Roger A. Pryor, LL.D.

IN WHOM LIVES ALL THAT WAS BEST
IN OLD VIRGINIA

CONTENTS

PART I

CHAPTER I

ILLUSTRATIONS

AUTHORITIES

Virginia Historical Magazine.

William and Mary Quarterly.

Virginia Historical Register.

Meade's Old Churches and Families of Virginia.

Campbell's History of Virginia.

Irving's Life of Washington.

Recollections and Private Memoirs of Washington. By George
Washington Parke Custis.

Cooke's Virginia.

The Bland Papers. By Campbell.

Howe's Virginia.

Journal of Philip Vickars Fithian.

Towers's Lafayette.

Creasy's Fifteen Decisive Battles.

Morse's Franklin.

Lecky's England in the Eighteenth Century.

Fiske's American Revolution.

Sparks's Diplomatic Correspondence.

Washington's Works.

Bancroft's History of the United States.

Life and Letters of George Mason. By Kate Mason Rowland.

Beaumarchais and his Times.

Edwardes's Translations of Lemonie.

Lives of the Chief Justices of England.

Twining's Travels in America.

Burnaby's Travels.

The Story of Mary Washington.   By Marion Harland.

Randall's Life of Jefferson.

Worthies of England.   By Thomas Fuller.

Foote's Sketches of Virginia.

Parton's Franklin.

A Study in the Warwickshire Dialect.   By Appleton Morgan, A.M., LL.B.

Maternal Ancestry of Washington.   By G. W. Ball.

NOTE

THE author has the honour to acknowledge the loan of portraits and engravings, and also valuable unpublished letters and diaries, from —

General G. W. Custis Lee,
Mrs. E. Parke Custis Lewis,
Mrs. William Key Howard of Kenmore,
Mr. Henry Tayloe of Mt. Airy,
Colonel Samuel M. Blackford,
Miss Kate Mason Rowland,
Rev. G. W. Beale,
Colonel George Washington Ball,
Mrs. Alice Morse Earle,
Mr. R. A. Lancaster, Jr.

PART I

The Mother of Washington and her Times

CHAPTER I

INTRODUCTORY

THE mothers of famous men survive only in their sons. This is a rule almost as invariable as a law of nature. Whatever the aspirations and energies of the mother, memorable achievement is not for her. No memoir has been written in this country of the women who bore, fostered, and trained our great men. What do we know of the mother of Daniel Webster, or John Adams, or Patrick Henry, or Andrew Jackson, or of the mothers of our Revolutionary generals?

When the American boy studies the history of his country, his soul soars within him as he reads of his own forefathers : how they rescued a wilderness from the savage and caused it to bloom into fruitful fields and gardens, how they won its independence through eight years of hardship and struggle, how they assured its prosperity by a wise Constitution and firm laws. But he may look in vain for some tribute to the mothers who trained his heroes. In his Roman history he finds Cornelia, Virginia, Lucretia, and Veturia on the same pages with Horatius, Regulus, Brutus, and Cincinnatus. If he be a boy of some thought and perception, he will see that the early seventeenth century women of his own land must have borne a similar relation to their country as these women to the Roman Republic. But our histories as utterly ignore them as if they never existed. The heroes of our Revolution might have sprung armed from the head of Jove for aught the American boy can find to the contrary.

Thus American history defrauds these noble mothers of their crown — not self-won, but won by their sons.

Letitia Romolino was known to few, while the fame of "Madame Mère" is as universal as the glory of Napoleon himself. But Madame Mère had her historian. The pioneer woman of America, who "broke the way with tears," retires into darkness and oblivion; while "many follow with a song" the son to whom she gave her life and her keen intelligence born of her strong faith and love.

Biographers have occasionally seemed to feel that something is due the mothers of their heroes. Women have some rights after all! And so we can usually find, tucked away somewhere, a short perfunctory phrase of courtesy, " He is said to have inherited many of his qualities from his mother," reminding us of " The Ladies — God bless 'em," after everybody else has been toasted at a banquet, and just before the toasters are ripe for the song, " We won't go home till morning ! "

But — if we are willing to be appeased by such a *douceur* — there is literature galore anent the women who have amused "great" men : Helen of Troy, Madame de Pompadour, Madame du Barry, Lady Hamilton, the Countess Guicciola, and such. We may comfort ourselves for this humiliating fact only by reflecting that the world craves novelty, and that these dames are interesting to the reading public, solely because they are exceptional, while the noble, unselfish woman, being the rule of motherhood, is familiar to every one of us and needs no historian.

It is the noble, unselfish woman who must shine, if she shine at all, by the light reflected from her son. *Her* life, for the most part, must be hidden by the obscurity of domestic duties. While herself thus inactive and retired, her son is developed for glory, and the world is his arena. It is only when he reaches renown that she becomes an object of attention, but it is then too late to take her measure in the plenitude of her powers. Emitting at best but a feeble ray, her genius is soon lost in the splendor of his meridian.

Nay more, her reputation is often the sport of a

love of contrast, and her simplicity and his magnificence the paradox of a gossiping public.

Mary Washington presents no exception to this picture. As the mother of the man who has hitherto done most for the good and glory of humanity, the details of her life are now of world-wide and enduring interest. Those details were lost in the seclusion and obscurity of her earlier years or else absorbed in the splendor of her later career. It is not deniable, too, that in the absence of authentic information, tradition has made free with her name, and has imputed to her motives and habits altogether foreign to her real character. The mother of Washington was in no sense a commonplace woman. Still less was she hard, uncultured, undignified, unrefined.

The writer hopes to trace the disparaging traditions, and to refute them by showing that all the known actions of her life were the emanations of a noble heart, high courage, and sound understanding.

"Characters," said the great Englishman who lived in her time, "should never be given by an historian unless he knew the people whom he describes, or copies from those who knew them." "A hard saying for picturesque writers of history," says Mr. Augustine Birrell, who knows so well how to be picturesque and yet faithful to the truth. Even he laments how little we can know of a dead man we never saw. "His books, if he wrote books, will tell us something; his letters, if he wrote any, and

they are preserved, may perchance fling a shadow
on the sheet for a moment or two; a portrait if
painted in a lucky hour may lend a show of sub-
stance to our dim surmisings; the things he did
must carefully be taken into account, but as a man
is much more than the mere sum of his actions
even these cannot be relied upon with great confidence. For the purpose, therefore, of getting at
any one's character, the testimony of those who
knew the living man is of all the material likely to
be within our reach the most useful."

How truly the words of this brilliant writer apply
to the ensuing pages will be apparent to every intelligent reader. No temptation has availed with
the compiler to accept any, the most attractive,
theory or tradition. The testimony of those who
knew Mary Washington is the groundwork of the
picture, and controls its every detail.

A few years ago an episode of interest was awakened in Mary Washington's life. There was a decided Mary Washington Renaissance. She passed
this way — as Joan of Arc — as Napoleon Bonaparte, Burns, Emerson, and others pass. A society
of women banded themselves together into a Mary
Washington Memorial Association. Silver and gold
medals bearing her gentle, imagined face were struck
off, and when the demand for them was at its
height, their number was restricted to six hundred,
to be bequeathed for all time from mother to daugh-

ter, the pledge being a perpetual vigil over the tomb of Mary Washington, thus forming a Guard of Honor of six hundred American women. The Princess Eulalia of Spain, and Maria Pilar Colon, a descendant of Christopher Columbus, were admitted into this Guard of Honor, and wear its insignia.

This "Renaissance" grew out of an advertisement in the Washington papers to the effect that the "Grave of Mary, the Mother of General Washington," was to be "sold at Public Auction, the same to be offered at Public Outcry," under the shadow of the monument erected in her son's honor, and in the city planned by him and bearing his name.

A number of the descendants of Mary Washington's old Fredericksburg neighbors assembled the next summer at the White Sulphur Springs in Virginia. It was decided that a ball be given at the watering-place to aid the noble efforts of the widow of Chief Justice Waite to avert the disaster, purchase the park, and erect a monument over the ashes of the mother of Washington. One of the guests was selected to personate her: General Fitzhugh Lee to represent her son George.

A thousand patrons assured the success of the ball. They wore Mary Washington's colors—blue and white — and assumed the picturesque garb of pre-Revolutionary days. The bachelor governor of New York, learning what was toward with these fair ladies, sent his own state flag to grace the occasion, and its snow-white folds mingled with the blue of the state banner contributed by the governor of Virginia.

The gowns of the Virginia beauties were yellow with age, and wrinkled from having been hastily exhumed from the lavender-scented chests; for when lovely Juliet Carter chose the identical gown of her great, great grandmother, — blue brocade, looped over a white satin quilted petticoat, — the genuine example was followed by all the rest. The Madam Washington of the hour was strictly taken in hand by the Fredericksburg contingent. Her kerchief had been worn at the Fredericksburg Peace Ball, her mob cap was cut by a pattern preserved by Mary Washington's old neighbors. There were mittens, a reticule, and a fan made of the bronze feathers of the wild turkey of Virginia. Standing with her son George in the midst of the old-time assembly, old-time music in the air, old-time pictures on the walls, Madam Washington received her guests and presented them to her son, whose miniature she wore on her bosom. "I am glad to meet your son, Madam Washington!" said pretty Ellen Lee, as she dropped her courtesy; "I always heard he was a truthful child!"

The lawn and cloister-like corridors of the large hotel were crowded at an early hour with the country people, arriving on foot, on horseback, and in every vehicle known to the mountain roads.

These rustic folk — weather-beaten, unkempt old trappers and huntsmen, with their sons and daughters, wives and little children — gathered in the verandas and filled the windows of the ball-room. When the procession made the rounds of the room the comments of the holders of the window-boxes were not altogether flattering. The quaint dress of "the tea-cup time of hoop and hood" was disappointing. They had expected a glimpse of the latest fashions of the metropolis.

" I don't think much of that Mrs. Washington," said one.

" Well," drawled another, a wiry old graybeard, " she looks quiet and peaceable! The ole one was a turrible ole woman! My grandfather's father used to live close to ole Mrs. Washington. The ole man used to say she would mount a stool to rap her man on the head with the smoke-'ouse key! She was that little, an' hot-tempered."

" That was *Martha* Washington, grandfather," corrected a girl who had been to school in Lewisburg. " *She* was the short one."

" Well, Martha or Mary, it makes no differ," grimly answered the graybeard. " They was much of a muchness to my thinkin'," and this was the first of the irreverent traditions which caught the ear of the writer, and led to investigation. They cropped up fast enough from many a dark corner!

About this time many balls and costume entertainments were given to aid the monument fund.
There were charming garden parties to

> " Bring back the hour
> Of glory in the grass and splendor in the flower,"

when the Mother of Washington was beautiful,
young, and happy. A notable theatrical entertainment, the " Mary Washington matinée," was arranged by Mrs. Charles Avery Doremus, the clever
New York playwright. The theatre was hung with
colors lent by the Secretary of the Navy, the order
therefor signed by " George Dewey." Everybody
wore the Mary Washington colors — as did Adelina
Patti, who flashed from her box the perennial smile
we are yet to see again. Despite the hydra-headed
traditions the Mother of Washington had her
apotheosis.

Brought face to face with my reader, and devoutly
praying I may hold his interest to the end, I wish I
could spare him every twice-told tale — every dull
word.

But " we are made of the shreds and patches of
many ancestors." What we are we owe to them.
God forbid we should inherit and repeat all their
actions ! The courage, the fortitude, the persistence,
are what we inherit — not the deeds through which
they were expressed. A successful housebreaker's
courage may blossom in the valor of a descendant

on the field who has been trained in a better school than his ancestor.

Dull as the public is prone to regard genealogical data, the faithful biographer is bound to give them. And therefore the reader must submit to an introduction to the Ball family, otherwise he cannot understand the Mother of Washington or Washington himself. One of them, perhaps the one most deserving eminence through her own beneficence, we cannot place exactly in our records. She was an English "Dinah Morris," and her name was Hannah Ball. She was the originator of Sunday-schools, holding her own school in 1772, twelve years before the reputed founder, Robert Raikes, established Sunday-schools in England.

CHAPTER II

THE family of Ball from which Mary, the mother of Washington, descended, can be traced in direct line only as far back as the year 1480. They came originally from " Barkham, anciently ' Boercham '; noted as the spot at which William the Conqueror paused on his devastating march from the bloody field of Hastings :[1] 'wasting ye land, burning ye towns and sleaing (*sic*) ye people till he came to Boerchum where he stayed his ruthless hand.' "

In the " History of the Ball family of Barkham, Comitatis Berks, taken from the Visitation Booke of London marked O. 24, in the College of Arms," we find that " William Ball, Lord of the Manor of Barkham, Com. Berks, died in the year 1480." From this William Ball, George Washington was *eighth* in direct descent.

The entry in the old visitation book sounds imposing, but Barkham was probably a small town nestled amid the green hills of Berkshire, whose beauty possibly so reminded the Conqueror of his

---

[1] *The Maternal Ancestry of Washington*, by George Washington Ball.

Normandy that "he stayed his ruthless hand." A century ago it was a village of some fifty houses attached to the estate of the Levison Gowers.

There is no reason to suppose that the intervening Balls in the line, — Robert, William, two Johns, — all of whom lived in Barkham, or the William of Lincoln's Inn, who became "attorney in the Office of Pleas in the Exchequer," were men of wealth or rank. The "getting of gear was never," said one of their descendants, "a family trait, nor even the ability to hold it when gotten"; but nowhere is it recorded that they ever wronged man or woman in the getting. They won their worldly goods honorably, used them beneficently, and laid them down cheerfully when duty to king or country demanded the sacrifice, and when it pleased God to call them out of the world. They were simply men "doing their duty in their day and generation and deserving well of their fellows."

They belonged to the Landed Gentry of England. This does not presuppose their estates to have been extensive. A few starved acres of land sufficed to class them among the Landed Gentry, distinguishing them from laborers. As such they may have been entitled to the distinction of "Gentleman," the title in England next lowest to "Yeoman." No one of them had ever bowed his shoulders to the royal accolade, nor held even the position of esquire to a baronet. But the title

"Gentleman" was a social distinction of value. "Ordinarily the King," says Sir Thomas Smith, "doth only make Knights and create Barons or higher degrees; as for *gentlemen*, they be made good cheap in this Kingdom; for whosoever studieth the laws of the realm, who studieth in the universities, who professeth the liberal sciences, he shall be taken for a gentleman; for gentlemen be those whom their blood and race doth make noble and known." By "a gentleman born" was usually understood the son of a gentleman by birth, and grandson of a gentleman by position. "It takes three generations to make a gentleman," we say to-day, and this seems to have been an ancient rule in England.

The Balls might well be proud to belong to old England's middle classes — her landed, untitled Gentry. A few great minds — Lord Francis Verulam, for instance — came from her nobility; and some gifted writers — the inspired dreamer, for instance — from her tinkers and tradesmen; but the mighty host of her scholars, poets, and philosophers belonged to her middle classes. They sent from their ranks Shakespeare and Milton, Locke and Sir Isaac Newton, Gibbon, Dryden, "old Sam Johnson," Pope, Macaulay, Stuart Mill, Huxley, Darwin, Wordsworth, Coleridge, Burke, Disraeli, Cowper, Sir William Blackstone, and nearly all of the Chief Justices of England. These are but a few of the great names that shine along the ranks of England's middle classes.

Many of these men were called to the foot of the throne by a grateful sovereign to receive some distinction, — so paltry by comparison with glory of their own earning, — and among them came one day an ancestor of the mother of George Washington. Who he was we know not, nor yet what had been his service to his country; but he was deemed worthy to bear upon his shield a lion rampant, the most honorable emblem of heraldry, and the lion's paws held aloft a ball! This much we know of him, — that in addition to his valor and fidelity he possessed a poet's soul. He chose for the motto, the *cri de guerre* of his clan, a suggestive phrase from these lines of Ovid : —

" He gave to man a noble countenance and commanded him to gaze upon the heavens, and to carry his looks upward to the stars."

CHAPTER III

THE BALL FAMILY IN VIRGINIA

THE first of the family of Ball to come to
Virginia was William Ball, who settled in
Lancaster County in 1650. He was the
son of the attorney of Lincoln's Inn. He emi-
grated, with other cavaliers because of the over-
throw of the royal house and the persecution of its
adherents.

Before this time one John Washington, an Englishman and a loyalist, had settled in Westmoreland.
He became a man of influence in the colony, rising
rapidly from major to colonel, justice of Westmoreland, and member of the House of Burgesses; accepting positions under the Commonwealth, as did others
of King Charles's adherents; doing their duty under
the present conditions, and consoling themselves by
calling everything — towns, counties, rivers, and their
own sons — after the " Martyred Monarch"; and in
rearing mulberry trees and silkworms to spin the
coronation robe of purple for the surely coming time
of the Restoration.

John Washington married three times, — two
Annes and one Frances, — and, innocently uncon-

scious of the tremendous importance to future historians of his every action, he neglected to place on record the date of these events.   In his day a woman appeared before the public only three times, — at her baptism, marriage, and death.   But one of Colonel Washington's wives emerges bravely from obscurity.   A bold sinner and hard swearer, having been arraigned before her husband, she was minded to improve her opportunity; and the Westmoreland record hath it that " Madam Washington said to ye prisoner, 'if you were advised by yr wife, you need not acome to this passe,' and he answered, having the courage of his convictions, '— — my wife!   If it were to doe, I would do it againe.'"

And so no more of Madam Washington!   This trouble had grown out of what was characterized as " ye horrid, traiterous, and rebellious practices " of a young Englishman on the James River, whose only fault lay in the unfortunate circumstance of his having been born a hundred years too soon.   Bacon's cause had been just, and he was eloquent enough and young and handsome enough to draw all men's hearts to himself, but his own was stilled in death before he could right his neighbors' wrongs.

And now, the Fates that move the pieces on the chess-board of life ordained that two prophetic names should appear together to suppress the first rebellion against the English government.   When the Grand Assembly cast about for loyal men and true to lay "a Levy in ye Northern Necke for ye charges in Raisinge ye forces thereof for suppressing ye late Rebellion," the lot fell on " Coll. John Washington and Coll : W^m. Ball," the latter journeying up from his home in Lancaster to meet Colonel Washington at Mr. Beale's, in Westmoreland.

Colonel Ball's Lancaster home was near the old White Chapel church, around which are clustered a large number of strong, heavy tombstones which betoken to-day "a deep regard of the living for the dead."

Almost all of them are inscribed with the name of Ball. In their old vestry books are stern records. A man was fined five thousand pounds of tobacco for profane swearing; unlucky John Clinton, for some unmentioned misdemeanor, was required four times to appear on bended knees and four times to ask pardon. As late as 1727 men were presented for drunkenness, for being absent one month from church, for swearing, for selling crawfish and posting accounts on Sunday. "And in addition to above," adds Bishop Meade, "the family of Ball was very active in promoting good things," as well as zealous in the punishment of evil. Overt acts — swearing, fishing on Sunday, absence from church — could easily be detected and punished. But how about drunkenness? There are degrees of intoxication. At what point was it punishable?

An old Book of Instructions settled the matter.

c

"Where ye same legges which carry a Man into a house cannot bring him out againe, it is Sufficient Sign of Drunkennesse."

The descendants of William Ball held good positions in the social life of the colony. Their names appear in Bishop Meade's list of vestrymen, as founders and patrons of the Indian schools, and fourteen times in the House of Burgesses. They intermarried with the leading families in Virginia; and the Balls, in great numbers, settled the counties of Lancaster, Northumberland, Westmoreland, and Stafford. They are not quoted as eminent in the councils of the time, or as distinguished in letters. That they were good citizens is more to their credit than that they should have filled prominent official positions; for high offices have been held by men who were not loyal to their trusts, and even genius — that beacon of light in the hands of true men — has been a torch of destruction in those of the unworthy.

They, like their English ancestors, bore for their arms a lion rampant holding a ball, and for their motto *Cælumque tueri*, taken, as we have said, from these lines of Ovid: —

> "Os homini sublime dedit, cælumque tueri
> Jussit, et erectos ad sidera tollere vultus."

The rampant lion holding the ball appears on an armorial document belonging to the first emigrant.

On the back of this document are the following words, written in the round, large script of those days, which, whatever it left undone, permitted no possible doubt of the meaning it meant to convey : —

"The Coat of Arms of Colonel William Ball, who came from England about the year 1650, leaving two sons — William of Millenbeck [the paternal seat] and Joseph of Epping Forest — and one daughter, Hannah, who married Daniel Fox. . . . Joseph's male issue is extinct."

George Washington was the grandson of this Joseph Ball through his youngest daughter Mary. She was born at Epping Forest, in Lancaster, Virginia, in 1708, and "not as is persistently stated by careless writers on Nov : 30th 1706 — a year before her parents were married."

1 Horace Edwin Hayden in *William and Mary Quarterly*, Vol. iii, p. 74.

CHAPTER IV

COAT ARMOR AND THE RIGHT TO BEAR IT

BISHOP Meade says of William Ball's coat of arms: "There is much that is bold about it: as a lion rampant with a globe in his paw, with helmet, shield and visor, and other things betokening strength and courage, but none these things suit of my work! There is, however, one thing that does. On a scroll are these words, *Cælum tueri!* May it be a memento to all his posterity to look upward and seek the things which are above!"

The Bishop attached, probably, more importance to the heraldic distinction than did the mother of Washington. Virginia families used the arms to which they had a right with no thought of ostentation — simply as something belonging to them, as a matter of course. They sealed their deeds and contracts with their family crest and motto, displayed their arms on the panels of their coaches, carved them on their gate-posts and on the tombstones of their people; for such had been the custom in the old country which they fondly called "home."

The pedigrees and coats of arms of the families, from which Mary Ball and her illustrious son descended, have been much discussed by historians. " Truly has it been said that all the glories of ancestral escutcheons are so overshadowed by the deeds of Washington that they fade into insignificance; that a just democracy, scornful of honors not self-won, pays its tribute solely to the man, the woman, and the deed; that George Washington was great because he stood for the freedom of his people, and Mary Washington was great because she implanted in his youthful breast righteous indignation against wrong, which must ever be the inspiration of the hero. And yet the insignia of a noble name, handed down from generation to generation, and held up as an incentive to integrity and valor, may well be cherished." The significance of the shield granted as reward, and the sentiment chosen as the family motto, are not to be ignored. The shield witnesses a sovereign's appreciation; the motto affords a key-note to the aspirations of the man who chose it. Not of the women! for only under limitations could women use the shield; the motto they were forbidden to use at all. Mottoes often expressed lofty sentiments. Witness a few taken from Virginia families of English descent: *Malo mori quam fœdari*. *Sperate et Virite Fortes* (Bland), *Sine Deo Cares* (Cary), *Ostendo non ostento* (Isham), *Rêve et Révéle* (Atkinson), etc.

At the present moment the distinction of a coat of arms is highly esteemed in this country. Families of English descent can always find a shield or crest on some branch, more or less remote, of the Family Tree. The title to these arms may have long been extinct — but who will take the trouble to investigate? The American cousin scorns and defies rules of heraldry! To be sure, he would prefer assuming a shield once borne by some ancestor, but if that be impossible, he is quite capable of marshalling his arms to suit himself. Is not "a shield of pretence" arms which a lord claims and which he adds to his own? Thus it comes to pass that the crest, hard won in deadly conflict, and the motto once the challenging battle-cry, find themselves embalmed in the perfume of a fine lady's tinted billet, or proudly displayed on the panels of her park equipage. Thus is many a hard-won crest and proud escutcheon of old England made to suffer the extreme penalty of the English law, " drawn and quartered,"and dragged captive in boastful triumph at the chariot wheels of the Great Obscure! They can be made to order by any engraver. They are used, unchallenged, by any and every body willing to pay for them.

It may, therefore, be instructive to turn the pages of old Thomas Fuller's "Worthies of England," and learn the rigid laws governing the use of arms by these " Worthies."

The "fixing of hereditary arms in England was a hundred years ancienter than Richard the Second" — in 1277, therefore.   Before his second invasion into France, Henry V issued a proclamation to the sheriffs to this effect: "Because there are divers men who have assumed to themselves arms and coat-armours where neither they nor their ancestors in times past used such arms or coat-armours, all such shall show cause on the day of muster why he useth arms and by virtue of whose gift he enjoyeth the same: those only excepted who carried arms with us at the battle of Agincourt;" and all detected frauds were to be punished "with the loss of wages, as also the rasing out and breaking off of said arms called coat-armours — and this," adds his Majesty, with emphasis, "you shall in no case omit."

By a later order there was a more searching investigation into the right to bear arms.   A high heraldic officer, usually one of the kings-at-arms, was sent into all the counties to examine the pedigrees of the landed gentry, with a view of ascertaining whether the arms borne by them were unwarrantably assumed.   The king-at-arms was accompanied on such occasions by secretaries or draftsmen.   The "Herald's Visitations," as they were termed, were regularly held as early as 1433, and until between 1686 and 1700.   Their object was by no means to create coats of arms but to reject the unauthorized, and confirm and verify those that were authentic. Thus the arms of the Ball and Washington families had been subjected to strict scrutiny before being registered in the Heralds' College. They could not have been unlawfully assumed by the first immigrant, nor would he, while living in England, have been allowed to mark his property or seal his papers with those arms nor use them in any British colony.

CHAPTER V

TRADITIONS OF MARY BALL'S EARLY LIFE

OF the ancestry of Mary Washington's mother nothing is known. She was the "Widow Johnson," said to have descended from the Montagus of England, and supposed to have been a housekeeper in Joseph Ball's family, and married to him after the death of his first wife. Members of the Ball family, after Mary Washington's death, instituted diligent search to discover something of her mother's birth and lineage. Their inquiries availed to show that she was an Englishwoman. No connection of hers could be found in Virginia. Since then, eminent historians and genealogists, notably Mr. Hayden and Mr. Moncure Conway, have given time and research "to the most important problem in Virginia genealogy, — Who and whence was Mary Johnson, widow, mother of Mary Washington?" The Montagu family has claimed her and discovered that the griffin of the house of Montagu sometimes displaced the raven in General Washington's crest; and it was asserted that the griffin had been discovered perched upon the tomb of one Katharine Washington, at Piankatank. To verify this, the editor of the *William and Mary Quarterly* journeyed to the tomb of Katharine, and found the crest to be neither a raven or a griffin but a wolf's head !

It matters little whether or no the mother of Washington came of noble English blood; for while an honorable ancestry is a gift of the gods, and should be regarded as such by those who possess it, an honorable ancestry is not merely a titled ancestry. Descent from nobles may be interesting, but it can only be honorable when the strawberry leaves have crowned a wise head and the ermine warmed a true heart. Three hundred years ago an English wit declared that " Noblemen have seldom anything in print save their clothes."

Knowing that Mary Johnson was an English-woman, we might, had we learned her maiden name, have rejoiced in tracing her to some family of position, learning, or wealth; for position and learning are desirable gifts, and wealth has been, and ever will be, a synonym of power. It can buy the title and command genius. It can win friendship, pour sunshine into dark places, cause the desert to bloom. It can prolong and sweeten life, and alleviate the pangs of death.

These brilliant settings, for the woman we would fain honor, are denied us. That she was a jewel in herself, there can be no doubt. We must judge of her as we judge of a tree by its fruits; as we

judge a fountain by the streams issuing therefrom. She was the mother of a great woman
" whose precepts and discipline in the education of
her illustrious son, himself acknowledged to have
been the foundation of his fortune and fame: — a
woman who possessed not the ambitions which are
common to meaner minds." This was said of her
by one who knew Mary, the mother of Washington, — Mary, the daughter of the obscure Widow
Johnson.

Indeed, she was so obscure that the only clew we
have to her identity as Joseph Ball's wife is found
in a clause of his will written June 25, 1711, a
few weeks before his death, where he mentions
" Eliza Johnson, daughter of my beloved wife."

Until a few months ago it was supposed that
Mary Ball spent her childhood and girlhood at
Epping Forest, in Lancaster County; that she had
no schooling outside her home circle until her
seventeenth year; that she visited Williamsburg with
her mother about that time; that in 1728 her
mother died, and she went to England to visit her
brother Joseph, a wealthy barrister in London.
Her biographers accepted these supposed facts and
wove around them an enthusiastic romance. They
indulged in fancies of her social triumphs in Williamsburg, the gay capital of the colony; of her
beauty, her lovers; how she was the " Rose of
Epping Forest," the " Toast of the Gallants of

her Day." They followed her to England, — whence also Augustine Washington was declared to have followed her, — sat with her for her portrait, and brought her back either the bride, or soon to become the bride, of Augustine Washington; brought back also the portrait, and challenged the world to disprove the fact that it must be genuine and a capital likeness, for had it not " George Washington's cast of countenance " ?

The search-light of investigation had been turned in vain upon the county records of Lancaster. There she had not left even a fairy footprint. What joy then to learn the truth from an accidental discovery by a Union soldier of a bundle of old letters in an abandoned house in Yorktown at the close of the Civil War! These letters seemed to lift the veil of obscurity from the youthful unmarried years of Mary, the mother of Washington. The first letter is from Williamsburg, 1722 : —

" Dear Sukey — Madam Ball of Lancaster and her sweet Molly have gone Hom. Mama thinks Molly the Comliest Maiden She Knows. She is about 16 yrs. old, is taller than Me, is verry Sensable, Modest and Loving. Her Hair is like unto Flax. Her Eyes are the colour of Yours, and her Chekes are like May blossoms. I wish You could see Her."

A letter was also found purporting to have been written by Mary herself to her brother in England;

defective in orthography, to be sure, but written in a plain, round hand : —

" We have not had a schoolmaster in our neighborhood until now in five years. We have now a young minister living with us who was educated at Oxford, took orders and came over as assistant to Rev. Kemp at Gloucester. That parish is too poor to keep both, and he teaches school for his board. He teaches Sister Susie and me, and Madam Carter's boy and two girls. I am now learning pretty fast. Mama and Susie and all send love to you and Mary. This from your loving sister,

" Mary Ball."

The fragment of another letter was found by the Union soldier. This letter is signed " Lizzie Burwell " and written to " Nelly Car —," but here, alas ! the paper is torn. Only a part of a sentence can be deciphered. " . . . understand Molly Ball is going Home with her Brother, a lawyer who lives in England. Her Mother is dead three months ago." The date is " May ye 15th, 1728," and Mary Ball is now twenty years old.

Could any admiring biographer ask more ? Flaxen hair, May blossoms — delightful suggestion of Virginia peach-blooms, flowering almond, hedge roses ! " Sensible, Modest, and Loving ! " What an enchanting picture of the girlhood of the most eminent of American women ! The flying steeds of imagination were given free rein. Away they went ! They bore her to the gay life in Williamsburg, then the provincial capital and centre of fashionable society in the Old Dominion. There she rode in the heavy coaches drawn by four horses, lumbering through the dusty streets : or she paid her morning visits in the sedan-chairs, with tops hitherto flat but now beginning to arch to admit the lofty head-dresses of the dames within. She met, perhaps, the haughty soldier ex-Governor, who could show a ball which had passed through his coat at Blenheim : and also her Serene Highness, Lady Spotswood, immortalized by William Byrd as " gracious, moderate, and good-humored." Who had not heard of her pier glasses broken by the tame deer and how he fell back upon a table laden with rare bric-a-brac to the great damage thereof! Along with the records of the *habeas corpus*, tiffs with the burgesses, the smelting of iron, the doughty deeds of the Knights of the Golden Horseshoe, invariable mention had been made of this disaster, and of the fact that the gracious Lady Spotswood " bore it with moderation and good-humor." This sublime example might have had some influence in moulding the manners of Mary Ball — one of whose crowning characteristics was a calm self-control, never shaken by the most startling events !

And then we took ship and sailed away with our heroine to England — Augustine Washington, as became an ardent lover, following ere long. Anon, we bore her, a happy bride, home again, bringing

with her a great treasure, — a portrait true to the
life, every feature bearing the stamp of genuineness.
Through how many pages did we gladly amplify
this, chilled somewhat by fruitless searches for
" Sister Susie " !   " Never," said an eminent geneal-
ogist, " never reject or lose tradition.   Keep it,
value it, record it *as tradition;*" but surely this was
not tradition.   It was documentary evidence,
but evidence rudely overthrown by another document, — a dry old yellow will lately found by the
Rev. G. W. Beale in the archives of Northumberland County, in Virginia.

CHAPTER VI

REVELATIONS OF AN OLD WILL

THE old will proves beyond all question that Mary Ball's girlhood was not passed in Lancaster, that she had ample opportunity for education, and was, therefore, not untaught until she was sixteen. She, probably, never visited Williamsburg when seventeen, — certainly never with her mother. There never was a Sister Susie! At the time the Williamsburg letter announced the recent death of her mother, that mother had for many years been sleeping quietly in her grave. Moreover, the letter of Mary herself had done a great injustice to Gloucester parish, which was not a "poor parish" at all — with an impecunious curate working for his board — but a parish erecting at that moment so fine a church that Bishop Meade's pious humility suffered in describing it.

From Dr. Beale's researches we learn that the "Rose of Epping Forest" was a tiny bud indeed when her father died; that before her fifth birthday her mother had married Captain Richard Hewes, a vestryman of St. Stephen's parish, Northumberland, and removed to that parish with her three children, John and Elizabeth Johnson, and our own little Mary Ball.

In 1713, Captain Hewes died, and his inventory was filed by his "widow, Mary Hewes," who also died in the summer of 1721. "It is seldom," says Dr. Beale,[1] commenting upon her last will and testament, "that in a document of this kind, maternal affection — having other and older children to share its bequests — so concentrates itself upon a youngest daughter, and she a child of thirteen summers. Perhaps of all the tributes laid at the feet of Mary Washington, none has been more heart-felt or significant of her worth than legacies of her mother's last will and testament, written as they were, all unconsciously of her future distinction." The will discovered by the Rev. G. W. Beale settles all controversies. For the benefit of those who must see in order to believe, we copy it verbatim.

"In the name of God Amen, the seventeenth Day December in the year of our Lord one thousand seven hundred and twenty.

"I Mary Hewes of St. Stephen's Parish, Northumberland County, widow, being sick and weak in body but of sound and perfect memory, thanks be to Almighty God for the same, and calling to mind the uncertain state of this transitory life, and that the flesh must yield unto Death, when it shall please God to call, do make and ordain this my last will and Testament.

[1] Rev : G. W. Beale in the *Virginia Historical Magazine.*

D

" First, I give and bequeath my soul (to God) that gave it me, and my body to the Earth to be buried in Decent Christian burial at the discretion of my executors in these presents nominated.   And as touching such Worldly estate which it hath pleased God to bestow upon me, I give, devise and dispose of in the following manner and form. *Imprimis,* I give and devise unto my Daughter Mary Ball one young likely negro woman to be purchased for her out of my Estate by my Executors and to be delivered unto her the said Mary Ball at the age of Eighteen years, but, my will is that if the said Mary Ball should dye without Issue lawfully begotten of her body that the said negro woman with her increase shall return to my loving son John Johnson to him, his heirs and assigns forever.

" *Item.* I give and bequeath unto my said Daughter Mary Ball two gold rings, the one being a large hoop and the other a stoned ring.

" *Item.* I give unto my said Daughter Mary Ball one young mare and her increase which said mare I formerly gave her by word of mouth.

" *Item.* I give and bequeath unto my said Daughter Mary Ball sufficient furniture for the bed her father Joseph Ball left her, vizt : One suit of good curtains and fallens, one Rugg, one Quilt, one pair Blankets.

" *Item.* I give and bequeath unto my said Daughter Mary Ball two Diaper Table clothes marked M. B. with inck, and one Dozen of Diaper napkins, two towels, six plates, two pewter dishes, two basins, one large iron pott, one Frying pan, one old trunk.

" *Item.* I give and bequeath unto my said Daughter Mary Ball, one good young Paceing horse together with a good silk plush side saddle to be purchased by my Executors out of my Estate.

"*Item.* I give and bequeath unto my Daughter Elizabeth Bonum one suit of white and black callico, being part of my own wearing apparel.

"*Item.* All the rest of my wearing apparel I give and bequeath unto my said Daughter Mary Ball, and I do hereby appoint her (to) be under Tutiledge and government of Capt. George Eskridge during her minority.

"*Item.* My will is I do hereby oblige my Executors to pay to the proprietor or his agent for the securing of my said Daughter Mary Ball her land Twelve pounds if so much (be) due.

"*Item.* All the rest of my Estate real and personal whatsoever and wheresoever I give and devise unto my son John Johnson, and to his heirs lawfully to be begotten of his body, and for default of such Issue I give and devise the said Estate unto my Daughter Elizabeth Bonum, her heirs and assigns forever.

"*Item.* I do hereby appoint my son John Johnson and my trusty and well beloved friend George Eskridge Executors of this my last will and Testament and also revoke and Disannul all other former wills or Testaments by me heretofore made or caused to be made either by word or writing, ratifying and confirming this to be my last Will and Testament and no other.

"In witness whereof I have hereunto sett my hand and seal the Day and Date at first above written.

"The mark and seal of Mary III Hewes. Sig. (Seal) Signed, Sealed and Published and Declared by Mary Hewes to be her last Will and Testament in presence of us.

"The mark of Robert ✕ Bradley.

"The mark of Ralph ✕ Smithurst

"David Stranghan."

The chief witness to this will was a teacher of no mean repute who lived near Mrs. Hewes, "And," says Dr. Beale, "others might be named who followed the same calling in Mary Ball's girlhood and near her home."

The son, John Johnson, named as joint executor in his mother's will, died very soon after her. His will and hers were recorded on the same day. The first bequest reveals his affection for his little half-sister.

"*Imprimis.* I give and bequeath unto my sister Mary Ball all my land in Stafford which my father-in-law Richard Hewes gave me, to the said Mary Ball and her heirs lawfully to be begotten of her body forever."

The will of Samuel Bonum, husband of the "Elizabeth" mentioned in Mrs. Hewes's will, was probated in Westmoreland, Feb. 22, 1726, and contains an item bequeathing "to my sister-in-law Mary Ball, my young dapple gray riding horse." Mary Ball was then eighteen years old.

So it appears that the mother of Washington, although not rich, according to the standard of that day or this, was fairly well endowed with Virginia real estate. Also that she owned three or more riding-horses, her own maid, a few jewels, and house plenishing sufficient for the station of a lady in her day and generation.

CHAPTER VII

MARY BALL'S CHILDHOOD

IT is easy to imagine the childhood of Mary Ball. Children in her day escaped from the nursery at an early age. They were not hidden away in convents or sent to finishing schools. There were no ostentatious débuts, no "coming-out teas." As soon as a girl was fairly in her "teens" she was marriageable.

Little girls, from early babyhood, became the constant companions of their mothers, and were treated with respect. Washington writes gravely of "Miss Custis," six years old. They worked samplers, learned to edge handkerchiefs with a wonderful imitation of needle-point, plaited lace-strings for stays, twisted the fine cords that drew into proper bounds the stiff bodices, knitted garters and long hose, took lessons on the harpsichord, danced the minuet, and lent their little hands to "clap muslins" on the great clearstarching days, when the lace "steenkirk," and ruffled bosoms, and ample kerchiefs, were "gotten up" and crimped into prescribed shape. No lounging, idleness, or loss of time was permitted. The social customs of the day enforced habits of self-control.   For long hours the little Mary was expected to sit upon high chairs, with no relenting pillows or cushions, making her manners as became a gentleman's daughter throughout the stated "dining days," when guests arrived in the morning and remained until evening.   Nor was her upright figure, clad in silk coat and mittens, capuchin and neckatees, ever absent from the front seat of the yellow chariot as it swung heavily through the sands to return these stately visits, or to take her mother and sister to old St. Stephen's church. Arriving at the latter, she might possibly have had a glimpse now and then of other little girls as she paced the gallery on her way to the high-backed family pew, with its "railing of brass rods with damask curtains to prevent the family from gazing around when sitting or kneeling."   Swallowed up in the great square pew she could see nothing.

From the viewpoint of a twentieth-century child, her small feet were set in a hard, if not thorny, path.   The limits of an early colonial house allowed no space for the nursery devoted exclusively to a child, and filled with every conceivable appliance for her instruction and amusement. There were no wonderful mechanical animals, lifelike in form and color, and capable of exercising many of their functions.   One stiff-jointed, staring, wooden effigy was the only prophecy of the enchanting   doll   family, — the   blue-eyed,   brown-eyed, flaxen-curled, sleeping, talking, walking, and dimpled darlings of latter-day children, — and the wooden-handled board, faced with horn and bound with brass, the sole representative of the child's picture-book of to-day. No children's books were printed in England until the middle of the eighteenth century; but one Thomas Flint, a Boston printer, appreciating the rhymes that his mother-in-law, Mrs. Goose, sang to his children, published them in book form and gave them a name than which none is more sure of immortality. This, however, was in 1719 — too late for our little Mary Ball. She had only the horn-

An Old Doll.

book as resource in the long, dark days when the fairest of all books lay hidden beneath the snows of winter — the horn-book, immortalized by Thomas Tickell as far back as 1636 : —

> "Thee will I sing, in comely wainscot bound,
> And golden verge enclosing thee around :

The faithful horn before, from age to age
Preserving thy invulnerable page ;
Behind, thy patron saint in armor shines
With sword and lance to guard the sacred lines.
The instructed handles at the bottom fixed
Lest wrangling critics should pervert the text.''

The "sword and lance" were in allusion to the one illustration of the horn-book. When the blue eyes wearied over the alphabet, Lord's prayer, and nine digits, they might be refreshed with a picture of St. George and the Dragon, rudely carved on the wooden back. The "instructed handle" clasped the whole and kept it together.

All orphans and poor children in colonial Virginia were provided with public schools under the care of the vestries of the parishes — "litle houses," says Hugh Jones in 1722, "built on purpose where are taught English, writing, etc." Parents were compelled to send their children to these schools, and masters to whom children were bound were required to give them schooling until "ye years of twelfe or thereabout" without distinction of race or sex. For instance, in the vestry book of Petsworth Parish, in Gloucester County, is an indenture dated Oct. 30, 1716, of Ralph Bevis to give George Petsworth, "a molattoe boy of the age of 2 years, 3 years' schooling; and carefully to instruct him afterwards that he may read well any part of the Bible." Having mastered the Bible, all literary possibilities were open to the said George. The gentry, however, employed private

Horn-book.

tutors in their own families, — Scotchmen or Englishmen fresh from the universities, or young curates from Princeton or Fagg's Manor in Pennsylvania. Others secured teachers by indenture.

"In Virginia," says the *London Magazine*, "a clever servant is often indentured to some master as a schoolmaster." John Carter of Lancaster directed in his will that his son Robert should have "a youth servant bought for him to teach him in his books in English or Latin." Early advertisements in the *Virginia Gazette* assured all "single men capable of teaching children to Read English, write or Cypher or Greek Latin and Mathematicks — also all Dancing Masters," that they "would meet with good encouragement" in certain neighborhoods.

But this was after Mary Ball's childhood. Days of silent listening to the talk of older people were probably her early school days. In Virginia there were books, true, but the large libraries of thirty years later had not yet been brought over. There was already a fine library at Stratford in Westmoreland. Colonel Byrd's library was considered vast when it attained to "3600 titles." Books were unfashionable at court in England. No power in heaven or earth has been yet found to keep the wise and witty from writing them, but in the first years of the eighteenth century it was very bad form to talk about them. Later, even, the first gentleman in England was always furious at the sight of books. Old ladies used to declare that "Books were not fit articles for drawing-rooms." "Books!" said Sarah Marlborough; "prithee,

don't talk to me about books! The only books
I know are men and cards."

But there were earnest talkers in Virginia, and
the liveliest interest in all kinds of affairs. It was a
picturesque time in the life of the colony. Things
of interest were always happening. We know this
of the little Mary, — she was observant and wise,
quiet and reflective. She had early opinions, doubtless, upon the powers of the vestries, the African
slave-trade, the right of a Virginia assembly to the
privileges of parliament, and other grave questions
of her time. Nor was the time without its vivid
romances. Although no witch was ever burnt in
Virginia, Grace Sherwood, who must have been
young and comely, was arrested "under suspetion
of witchcraft," condemned by a jury of old women
because of a birth-mark on her body, and sentenced
to a seat in the famous ducking-stool, which had
been, in the wisdom of the burgesses, provided to
still the tongues of "brabbling women," — a sentence never inflicted, for a few glances at her tearful eyes won from the relenting justice the order
that this ducking was to be "in no wise without her
consent, *or if the day should be rainy*, or in any way
to endanger her health!"

Stories were told around the fireside on winter
nights, when the wooden shutters rattled — for
rarely before 1720 were "windows sasht with crystal glass." The express, bringing mails from the

north, had been scalped by Indians.   Four times in
one year had homeward-bound ships been sunk
by pirates.   Men, returning to England to receive
an inheritance, were waylaid on the high seas,
robbed, and murdered.   In Virginia waters the
dreaded "Blackbeard" had it all his own way for
a while.   Finally, his grim head is brought home on
the bowsprit of a Virginia ship, and a drinking-cup,

Ducking-stool.

rimmed with silver, made of the skull that held his
wicked brains.   Of course, it could not be expected
that he could rest in his grave under these circumstances, and so, until fifty years ago (when possibly
the drinking-cup was reclaimed by his restless spirit),
his phantom sloop might be seen spreading its ghostly
sails in the moonlight on the York River and putting into Ware Creek to hide ill-gotten gains in the
Old Stone House.   Only a few years before had

the dreadful Tuscaroras risen with fire and toma-
hawk in the neighbor colony of North Carolina.

Nearer home, in her own neighborhood, in fact,
were many suggestive localities which a child's fears
might people with supernatural spirits. Although
there were no haunted castles with dungeon, moat,
and tower, there were deserted houses in lonely

The Old Stone House.

places, with open windows like hollow eyes, grave-
yards half hidden by tangled creepers and wept over
by ancient willows. About these there sometimes
hung a mysterious, fitful light which little Mary,
when a belated traveller in the family coach, passed
with bated breath, lest warlocks or witches should
issue therefrom, to say nothing of the interminable
stretches of dark forests, skirting ravines fringed

with poisonous vines, and haunted by the deadly rattlesnake. People talked of strange, unreal lights peeping through the tiny port-holes of the old Stone House on York River — that mysterious fortress believed to have been built by John Smith — while, flitting across the doorway, had been seen the dusky form of Pocahontas, clad in her buckskin robe, with a white plume in her hair: keeping tryst, doubtless, with Captain Smith, with none to hinder, now that the dull, puritanic John Rolfe was dead and buried; and, as we have said, Blackbeard's sloop would come glimmering down the river, and the bloody horror of a headless body would land and wend its way to the little fortress which held his stolen treasure. Moreover, Nathaniel Bacon had risen from his grave in York River, and been seen in the Stone House with his compatriots, Drummond, Bland, and Hansford.

Doubtless such stories inspired many of little Mary's early dreams, and caused her to tremble as she lay in her trundle-bed, — kept all day beneath the great four poster, and drawn out at night, — unless, indeed, her loving mother allowed her to climb the four steps leading to the feather sanctuary behind the heavy curtains, and held her safe and warm in her own bosom.

CHAPTER VIII

GOOD TIMES IN OLD VIRGINIA

DESPITE the perils and perplexities of the
time; the irreverence and profanity of the
clergy; the solemn warning of the mis-
sionary Presbyterians; the death of good Queen
Anne, the last of the Stuarts, so dear to the hearts
of loyal Virginians; the forebodings on the acces-
sion to the throne of the untried Guelphs; the total
lack of many of the comforts and conveniences of
life, Virginians love to write of the early years of
the century as "the golden age of Virginia." These
were the days known as the "good old times in old
Virginia," when men managed to live without tele-
graphs, railways, and electric lights. "It was a happy
era!" says Esten Cooke. "Care seemed to keep
away and stand out of its sunshine. There was a
great deal to enjoy. Social intercourse was on the
most friendly footing. The plantation house was
the scene of a round of enjoyments. The planter
in his manor house, surrounded by his family and
retainers, was a feudal patriarch ruling everybody;
drank wholesome wine — sherry or canary — of his
own importation; entertained every one; held great

47

festivities at Christmas, with huge log fires in the great fireplaces, around which the family clan gathered. It was the life of the family, not of the world, and produced that intense attachment for the soil which has become proverbial. Everybody was happy! Life was not rapid, but it was satisfactory. The portraits of the time show us faces without those lines which care furrows in the faces of the men of to-day. That old society succeeded in working out the problem of living happily to an extent which we find few examples of to-day."

"The Virginians of 1720," according to Henry Randall, "lived in baronial splendor; their spacious grounds were bravely ornamented; their tables were loaded with plate and with the luxuries of the old and new world; they travelled in state, their coaches dragged by six horses driven by three postilions. When the Virginia gentleman went forth with his household his cavalcade consisted of the mounted white males of the family, the coach and six lumbering through the sands, and a retinue of mounted servants and led horses bringing up the rear. In their general tone of character the aristocracy of Virginia resembled the landed gentry of the mother country. Numbers of them were highly educated and accomplished by foreign study and travel. As a class they were intelligent, polished in manners, high toned, and hospitable, sturdy in their loyalty and in their adherence to the national church."

Another historian, writing from Virginia in 1720, says: "Several gentlemen have built themselves large brick houses of many rooms on a floor, but they don't covet to make them lofty, having extent enough of ground to build upon, and now and then they are visited by winds which incommode a towering fabric. Of late they have sasht their windows with crystal glass; adorning their apartments with rich furniture. They have their graziers, seedsmen, brewers, gardeners, bakers, butchers and cooks within themselves, and have a great plenty and variety of provisions for their table; and as for spicery and things the country don't produce, they have constant supplies of 'em from England. The gentry pretend to have their victuals served up as nicely as the best tables in England."

A quaint old Englishman, Peter Collinson, writes in 1737 to his friend Bartram when he was about taking Virginia in his field of botanical explorations: "One thing I must desire of thee, and do insist that thee oblige me therein: that thou make up that drugget clothes to go to Virginia in, and not appear to disgrace thyself and me; for these Virginians are a very gentle, well-dressed people, and look, perhaps, more at a man's outside than his inside. For these and other reasons pray go very clean, neat and handsomely dressed to Virginia. Never mind thy clothes: I will send more another year."

E

Those were not troublous days of ever changing fashion.   Garments were, for many years, cut after the same patterns, varying mainly in accordance with the purses of their wearers.   "The petticoats of sarcenet, with black, broad lace printed on the bottom and before; the flowered satin and plain satin, laced with rich lace at the bottom," descended from mother to daughter with no change in the looping of the train or decoration of bodice and ruff. There were no mails to bring troublesome letters to be answered when writing was so difficult and spelling so uncertain.   Not that there was the smallest disgrace in bad spelling!   Trouble on that head was altogether unnecessary.

There is not the least doubt that life, notwithstanding its dangers and limitations and political anxieties, passed happily to these early planters of Virginia. The lady of the manor had occupation enough and to spare in managing English servants and negroes, and in purveying for a table of large proportions. Nor was she without accomplishments.   She could dance well, embroider, play upon the harpsichord or spinet, and wear with grace her clocked stockings, rosetted, high-heeled shoes and brave gown of "taffeta and moyre" looped over her satin quilt.

There was no society column in newspapers to vex her simple soul by awakening unwholesome ambitions.   There was no newspaper until 1736.   She had small knowledge of any world better than her

own, of bluer skies, kinder friends, or gayer society.
She managed well her large household, loved her
husband, and reared kindly but firmly her many
sons and daughters. If homage could compensate
for the cares of premature marriage, the girl-wife
had her reward. She lived in the age and in the
land of chivalry, and her "amiable qualities of mind
and heart" received generous praise. As a matron
she was adored by her husband and her friends.
When she said, "Until death do us part," she
meant it. Divorce was unknown; its possibility
undreamed of. However and wherever her lot was
cast she endured to the end; fully assured that
when she went to sleep behind the marble slab in
the garden an enumeration of her virtues would
adorn her tombstone.

In the light of the ambitions of the present day,
the scornful indifference of the colonists to rank,
even among those entitled to it, is curious. Very
rare were the instances in which young knights and
baronets elected to surrender the free life in Virginia and return to England to enjoy their titles and
possible preferment. One such embryo nobleman
is quoted as having answered to an invitation from
the court, "I prefer my land here with plentiful
food for my family to becoming a starvling at court."

Governor Page wrote of his father, Mason Page
of Gloucester, born 1718, "He was urged to pay
court to Sir Gregory Page whose heir he was sup-

posed to be but he despised title as much as I do; and would have nothing to say to the rich, silly knight, who finally died, leaving his estate to a sillier man than himself — *one Turner*, who, by act of parliament, took the name and title of Gregory Page."

Everything was apparently settled upon a firm, permanent basis. Social lines were sharply drawn, understood, and recognized. The court "at home" across the seas influenced the mimic court at Williamsburg. Games that had been fashionable in the days of the cavaliers were popular in Virginia. Horse-racing, cock-fighting, cards, and feasting, with much excess in eating and drinking, marked the social life of the subjects of the Georges in Virginia as in the mother country. It was an English colony, — wearing English garments, with English manners, speech, customs, and fashions. They had changed their skies only.

Cælum, non animum, qui trans mare currunt.

It is difficult to understand that, while custom and outward observance, friendship, lineage, and close commercial ties bound the colony to England, forces, of which neither was conscious, were silently at work to separate them forever. And this without the stimulus of discontent arising from poverty or want. It was a time of the most affluent abundance. The common people lived in the greatest comfort, as far as food was concerned. Fish and flesh, game, fruits, and flowers, were poured at their feet from a liberal horn-of-plenty. Deer, coming down from the mountains to feed upon the mosses that grew on the rocks in the rivers, were shot for the sake of their skins only, until laws had to be enforced lest the decaying flesh pollute the air. Painful and hazardous as were the journeys, the traveller always encumbered himself with abundant provision for the inner man.

When the Knights of the Golden Horseshoe accomplished the perilous feat of reaching the summit of the Blue Ridge Mountains, they had the honor of drinking King George's health in "Virginia red wine, champagne, brandy, shrub, cider, canary, cherry punch, white wine, Irish usquebaugh, and two kinds of rum," — all of which they had managed to carry along, keeping a sharp lookout all day for Indians, and sleeping on their arms at night. A few years later we find Peter Jefferson ordering from Henry Wetherburn, innkeeper, the biggest bowl of arrack punch ever made, and trading the same with William Randolph for two hundred acres of land.

We are not surprised to find that life was a brief enjoyment. Little Mary Ball, demurely reading from the tombstones in the old St. Stephen's church, had small occasion for arithmetic beyond the numbers of thirty or forty years — at which age, having "Piously lived and comfortably died, leaving the sweet perfume of a good reputation," these light-hearted good livers went to sleep behind their monuments.

Of course the guardians of the infant colony spent many an anxious hour evolving schemes for the control of excessive feasting and junketing.   The clergy were forced to ignore excesses, not daring to reprove them for fear of losing a good living.   Their brethren across the seas cast longing eyes upon Virginia. It was an age of intemperance.   The brightest wits of England, her poets and statesmen, were "hard drinkers."   "All my hopes terminate," said Dean Swift in 1709, "in being made Bishop of Virginia." There the Dean, had he been so inclined, could hope for the high living and hard drinking which were in fashion.   There, too, in the tolerant atmosphere of a new country, he might — who knows ? — have felt free to avow his marriage with the unhappy Stella.

In Virginia the responsibility of curbing the fun-loving community devolved upon the good burgesses, travelling down in their sloops to hold session at Williamsburg.   We find them making laws restraining the jolly planters.   A man could be presented for gaming, swearing, drunkenness, selling crawfish on Sunday, becoming engaged to more than one woman at a time, and, as we have said, there was always the ducking-stool for " brabbling women who go about from house to house slandering their neighbors : — a melancholy proof that even in those Arcadian days the tongue required control."

CHAPTER IX

MARY BALL'S GUARDIAN AND HER GIRLHOOD

EXCEPT for the bequest in her brother-in-law's will, nothing whatever is known of Mary Ball for nine years — indeed, until her marriage with Augustine Washington in 1730. The traditions of these years are all based upon the letters found by the Union soldier, — genuine letters, no doubt, but relating to some other Mary Ball who, in addition to the flaxen hair and May-blossom cheeks, has had the honor of masquerading, for nearly forty years, as the mother of Washington, and of having her story and her letters placed reverently beneath the corner-stone of the Mary Washington monument.

Mary Ball, only thirteen years old when her mother died, would naturally be taken to the Westmoreland home of her sister Elizabeth, wife of Samuel Bonum and only survivor, besides herself, of her mother's children. Elizabeth was married and living in her own house seven years before Mrs. Hewes died. The Bonum residence was but a few miles distant from that of Mrs. Hewes, and a mile and a half from Sandy Point, where lived the

" well-beloved and trusty friend George Eskridge."
Major Eskridge " seated " Sandy Point in Westmoreland about 1720.   The old house was standing
until eight years ago, when it was destroyed by fire.
He had seven children; the fifth child, Sarah, a
year older than Mary Ball and doubtless her friend
and companion.

Under the " tutelage and government " of a man
of wealth, eminent in his profession of the law, the
two little girls would naturally be well and faithfully instructed.   We can safely assume, considering all these circumstances, that Mary Ball's girlhood
was spent in the " Northern Neck of Virginia,"
and at the homes of Major Eskridge and her only
sister; and that these faithful guardians provided
her with as liberal an education as her station demanded and the times permitted there cannot be
the least doubt.   Her own affectionate regard for
them is emphatically proven by the fact that she
gave to her first-born son the name of George
Eskridge, to another son that of Samuel Bonum,
and to her only daughter that of her sister Elizabeth.

Tradition tells us that in the latter part of the
seventeenth century, George Eskridge, who was a
young law student, while walking along the shore
on the north coast of Wales, studying a law-book,
was suddenly seized by the Press Gang, carried
aboard ship and brought to the colony of Virginia.

As the custom was, he was sold to a planter for a term of eight years. During that time, he was not allowed to communicate with his friends at home. He was treated very harshly, and made to lodge in the kitchen, where he slept, because of the cold, upon the hearth.

On the day that his term of service expired he rose early, and with his mattock dislodged the stones of the hearth. Upon his master's remonstrance, he said, " The bed of a departing guest must always be made over for his successor;" and throwing down his mattock he strode out of the house, taking with him the law-book which had been his constant companion during his years of slavery.

He returned to England, completed his law studies, was admitted to the bar, and, returning to Virginia, was granted many thousand acres of land, held several colonial positions, and became eminent among the distinguished citizens of the " Northern Neck," — the long, narrow strip of land included between the Potomac and the Rappahannock rivers. His daughter, Sarah, married Willoughby Newton, and lived near Bonum Creek in Westmoreland. The family intermarried, also, with the Lee, Washington, and other distinguished families in the Northern Neck.

CHAPTER X

YOUNG MEN AND MAIDENS OF THE OLD DOMINION

THE social setting for Mary Ball — now a young lady — is easily defined. It matters little whether she did or did not visit her brother in England. She certainly belonged to the society of Westmoreland, "the finest," says Bishop Meade, "for culture and sound patriotism in the Colony." Around her lived the families of Mason, Taliaferro, Mountjoy, Travers, Moncure, Mercer, Tayloe, Ludwell, Fitzhugh, Lee, Newton, Washington, and others well known as society leaders in 1730. If she was, as her descendants claim for her, "The Toast of the Gallants of Her Day," these were the "Gallants," — many of them the fathers of men who afterward shone like stars in the galaxy of revolutionary heroes.

The gallants doubtless knew and visited their tide-water friends, — the Randolphs, Blands, Harrisons, Byrds, Nelsons, and Carters, — and, like them, followed the gay fashions of the day. They wrote sonnets and acrostics and valentines to their Belindas, Florellas, Fidelias, and Myrtyllas — the real names of Molly, Patsy, Ann, and Mary being

WILLIAM AND MARY COLLEGE.

reckoned too homespun for the court of Cupid. These gallants wore velvet and much silk; the long vests that Charles the Second had invented as "a fashion for gentlemen of all time"; curled, powdered wigs, silver and gold lace; silken hose and brilliant buckles. Many of them had been educated abroad, or at William and Mary College, — where they had been rather a refractory set, whose enormities must be winked at, — even going so far as to "keep race-horses at ye college, and bet at ye billiard and other gaming tables." Whatever their sins or shortcomings, they were warm-hearted and honorable, and most chivalrous to women. It was fashionable to present locks of hair tied in true-lovers' knots, to tame cardinal-birds and mocking-birds for the colonial damsels, to serenade them with songs and stringed instruments under their windows on moonlight nights, to manufacture valentines of thinnest cut paper in intricate foldings, with tender sentiments tucked shyly under a bird's wing or the petal of a flower.

With the youthful dames themselves, in hoop, and stiff bodice, powder and "craped" tresses, who cut watch-papers and worked book-marks for the gallants, we are on terms of intimacy. We know all their "tricks and manners," through the laughing Englishman, and their own letters. An unpublished manuscript still circulates from hand to hand in Virginia, under oath of secrecy, for it contains a tragic secret, which reveals the true character of the mothers of Revolutionary patriots. These letters express high sentiment in strong, vigorous English, burning with patriotism and ardent devotion to the interests of the united colonies — not alone to Virginia. The spelling, and absurdly plentiful capitals, were those of the period, and should provoke no criticism. Ruskin says, " no beauty of execution can outweigh one grain or fragment of thought." Beauty of execution and good spelling, according to modern standards, do not appear in the letters of Mary Ball and her friends, but they are seasoned with many a grain of good sense and thought.

Of course we cannot know the names of her best friends. Her social position entitled her to intimacy with the sisters of any or all of the " gallants" we have named. She might have known Jane Randolph, already giving her heart to plain Peter Jefferson, and destined to press to her bosom the baby fingers that grew to frame the Declaration of Independence; or Sarah Winston, whose brilliant talents flashed in such splendor from the lips of Patrick Henry; or ill-starred Evelyn Byrd, whose beauty had fired the sluggish veins of George II and inspired a kingly pun upon her name, " Much have I heard, lady, of thy fair country, but of the beauty of its birds I know but now," — all these and more; to say nothing of the mother of

Sally and Molly Cary, of Lucy Grymes, of Betsy Fauntleroy, and of Mary Bland, each of whom has been claimed by Lossing and others to be the Lowland beauty, to whom her illustrious son wrote such wonderful sonnets, but quite impossible in the case of Mary Bland, seeing she was born in 1704, and was some years older than his mother.

They were a light-hearted band of maidens in these pre-Revolutionary days in the "Old Dominion!" They had no dreams sadder than mystic dreams on bride's cake, no duties except those imposed by affection, no tasks too difficult, no burdens too heavy. They sang the old-time songs, and danced the old-time dances, and played the old-time English games around the Christmas fires, burning nuts, and naming apple seeds, and loving their loves "with an A or a B," even although my Lady Castlemaine, of whom no one could approve, had so entertained her very doubtful friends a hundred years before. They had the Pyrrhic dances, but they had the Pyrrhic phalanx as well! The "nobler and manlier lessons" were not forgotten in all the light-hearted manners of the age.

CHAPTER XI

OF the " Mistress Mary Ball's " personal appearance we know nothing, unless we can
guide our imaginations by the recollections
of old Fredericksburg neighbors who knew her after
she had passed middle age. Washington Irving says
she was a beauty and a belle. He had only one
source of information, George Washington Parke
Custis, the sole eye-witness who wrote of her personal
appearance in middle life. Sparks, Lossing, and all
the rest who have described her, had no other.
Parson Weems, of course, had something to say;
but we do not know that he ever saw her. Any
pen-portrait made of her to-day can boast only an
outline of truth. Probability and imagination must
fill in the picture. It is *certain* that she was
" finely formed, her features pleasing, yet strongly
marked." That is all! Has not some one said
" her eyes were blue "? Well, then, fair hair and
fair complexion would match the blue eyes. She
was purely English. Her mother was probably
born in England, her grandmother and grandfather were certainly born and reared there. Her

OLD YEOCOMICO CHURCH.

type was that of an athletic, healthy Englishwoman, to whom an upright carriage and much out-of-door life gave a certain style.   I, for one, am assured that she was handsome and distingué, — a superb woman in every particular.   She possessed a pure, high spirit, and

> " Every spirit as it is most pure
> And hath in it the more of heavenly light —
> So it the fairer bodie doth procure
> To habit in."

Imagination and probability join hands in picturing her on horseback.   She was a fearless and expert horsewoman.   At thirteen years of age she had owned her own mount, her own plush saddle. Now, at twenty, we find her in "habit, hat, and feather" at home on her own dapple-gray, her brother-in-law's gift — she was too good a horse- woman for mad gallops — "pacing" through the lanes in Westmoreland to and fro from Bonum Creek to Sandy Point, or to Yeocomico church, or to superintend her own fields.   Her English habit is of scarlet cloth, long and flowing as to the skirt and tightly fitted as to the bodice.   Her hat is of beaver, and hat and floating plume alike are black.

This is a pleasing picture of the mother of our adored Washington, and it is as true a picture as we have authority for drawing.   It would have helped much if we could have accepted any one of the portraits claiming to be genuine, although no one of them expresses the type which we may reasonably suppose to have been hers.   Her own descendants and the wisest historians declare she left no portrait.   A picture, claiming to be such, hangs to-day in Lancaster court-house — one that was genuine was burned in the home of her early married life.   Handsome and stately she certainly was.   Nor can we suppose from the character developed in her early maternal life, that she mingled to any extent in the gayeties of her time.   In no letter, no record of any kind, is her name mentioned until her marriage.   She was doubtless always grave, always thoughtful, concerning herself much with her religious duties, industrious in womanly occupations, reverently attentive to the services at Yeocomico church, of which the Eskridge family were members.

We may be sure she was instructed in dancing — the universal accomplishment of the time. The saintly blind preacher, James Waddell, had his daughters, to the great scandal of his Presbyterian followers, taught to dance; his defence being that "no parent has a right to make his children unfit for polite society."   Members of the Lee, Corbyn, and other influential families of her neighborhood urged the building of a "Banquetting House" — a rustic casino — in Pickatown's Field in Westmoreland, according to contracts made years before, "to make an Honourable treatment fit to entertain the undertakers thereof, their wives, mistresses (sweethearts) and friends, yearly and every year;" and the "yearly and every year" was likely to be construed, as the merry colonists knew well how to construe all opportunities for pleasure. For despite Francis Makemie, James Waddell, and the truly evangelical priests of the Established Church — of whom there were still some — the times went merrily in old Virginia; and the waters of the York had cooled long ago the fevered blood of the first martyr to freedom; and Benjamin Franklin was composing ballads upon " Blackbeard, the pyrate," to say nothing of rollicking rhymes fit no longer for ears polite; and Patrick Henry, and Richard Henry Lee, and George Washington were yet unborn.

The veil of obscurity which hangs over the unmarried life of Mary Ball will never be lifted. The evidence is all in, the testimony all taken. It is certain that she could hardly escape the social round in the gay society of Westmoreland, and quite as certain that she was not a prominent part of it. When the gardener desires the perfecting of some flower, to bloom but once in a twelve-month, he keeps it secluded in some cool, dark spot — only when well rooted bringing it forth into the sunlight. Thus the mind and character grow best in quiet and seclusion, becoming serene, strong, and superior to petty passions. When Mary Ball's hour was come,

F

when her high vocation was pressed upon her, she was rooted and grounded in all things requisite for her exalted but difficult lot.

The years of which we have no record included the formative period of her life. They were dark years in the religious history of the colony. She could have small help from the clerical guides of the day. Even at the best, a church service was mainly a social function, — prayers hurriedly read, perfunctory sermon of short duration, followed by a social half-hour for the purpose of giving and accepting invitations to dinner. The dinner ended with the inevitable punch bowl, over which the clergyman was often the first to become incapable of pursuing his journey home. It had not been so very long since a rector of the Wicomoco church had reached the limit of irreverence. While administering the Communion of the Lord's Supper, upon tasting the bread, he had cried out to the church warden, "George, this bread is not fit for a dog." [1]

A more unwilling witness against the clergy than good Bishop Meade can hardly be imagined. He tells of one who was for years the president of a jockey club; of another who was an habitué of the bar of a country tavern, often seen reeling to and fro with a bowl of "toddy" in his hands, challenging the passers-by to "come in and have a drink";

---

[1] Foote's "Sketches of Virginia."

of still another who indulged in a fisticuff with some
of his vestrymen, floored them, and next Sunday
preached a sermon from Nehemiah, "And I con-
tended with them and cursed them and smote certain of them, and plucked off their hair!" (Let us
hope they were "Gentlemen" and therefore wore
the wigs fashionable in their day. "Plucked off"
seems to imply as much.)   One of these recreant
rectors fought a duel within the grounds of his own
church ; all of them, according to a report made to
the Bishop of London, were either "slothful and
negligent" or "debauched and bent on all manner
of vices."

No one of the Established Church ever *gave* his
services. They were paid for by the piece or dozen
like any other merchantable article. In St. Stephen's
parish the vestry book, in 1712, records the price
of sermons, for instance, to "Rev. John Bell for
eight sermons 450 pounds of tobacco apiece." The
Rev. Mr. Lechardy rated his eloquence at a lower
figure, "for two sermons 600 pounds of tobacco,"
etc.   Notwithstanding the velvet and lace, the powder, perfume, and high-flown compliments of "the
gallants of the early eighteenth century" license of
speech was universal. Colonel Byrd, the courtly
master of Westover, wrote letters too gross for the
pages of a reputable magazine. Swearing among
women was as common as in the "spacious times
of great Elizabeth."   From all this, no tutelage and

government, however careful, could insure escape. In spite of all this and more, Mary Ball acquired the refinement and moderation of speech by which she was characterized.

CHAPTER XII

HER MARRIAGE AND EARLY LIFE

"THE 'Rose of Epping Forest,'" says one of her descendants, "and 'reigning Belle of the Northern Neck,' as she was universally styled, would, in common parlance, be called 'hard to please,' in that, in times when marriages were early she did not resign her sceptre until she had attained the then ripe age of twenty-two — not 'love-inspiring sixteen,' as Parson Weems would have us believe. In this she exhibited that consummate wisdom, calm equipoise of soul, and perfect self-control so strikingly displayed throughout her subsequent career."

She was blessed then with the priceless gift of a long and happy girlhood — that sweet fountain of pure waters, the memory of which has cheered so many women throughout a long and difficult life. In her day so late a marriage was not only eccentric but something to be condemned as unwise. The reluctant Virginia belle was warned that those who "walked through the woods with a haughty spirit would have to stoop at last and pick up a crooked stick." That women could stand alone was unthinkable in those days. A staff was essential, and she who scorned the stately saplings of the forest would surely be forced at last to accept some inferior windfall.

But Mary Ball chose wisely and well; of this we may be sure. Augustine Washington died before he could earn the honor of impressing her life or that of his illustrious son.

He belonged to an old English family which had sent two of its members to Virginia early in the seventeenth century, and, as we have seen, his grandfather held positions of honor and trust in the colony.

With the origin of his crest, — the closed visor, the soaring raven, — with the motto *Excitus acta probat*, we need not concern ourselves. The shield itself is more to our purpose, for it furnished the pattern for the Stars and Stripes of this country; and is surely of all insignia the most distinguished, since in all lands, on all waters, amid all the emblems of the pride of the world, it stands preëminent as the emblem of freedom won by valor.

It should be quite enough for us to know, " He was a gentleman of high standing, noble character, large property and considerable personal attractions, being of fair complexion, tall stature, commanding presence and an age not disproportioned to her own." He was a neighbor of Major George Esk-ridge, although their homes were fifteen or twenty miles distant from each other. We have all supposed that he followed Mary Ball to England and was married there. Possibly, not probably. He was a plain Virginia planter, immersed in business and domestic cares, and it is not probable that he went to England in quest of Mary Ball. Why should he cross the ocean to gather the flower that grew at his threshold?

It is much more likely that he rode over to attend service in the handsome, recently erected Yeocomico church, and to visit George Eskridge at Sandy Point, coming with his first wife and their little boys, Lawrence and Augustine. Elizabeth Bonum lived a mile and a half from Sandy Point. It is quite certain that all the families in this hospitable region knew and visited each other. Mary Ball probably knew Augustine Washington well, long before he was a widower.

All this seems prosaic by contrast with the legend that "the fair American" met her future husband while she was visiting her half-brother in a Berkshire town in England; that one day a gentleman was thrown from his travelling chariot in front of her brother's gate, was seriously injured, brought in and nursed by the fair hands of Mary herself; that love and marriage followed in short order; that the pair lived several years in a villa at Cookham. All this is so much more attractive than a plain story of propinquity and old-fashioned neighborhood friendship, blossoming into a temperate, middle-aged, old-fashioned widower-love and marriage !   But we are constrained to accept the latter, having no proof of anything better.   Besides, where were Lawrence and Augustine during all those halcyon years ? Who was looking after those lambs while the Shepherd was disporting himself at villas in Cookham ?

The snows had melted from the violet beds, and the " snow-birds " were nesting in the cedars when our Mary left her girlhood's home to become the wife of Augustine Washington.   Her new home was a large, old-fashioned house on the banks of the Potomac — one of those dwellings with great low-stretching roof, which always reminds me of a gigantic fowl brooding with expanded wings over its young.   It was not one of the imposing colonial houses just then (March 6, 1730) in process of erection.   Marion Harland says, in her reverent " Story of Mary Washington ": " Augustine Washington's plantation of Wakefield rested upon the Potomac, and was a mile in width.   Wakefield comprised a thousand acres of as fine wood and bottom land as were to be found in a county that by reason of the worth, talents and patriotism that adorned it was called the Athens of Virginia.   The house faced the Potomac, the lawn sloping to the bank between three and four hundred yards distant from the ' porch,' running from corner to corner of the old dwelling. There were four rooms of fair size upon the first floor, the largest in a one-story extension in the back being the chamber. The high roof above the main building was pierced by dormer windows that lighted a large attic. At each end of the house was a chimney built upon the outside of the frame dwelling and of dimensions that made the latter seem disproportionately small. Each cavernous fireplace would hold half a cord of wood. About the fireplace in the parlor were the blue Dutch tiles much affected in the decorative architecture of the time." Here we can fancy the bride, covertly exploring her new home and scanning the footprints of her predecessor ; keeping her own counsel, but instructing herself as to what manner of woman had first enthroned herself in the bosom of her lord.

It appears she was arrested in this voyage of discovery by a small but rare treasure of books. Standing before the diamond-paned " secretary," she examined one volume after another. Finally, turning over the leaves of one, she read : "On Moderation and Anger," "On Self-Denial," "On ye Vanity and Vexation which ariseth from Worldly Hope and Expectation." These seemed to her words of wisdom by which one might be guided. The title-page announced " Sir Matthew Hale's Contemplations," the fly-leaf revealed the name of the owner, the first wife, " Jane Washington." Finding the ink-horn, she wrote firmly beneath,

"And Mary Washington" — probably the first time she had written the new name. We all know the rest : how this book of England's learned Judge never left her side ; how she read it to her stepsons and her own sons ; how it was reverenced by George Washington ; how it is treasured to-day at our National Mecca, Mount Vernon.

CHAPTER XIII

AT the Wakefield house was born, Feb. 22, 1732, the eldest son of this superb specimen of young American womanhood. There is not the least doubt that he was in every respect "a fine boy" and worthy of the best name his mother could give him.

Monument at Wakefield marking the Birthplace of George Washington.

She did not follow the invariable custom of colonial Virginians. He was not called "John" or "Augustine" or "Joseph" after his father or grandfathers. He was given the first name of the "Trusty and well-beloved George Eskridge," — a fact which has hitherto escaped the notice of biographers, —

75

and no more significant tribute could have been
paid to faithful guardianship. According to Virginia customs, her only daughter would naturally
have been named for her mother and grandmother,
but here, again, affectionate gratitude for an elder
sister's love to a motherless girl decided the name.

The old house with the brooding wings burned
down soon after — the thrifty young housewife setting fire to it, not by "warming her posset," but in
her zealous burning up of the leaves and débris of
her garden. Her husband was absent at the time,
but she saved some furniture and Sir Matthew Hale
— and we read that the family "dined that day" in
apparent content "in the kitchen." It is certain
there was no great loss of pictures, hangings, bric-a-
brac, bibelots, and the ten thousand trifles with
which the housewife of a later day would have been
encumbered. In the old wills, after disposition
had been made of the bed, furniture, and "Rugg,"
there seems to have been little worth the dignity of a
bequest. The rug — always included with the bed
and its belongings — was the only carpet in general
use in 1730. Besides these, a chamber could boast
of little except a tall table surmounted by a small
mirror, before which one must stand in arranging
the head-dress only (for no part of the person
lower than the head could be reflected), and a
grandfather chair drawn near the ample fireplace.
Both table and chair were covered in white linen or

Virginia cotton cloth, — the toilet cover embroidered by the ladies of the family.   Similar embroidery or a bit of brocade adorned the pin-cushion, which was an important article, conserving as it did the scarce, imported English pins — clumsy, blunt affairs, with a bit of twisted wire for the head which was always coming off.

Furniture was hard, stiff, and unyielding, not one whit more luxurious in shape and cushioning than the furniture of the Greeks, and without the charm of grace or beauty.

Moreover, it was, unhappily, built to last forever. Backs might break on the hard chairs, but the chairs never!   Beds, however, were piled high with feathers, bolster, and pillows, and bed-curtains were *de rigueur*.   Dickens complained, among the horrors of his early days in America, that he actually had no bed-curtains.   Poor indeed must be the house that could not afford " fallens," *i.e. valence*, around the " tester " and the bottom of the bedstead.   This ancient appanage of a man of quality, as early as in Chaucer's time, was sometimes richly embroidered with pearls.

> " Now is Albano's marriage-bed new hung
>   With fresh rich curtaines !   Now are my Valence up
>   Imbost with orient pearles."

Losing her bed and valence, Mary Washington would have lost everything!   Her dining-table and

chairs were of the plainest. There were no sideboards in her day anywhere — no mahogany until
1747. As to her best room, her parlor, she probably was content with a harpsichord, a table, and
chairs. Great fires glorified every room in winter,
and in summer the gaping, black fireplace was filled
with cedar boughs and plumy asparagus.

The colonial Virginian lived much out of doors.
Driven in by a storm he would find shelter in his
" porch " and remain there until the storm was over.
His house was a good enough place to eat and sleep
in, but beauty in house-furnishing never inspired
ambition. *That* was fully gratified if he could welcome a guest to a good dinner, and interest him
afterwards in a fine horse or two and a pack of fox-
hounds.

That Augustine Washington's house should burn
down was perfectly consistent and natural. Everything in colonial Virginia was burned sooner or
later, — dwelling-houses, court-houses with their
records, tobacco-houses with their treasures of Ori-
noko or Sweet-scented. Nearer than the spring at
the foot of the hill was no water, and, except the
pail borne on the head of the negro, no extinguish-
ing appliance whatever. Churches did not burn
down for the very good reason that they were never
lighted or heated ; thus insuring that mortification
of the body so good for the health of the soul. In
winter little stoves of perforated tin, containing coals

or heated bricks, were borne up the aisles by foot-men and placed beneath the feet of the colonial dames. Otherwise the slippered feet would surely have frozen!

It has been a favorite fashion with historians to picture the Wakefield house as an humble four-roomed dwelling. Americans love to think that their great men were cradled in poverty, but exca-vations have been recently made which develop the foundations of a large residence. One is inclined to wonder when and by whom the pictures were made of the birthplace of Washington, which was destroyed by fire before there was a newspaper to print a description or picture in Virginia. That the sketch of any visitor or member of the family should have been preserved nearly two hundred years is impossible. Why should it have been made at all? Nobody living in the unpretending house had then interested the world. Every such picture is from the imagination, pure and simple, of Mr. Prud-homme, who made the first for a New York pub-lishing house. He was probably as accurate as he could be, but the house faced the road, not the river, and the latter flowed at the bottom of a hill in the rear of the mansion.

In the town of Quincy, in Massachusetts, the old home of John and Abigail Adams still stands, built in 1716, according to "a truthful brick found in the quaint old chimney." Pious hands have preserved

this house, restored it, filled it with just such furniture and draperies and garments as were preserved
by those who lived in the year 1750.   There the
house stands — an object lesson to all who care for
truth about the old colonial farm-houses.   Beauty,
genius, and patriotism dwelt in this house.   From
it the master went forth to the courts of France and
England and to become the President of the
United States; and on the little table in the front
room Abigail, the accomplished lady of beauty and
talent, wrote, "This little Cottage has more comfort and satisfaction for you than the courts of
Royalty."

The colonial houses of Virginia were larger, but
yet were modest dwellings.   They became more
ambitious in 1730, but Augustine Washington's
home had made a history of happiness and sorrow,
birth and death, before our Mary entered it.

The universal plan of the Virginia house of 1740
included four rooms, divided by a central "passage"
(never called a "hall") running from front to rear
and used as the summer sitting room of the family.
From this a short staircase ascended to dormer-
windowed rooms above.   As the family increased in
numbers one-story rooms and "sheds" were tacked
on wherever they were needed, without regard to
architectural effect, growing around a good chimney
and even enclosing a tree valued for its shade.   The
old house rambled about, as the land lay, so rooms

were often ascended by one or more steps. I fancy this was the case with the Wakefield house — Mary Washington, her fast-coming babies, and her very large family connection demanding more room than did Jane with her two little boys.

The iron bar across the front folding-door of a colonial Virginian house was never put up in summer except in a thunder-storm. The door stood open, and proud and happy were master, mistress, children, and servants when it was thronged with friendly neighbors or wandering tourists from abroad. They were welcome to come, and to stay! One instance of a visit lasted three years; another thirteen years! Not once was the contented guest ever reminded that he had worn out his welcome! One marvels that time was found for all this hospitality. It was simply the prime occupation and duty of life; and then fashions in garments were not always changing, and the housewife had no bric-a-brac to dust and keep in order.

The Wakefield house, be it large or small, well or poorly appointed, had the honor of being the birthplace of our adored Washington, and there, or at the nearest church, he was baptized. Mildred Gregory, Augustine Washington's sister, held him in her arms and renounced for him "the devil and all his works, the vain pomp and glory of the world" and all the "sinful desires of the flesh," promising that he would "obediently keep God's

G

holy will and commandments and walk in the same all the days of his life."

George Washington's Apron.

His baptismal robe is still in existence — or was, on the 22d of February, 1850, when Virginia's monument in his honor was unveiled in Richmond.

BEWDLEY.

The Masonic orator of the day, Mr. R. G. Scott, exhibited, with Washington's sash, apron, and gloves, the small silk mantle in which he was baptized, — a sacred relic still preserved, no doubt, by the Masonic Lodge of Richmond or Fredericksburg.

Mildred Gregory was then a widow. Her three beautiful daughters (destined to take and keep the hearts of a family of Thorntons) were present at the christening and full of interest in their Aunt Mary and her first boy. Uncle Augustine did not signify! He had two boys already. Were they not ordinary, commonplace fellows — their own everyday playmates?

The proud young mother hastened to present her fine boy to her own kindred, and when he was a month old she took him to visit her cousin, Major James Ball at "Bewdley," in Lancaster County. The house still stands that sheltered George Washington in infancy.

If any one wishes to know the probable appearance and extent of the house in which he was born, the two-hundred-year-old house at Bewdley will perhaps furnish the most accurate example. The steep, double-storied roof, the heavy, outside chimneys, the old kitchen in the yard, are all characteristics.

Probably the Wakefield house was never rebuilt. Fifty years ago a solitary chimney, and a small, engraved stone marked the birthplace of George

Washington ; the stone, the first monument ever dedicated to his memory, having been placed there by the pious hands of George Washington Parke Custis.   A better stone, protected by an iron railing, now marks the spot.

CHAPTER XIV

THE CHERRY TREE AND LITTLE HATCHET

WHETHER the immortal cherry tree grew at this home on the Potomac, or on the farm on the Rappahannock to which the family moved, we are not instructed by the imaginings of "Parson Weems," Washington Irving, and others; but the hatchet, if the cherry tree grew in Westmoreland, must have been a very "little hatchet," indeed, for Augustine Washington removed to a seat opposite Fredericksburg when George was a small boy.

And just here the writer begs leave to enter a plea for the life of this cherry tree! Irreverent biographers sneer at it as "a myth." We have sacrificed much to truth. We have wiped from our canvas all the "gay gallants" of Williamsburg, the love-lorn wandering curate, "Sister Susie," the life in England, the charming portrait! Really, we cannot give up our cherry tree! It is deeply rooted. It has flourished more than one hundred and fifty years. Its lessons and its fruits are the crowning glory of the board on the twenty-second day of February. We positively decline to bury the little hatchet or uproot the cherry tree!

" Parson Weems," who first told the story of
the little hatchet, was an Episcopal clergyman well
known to General Washington. His " Life of Washington " appeared several years before the great man's
death. " It was read by him and mildly com-

Pohick Church, Mount Vernon, Virginia.

mended," says one writer. Certainly it was never
contradicted. Parson Weems was an eccentric
character, but so kind and charitable that his
" oriental imagination " was indulgently condoned
by his neighbors. He claimed to have been rector
of Pohick church which was attended by General
Washington. Not even this was contradicted at

the time, and is given the benefit of a doubt by
the accurate old Bishop Meade himself.   He loved
to make people happy.   He would preach to the
poor negroes and then fiddle for them to dance.
He probably believed with George Herbert that : —

> " A verse may find him who a sermon flies
>   And turn delight into a sacrifice."

He was a charming historian.   If there were no
interesting facts to mitigate the dryness of a narrative, why then, of course, something must be invented !   So " his books have been read," says
Bishop Meade, " by more persons than those of
Marshall, Ramsey, Bancroft and Irving put together."   Evidently the good bishop at heart liked
him.   He thought him probably " too good for
banning, too bad for blessing," but he admired,
nevertheless, " the pathos and elegance of his writ-
ings."   Now, if General Washington did not
stamp the cherry-tree story as a falsehood, and
if Bishop Meade does not contradict it, we may
leave it, as they did, to flower and fruit for the
teaching of American children.

The title of the clergyman's book was, " The
Life of George Washington ; With Curious Anec-
dotes, Equally Honourable to Himself and Exem-
plary to His Young Countrymen.   By M. L.
Weems, Formerly Rector of Mount Vernon
Parish."   It may be interesting to relate the origi-

nal cherry-tree story as it appeared in this quaint little book. The author says it was communicated to him by " an aged lady who was a distant relative, and who, when a girl, spent much of her time in the family." How convenient the aged lady, the distant relative, has always been in tradition !

" When George was about six years old he was made the wealthy master of a hatchet; of which, like most little boys, he was immoderately fond, and was constantly going about chopping everything that came in his way. One day in the garden, where he often amused himself hacking his mother's pea sticks, he unluckily tried the edge of his hatchet on the body of a beautiful young English cherry tree, which he barked so terribly that I don't believe the tree ever got the better of it. The next morning the old gentleman, finding out what had befallen this tree, which, by the way, was a great favorite, came into the house, and with much warmth asked for the mischievous author, declaring at the same time that he would not have taken five guineas for the tree. Nobody could tell him anything about it. Presently George and his hatchet made their appearance. 'George,' said his father, 'do you know who killed that beautiful little cherry tree yonder in the garden ? ' This was a tough question and George staggered under it for a moment, but quickly recovered himself, and looking at his father with the sweet face of youth, brightened with the inexpressible charm of all-conquering truth, he bravely cried out, ' I can't tell a lie, Pa, you know I can't tell a lie.   I did cut it with my little hatchet.' ' Run to my arms, you dearest boy,' cried his father in transports ; ' run to my arms ; glad am I, George, that you killed my tree, for you have paid me for it a thousand fold.   Such an act of heroism in my son is worth more than a thousand trees, though blossomed with silver and their fruits of purest gold.'

" It was in this way," adds Parson Weems, tagging on his moral, " by interesting at once both his head and heart, that Mr. Washington conducted George with great ease and pleasure along the happy paths of pleasure."

CHAPTER XV

THE YOUNG WIDOW AND HER FAMILY

AUGUSTINE Washington selected a fine site on the banks of the Rappahannock opposite Fredericksburg, and near "Sting Ray Island," where the very fishes of the stream had resented the coming of Captain John Smith. The name of this home was Pine Grove. "The situation was commanding [1] and the garden and orchard in better cultivation than those they had left. The house was like that at Wakefield, broad and low with the same number of rooms upon the ground floor, one of them in the shed-like extension at the back; and the spacious attic was over the main building. It had its name from a noble body of trees near it, but was also known by the old neighbors as 'Ferry Farm.' There was no bridge over the Rappahannock and communication was had with the town by the neighboring ferry." "Those who wish to associate Washington," says another writer, "with the grandeurs of stately living in his youth, would find all their theories dispelled by a glimpse of the modest dwelling where he spent his boyhood years. But

---

[1] "Story of Mary Washington," Marion Harland.

nature was bountiful in its beauties in the lovely landscape that stretched before it.   In Overwharton parish, where it was situated, the family had many excellent neighbors, and there came forth from this little home a race of men whose fame could gather no splendor had the roofs which sheltered their childhood been fretted with gold and blazoned with diamonds.   The heroic principle in our people does not depend for perpetuity on family trees and ancestral dignities, still less on baronial mansions."

Augustine Washington died in 1743, at the age of forty-nine, at Pine Grove, leaving two sons of his first wife, and four sons and one daughter our Mary had borne to him, little Mildred having died in infancy.   We know then the history of those thirteen years, the birth of six children, the death of one, finally the widowhood and desolation of the mother.

At the time of his father's death, George Washington was only ten years of age.   He had been heard to say that he knew little of his father except the remembrance of his person and of his parental fondness.   To his mother's forming care he himself ascribed the origin of his fortune and his fame.

Mary Washington was not yet thirty-six, the age at which American women are supposed to attain their highest physical perfection.   Her husband had left a large estate under her management to be surrendered in portions as each child reached majority.

Their lands lay in different parts of the country, — Fairfax, Stafford, King George, and Westmoreland. She found herself a member of a large and influential society, which had grown rapidly in wealth, importance, and elegance of living since her girlhood and early married life in Westmoreland. Her stepson, Lawrence, married a few months after his father's death, and she was thus allied to the Fairfaxes of Belvoir — allied the more closely because of the devotion of Lawrence to her own son George. Lawrence, with his pretty Anne Fairfax, had gone to live on his inherited estate of "Hunting Creek," which he made haste to rechristen in honor of an English admiral, famous for having recently reduced the town and fortifications at Porto Bello; famous also for having reduced the English sailors' rum by mixing it with water. He was wont to pace his decks wrapped in a grogram cloak. The irate sailors called him, and the liquor he had spoiled, "Old Grog." The irreverent, fun-loving Virginians at once caught up the word, and henceforth all unsweetened drinks of brandy or rum and water were "grog," and all unstable partakers thereof "groggy."

Mary Washington, young, handsome, and the mistress of a fine estate, was closely connected by ties of kindred with nearly all of the families we shall describe hereafter. She could have elected for herself a gay life of social pleasure, and could have been a prominent figure in that life. The pictures we have of her were nearly all drawn by George Washington Parke Custis, whose authorities were the old neighbors who knew and remembered her well at a later day, and in their turn had gathered impressions from the companions of her early womanhood.

"She is the most excellent woman," says Goethe, "who when the husband dies, becomes as a father to the children."

This was the part which Mary Washington, in her thirty-sixth year, elected to perform for her five fatherless children, — George, Elizabeth, Samuel, John Augustine, and Charles. Pleasing stories are told of how the young widow would gather her brood around her, reading them lessons from some good book, and then repairing to her domestic tasks. She exacted the strictest obedience from her children. She directed alike their amusements and their education, manifesting in her administration of family affairs great good sense, resolution, and business capacity.

Mr. Custis often visited her in his childhood, and although too young to appreciate her, has gathered material for a noble tribute to the youthful matron, which is best given in his own words : —

"Bred in those domestic and independent habits which graced the Virginia matrons in the old days of Virginia," says Mr. Custis, "this lady, by the death of her husband, became involved in the cares of a young family, at a period when those cares seem more especially to claim the aid and control of the stronger sex. It was left for this eminent woman, by a method the most rare, by an education and discipline the most peculiar and imposing, to form in the youth-time of her son those great and essential qualities which gave lustre to the glories of his after-life. If the school savored the more of the Spartan than the Persian character, it was a fitter school to form a hero, destined to be the ornament of the age in which he flourished, and a standard of excellence for ages yet to come.

"The home of Mrs. Washington, of which she was always mistress, was a pattern of order. There the levity and indulgence common to youth were tempered by a deference and well-regulated restraint, which, while it neither suppressed nor condemned any rational enjoyment used in the springtime of life, prescribed those enjoyments within the bounds of moderation and propriety. Thus the chief was taught the duty of obedience, which prepared him to command. Still the mother held in reserve an authority which never departed from her, even when her son had become the most illustrious of men. It seemed to say, ' I am your mother, the being who gave you life, the guide who directed your steps when they needed a guardian : my maternal affection drew forth your love ; my authority constrained your spirit ; whatever may be your success or your renown, next to your God, your reverence is due to me.' Nor did the chief dissent from the truths ; but to the last moments of his venerable parent, yielded to her will the most dutiful and implicit obedience, and felt for her person and character the highest respect, and the most enthusiastic attachment.

"Such were the domestic influences under which the mind of Washington was formed ; and that he not only profited by, but fully appreciated, their excellence and the character of his mother, his behavior toward her at all times testified."

It was of the first importance that she should take care of the inheritance of her children. She must keep the land together and glean from it maintenance and education for her four boys and her daughter.

Virginians were taught to hold their land at any sacrifice. " Never part from your land, boys ! " said Frances Bland Randolph to John Randolph and his brother. " Keep your land and your land will keep you ! " And yet this plan did not insure competence. Land would keep the family, it is true, but afford small margin for education. Mary Washington realized this and wisely prepared her sons to earn their own living.

She sent George to an old-field school of Master Hobby, the sexton of the parish church, and then under his brother Lawrence's guidance to Master Williams. During one winter he rode on horseback ten miles to school every morning, returning home at night to prepare his tasks for the next day. At another time he ferried himself across the Rappahannock to his " day-school," — the old academy at Fredericksburg, afterwards attended by Madison and Monroe. He was never sent, like other gentlemen's sons, to a college or university at home or abroad. Conscious of this, he was probably the more diligent to overcome by his own industry all deficiencies of opportunity.

He proved an apt scholar, and soon possessed the rudiments of a practical education, which was expanded in later life by reading into scholarly accomplishments. But it was she, the mother, who first cast his mind and heart in the right mould.

This schooling, supplemented by his own study and experience, was his only foundation for that "thorough knowledge of the technical part of his profession, that skill in military combinations, and extraordinary gifts of military administration," which has won the unstinted praise of England's brilliant historian. But it was from the training of early habits by his watchful mother that he became, as Lecky adds, " punctual, methodical, and exact in the highest degree, managing the minute details so essential to the efficiency of an army." From his mother he inherited qualities which she herself possessed in an eminent degree, — " a rare form of courage which can endure long-continued suspense, bear the weight of great responsibility, and encounter, without shrinking, risks of misrepresentation and unpopularity."

She early proved herself to be a strong, self-reliant woman, with executive ability and a supreme power of awing and governing others. Her life was given to her children and to the care of a thriving plantation ; to sowing, and planting, and reaping ;

to the rearing of fine, blooded cattle.   Her children
had a plain, abundant, comfortable home, and led
healthy out-of-door lives.   She made Truth and
Honor her handmaidens, and in their defence ruled
her house with austerity, that "austerity in woman
so often the accompaniment of a rare power of loving, causing love to be piety, tenderness, religion,
devotion strong as death."

Surrounding her children with all the comforts of
a well-governed household, she loved them, taught
them, persuaded them.   If all failed, if Sir Matthew
Hale was in vain, and headlong youth yielded not
when the right was at issue, she did not disdain to
command another influence, pliant, pungent, prompt,
and most convincing, — a bundle of keen rods
gathered daily from the friendly peach tree!   This
lay always upon her historic table, or found place in
her capacious pockets when she went abroad.   It was
the presence of this ally, offensive and defensive,
which made harder the telling of the truth and enhanced the sublimity of virtue.

Tradition insists that she possessed a high spirit,
passionate, lofty, intense, and yet under the most
magnificent control; that her feelings were so deep
and strong she durst not show them, durst not even
recognize them, lest they should master her.   "A
lady," says Andrew Lang, "is a woman of high
breeding, high passion and high courage."   Mary
Washington was a lady!   She was tender, gracious,

H

and courteous to her neighbors in humble station, but to them as to others she made hard the way of the transgressor. Yet she knew how to excuse and forgive.

Tradition relates that when George was a fine, big boy of twelve, he was fired with ambition to conquer the spirit of an exceedingly valuable colt which had never permitted the near approach of man or boy. One morning early this feat was achieved. George with his brothers having chased the rebel into a corner of the pasture, he vaulted upon the back of the dangerous animal, which plunged forward so madly that a blood-vessel was ruptured, dying, like the Indian, with a broken heart sooner than submit.

There were five anxious faces around the breakfast table that morning! Presently the mother forced matters to an issue by asking: "Boys, have you seen my fine sorrel colt lately? Is he as big as his sire?"

Four pairs of eyes were turned to George, who unhesitatingly answered: "Madam, that horse possessed an ungovernable spirit which had to be conquered. I mounted him this morning, and he plunged violently and killed himself." The mother's face flushed for a moment, and then she said quietly: "That seems to be a pity! But I am proud and grateful for my brave, truthful son!"

This son was always a prince among boys, as he

was afterwards a king among men. Strong, brave, athletic, with a grand air, he became the prime favorite of his aristocratic brother Lawrence, whom he often visited at Mount Vernon, and who desired to place him in the service of the crown. In 1747, when George was in his fourteenth year, a midshipman's warrant was obtained for him by his brother Lawrence, and he embraced with boyish ardor the idea of going to sea.

While the matter was in doubt, however, his English uncle, Joseph Ball, wrote to his sister: " I understand that you have been advised to put your son George to sea. I think he had better be apprentice to a tinker; for a common sailor before the mast has by no means the liberty of a subject; for they will cut and slash him and use him like a negro, or rather like a dog. He must not be too hasty to be rich, but go on gently with patience as things will naturally go, without aiming to be a fine gentleman before his time," etc. The ship that was to carry him into the service of his most Gracious Majesty, George the Second, was riding at anchor in the Potomac with the young midshipman's luggage on board, but when the hour came for him to sail his mother braved the chance of Lawrence's displeasure, and forbade him to go!

The great trials of her life were henceforth to come through her crowning glory and pride. Her splendid boy, only fifteen years old, entered, as surveyor to Lord Fairfax, a life of hardship and peril, exposed to hourly danger from the Indians, and to the rigors of inclement winters. The eaglet had flown from the nest, never to return. Henceforth her straining eyes might strive to follow — they could never recall him.

Mrs. Washington persuades George not to go to Sea.

The lands to be surveyed lay in the wilderness beyond the Blue Ridge. There the boy of sixteen matched himself against fatigue, danger, and privations of every kind, and found himself equal to them all. He became familiar with the frontier people — the Indians and settlers. There he unconsciously trained himself for his future career.

Just at this time, when Fate sent him into the wilderness as preparation for the stern life ordained for him, the gentle god of Love was experimenting with his virgin heart. Among the yellow papers, which were tied in bundles and preserved in the deep drawers of the old secretary at " Pine Grove," behold the following acrostic, dated 1747, when the lad was fifteen : —

> " From your bright sparkling eyes I was undone.
> Rays you have — more transparent than ye Sun
> Amidst its Glory in ye Rising Day.
> None can you equal in y^r bright array.
> Constant in y^r Calm, Unspotted Mind —
> Equal toe all, will toe none Prove kind.
> Soe knowing, seldom One soe young you'll find."

Who was Frances ? Was she responsible for the " hurt of the heart uncurable," of which he wrote a few months later? Alas, we shall never know! Her Rays were all dimmed before Parson Weems appeared to take notes and print them.

At least we have this fragment of boyhood love, and can enrol her name as the *first* of his five sweethearts.

There is also a relic of his work for Lord Fairfax. Underneath the veranda at Capon Springs in West Virginia lies the trunk of one of the trees that the young surveyor marked with his hatchet. At least, it was there ten years ago!

CHAPTER XVI

BETTY WASHINGTON, AND WEDDINGS IN OLD VIRGINIA

IN 1746 young Fielding Lewis came up from his family seat at Marmion, bringing General Washington's aunt, Catharine Washington, as his wife, and made his home at Kenmore in Fredericksburg. They were married just one year before the birth of little John Lewis, and Mrs. Henry Lee (the mother of "Light-horse Harry") and Mrs. Mary Washington were godmothers. (Five times was this little fellow destined to be married, and if a problem of involved relationship be in order, he could furnish it. His first two wives were the granddaughters of his great-aunt, Mildred Gregory, and his *last* wife great-granddaughter of *her* last husband!) But to return to Fielding Lewis and Catharine (Washington) Lewis: the next year (1748) Frances was born, George Washington (aged sixteen), godfather — the next year (1749) the third child was born, and then the poor young mother, having borne a child every year, was gathered to her fathers and her children (January, 1750). All these events were of keen interest to the family at " Pine Grove." In all these functions nobody was more sympathetic than Betty Washington, now a handsome maiden of seventeen. She took her little orphan cousins to her heart, and in two months she comforted also the forlorn widower, and became his wife.

Kenmore House.

There is not the least doubt that she was given away by her brother George, now eighteen years of age, and that Samuel, John Augustine, and Charles, handsome, well-grown lads, were present at her wedding. Charles was twelve years old ; Samuel, sixteen. Elizabeth was "a fine young woman." Describing her, Mr. Custis used a favorite word of the day. Majesty being the highest of all places, "Majestic" was the highest of all praise. Colonial beauties were rarely described as "graceful," "winsome," "exquisite," "lovely"; they were "stately," "majestic," "queenly." They wore stately garments, — paduasoy, from *soie de Padua*, where the strong, lustrous silk so much worn by men and women was manufactured, or "tabby" velvet and silk, the rich watered oriental fabric manufactured in Attabya, a quarter in Bagdad. These were the grandest, the most sumptuous fabrics known. The wife of Goldsmith's Vicar was proud of her crimson paduasoy (the silk had given its name to a garment). Samuel Pepys could not afford the genuine article, but he boasted a "wastecoat of false tabby." Of course, a majestic woman wore these rich materials, "silk gowns wad stand on end" like the gowns of Dumbiedike's grandmother. Who could be majestic in clinging, willowy chiffon? Elizabeth Washington, known by the diminutive "Betty," undoubtedly enhanced her majesty by one or more of these gowns made in the fashion invented by the artist Watteau.

As to the rest, we know she was "mannerly." Stately gowns befitted stately manners. People "Sirred and Madamed" each other in true Johnsonian style, with many a low courtesy, veiling the bosom with outspread fan, and many a profound bow with hand on heart.   There was leisure for all this before the day of the trolley car and steam car, or even the stage and omnibus ; when in towns visits were made at ten in the morning, and the visitors sent hither and thither in sedan-chairs. Young ladies of her day were expert horsewomen. Those of us who saw the portrait of Betty Washington at the Centennial in New York can imagine her handsome figure on horseback.   " She was a most majestic woman," said Mr. Custis, adding that he perfectly well remembered her, " and was so strikingly like the Chief her brother, that it was a matter of frolic to throw a cloak around her, and then place a military cap on her head : and such was the perfect resemblance that had she appeared on her brother's steed, battalions would have presented arms, and senates risen to do homage to the chief." She adored her brother, and was proud to be so like him.   " Be good," she would say to her young friends in after life, " and I will be General Washington for you ! "   Tying her hair in a cue, and crowning it with a cocked hat, she would take a sword and masquerade to their infinite amusement.   She and her brother closely resembled their mother in form, carriage, and the contour of their faces.   They inherited her splendid health, her mental strength, and her sterling virtues — but *not* her seriousness which grew to be a settled sadness.   Betty Washington was as merry-hearted a maiden as might be found in that merry time.

If somebody had only thought of us at the great wedding at " Pine Grove," when stately Elizabeth Washington was given in marriage to the dignified, handsome Colonel Fielding Lewis, if somebody had only described it for our sakes, we should not be obliged to imagine it! The three great social occasions of domestic life were weddings, christenings, and funerals. These were solemnized, if not too distant, in churches. The bride on the large isolated estates made her vows in her own home, in her own home consecrated her offspring, from her own home was borne at last to her final resting-place. A wedding lasted many days, during which the house was filled with feasting kindred, coming from far and near. Social usage varied so little in colonial Virginia that we are quite safe in noting some features of Betty Washington's wedding. Of some things we may be sure, — first, there is not the least doubt that she chose her own husband.

One of the first fruits of the spirit of freedom was the American girl's determination henceforth to choose her husband. She made mistakes sometimes, poor child, but was probably silenced by the reflection that she had no one to blame but herself. She was much under the influence of French fashions, but had a prejudice against the French manner of conducting matrimonial alliances, while the French at once conceived a horror of the American departure. "We must marry our daughters as soon as possible," said a Frenchwoman to an easy-going American husband. "If we do not take care, she will be like your terrible Americans, and end by joining in the '*hount for housband*'!" dropping her French to quote the enormity in its own appropriate tongue.

Something of the old-time English customs in contracting parties remained in the formal correspondence of the prospective bridegroom's father with the father of the bride-elect, presumably before the young lady had been consulted. The former stated that his son proposed "paying his addresses," and he therefore announced the number of acres and slaves, and the kind of house he could give his son, and, without any expression of romance or sentiment, politely requested a similar statement from the "party of the second part." This party informs the other that his son has applied for "leave to make his addresses," and states what *he* can do.

Of course, it sometimes happened that the matter rested just here — the ideas on one side or the other being unsatisfactory. Then it was that Cupid had his opportunity! More than one lover has hidden in the close-screened, cedar summer-house, and more than one maiden has stolen in the gray dawn from her back door, disguised as her own maid, to join him in an early horseback ride to Gretna Green.

Moreover, more than one such maiden was "cut off with a shilling" by an injured father, and went through her life stoutly declaring herself the happiest woman in the world, albeit not as rich in worldly goods as her dutiful sisters!

Betty Washington's wedding-dress we must imagine. It was probably not unlike Martha Custis's wedding-gown a few years later. This was thus described by one of her guests: a white satin quilt, over which a heavy white silk, interwoven with threads of silver, was looped back with white satin ribbons, richly brocaded in a leaf pattern. Her bodice was of plain satin, and the brocade was fastened on the bust with a stiff butterfly bow of the ribbon. Delicate lace finished the low, square neck. There were close elbow-sleeves revealing a puff and frill of lace. Strings of pearls were woven in and out of her powdered hair. Her high-heeled slippers were of white satin, with brilliant buckles. Just this dress, in style if not material, was certainly worn by Betty.

Her mother being a devout churchwoman, she was probably married at church. And if Colonel Lewis chose to follow the fashion of the day, he was brave indeed in a white satin vest, a suit of fine cloth lined with crimson satin, fine lace at wrist and throat, and diamond (or was it paste?) buckles at knee and shoe top.

Our forefathers and foremothers wore good clothes in 1750!

We may be sure that none of the orthodox wedding customs and ceremonies were omitted by Mary Washington at her daughter's marriage. There were certainly bride's favors, wedding-cake, ring, and thimble, and, alas! the slipper and rice. The bride was duly provided, for her bridal costume, with

"Something old, and something new,
Something borrowed and something blue."

The "old" was oftenest an heirloom of lace; the "borrowed," an orange blossom or two which had been worn by other brides; the "blue," a tiny knot of ribbon on the garter.

These ceremonies were full of significance, and in observing them, the bride linked herself in the long chain which stretches back to the early stages of the world. The wedding-ring, and the choice of the third finger as being connected with the heart, are mentioned in old Egyptian literature. The blue ribbon, whether worn as a badge, or order, or at bridals, comes down from the ancient Israelites, who were bidden to put upon the borders of their fringed garments a "ribband of blue" — blue, the color of purity, loyalty, and fidelity. Bridesmaids were a relic of the ten witnesses of old Roman weddings. Bride's cake and rice, of the aristocratic Roman *confarreatio*. The Spanish custom of wearing fragments cut from the bride's ribbons, first introduced into England when Charles II brought home his Katharine of Portugal to be England's queen, survived in the enormous white satin rosettes (bride's favors) worn by the groomsmen, and survives to-day in the boutonnières of the bride's flowers. The old and the new symbolize her past and future — not divided, but united. The "something borrowed" signifies a pledge to be redeemed. Nothing is without significance, which accounts for the fact that all these old-time customs continue from century to century, and are so jealously observed to-day.

One of the eighteenth-century customs, has, however, been lost in the hurry and rush of our own time. The "infair," the faring into the house of the bridegroom's parents, was quite as lengthy and important a function as the wedding. This great housewarming entertainment to celebrate the reception into the bridegroom's family was an ancient English custom, religiously observed in Virginia until the middle of the nineteenth century.

The quantity of wedding-cake made in the Virginia kitchens was simply astounding! It was packed in baskets and sent all over the country to be eaten by the elders and "dreamed on" by the maidens.

What would Betty Washington and Colonel Lewis have thought of a wedding reception of an hour, and then a flitting to parts unknown, leaving the world to comfort itself with a small square of

cake in a pasteboard box? Such behavior would
have been little less than " flat burglary," defrauding
people of their just dues.

Colonel Fielding Lewis, although young, was
already a merchant of high standing and wealth, a

The Hall at Kenmore, showing the Clock which belonged to Mary
Washington.

vestryman, magistrate, and burgess. Kenmore, near
Fredericksburg, was built for him, that his wife
might be near her mother. The mansion, still kept
in excellent repair, was reckoned a fine one at the
time. It was built of brick and skilfully decorated
by Italian artists. Betty wrote to her brother
George that their " invention had given out," and

invited him to contribute something. It is said that he designed the decoration illustrating Æsop's fable of the Crow and the Fox, which adorns the drawing-room mantel to-day. It is in stucco, and besides illustrating the fable of the wheedling fox who seeks to gain booty by a smooth tongue, another fable — the wolf accusing the lamb of fouling the water — is represented. The story told at Kenmore is of Italians captured in the French army as prisoners of war, who were led by choice or necessity to remain in America, where they plied their trade of decorators.

Nine months after Betty Washington's wedding, on St. Valentine's day, 1751, another Fielding Lewis was born, and George Washington, just nineteen, was godfather, his mother, godmother. Having done her duty to her husband, Betty in 1752 named her next son John Augustine, and her brother Charles, fourteen years old, was godfather. A third boy was born, 1755, and Charles was again godfather. In 1757 she named a fourth son George Washington, and, in 1759, Mary Washington was sponsor for a little Mary Lewis, and Samuel Washington, godfather. Then, in 1760, a year after his own marriage, we find George Washington and his mother sponsors for a Charles Lewis. Samuel and Betty were born respectively in 1763 and 1765, and in April, Lawrence, the lucky, — destined to win " the nation's pride," lovely Nellie

NELLIE CUSTIS.

Custis, the adopted daughter of General Washington. Then Robert and Howell were born. Again, and yet again, was the traditional gown of black brocade brought forth by the proud grandmother, as Betty claimed her mother and brothers for the important and solemn office of sponsors for her splendid boys — boys that followed their illustrious uncle all through the war of the Revolution, and to whom he was ever the most faithful of friends and guardians.

CHAPTER XVII

DEFEAT IN WAR: SUCCESS IN LOVE

WASHINGTON was only nineteen when Virginia appointed him one of her adjutants-general. He was "Major Washington" now when he visited his mother at "Ferry Farm," *visiting* her only, because the failing health of his brother Lawrence demanded his care. His mother gladly surrendered him for the comfort of this, her devoted stepson, to whom she had always deferred as the head of the family. He went with this brother to try the warmer climate of Barbados, bringing him back ere long to die at Mount Vernon.

In 1752 Governor Dinwiddie had information about the French. They had commenced establishing forts in the territory on the banks of the Ohio claimed by Virginia. The governor needed some trusty messenger to send to the Chevalier Le Gardeur de St. Pierre, the French commander, to claim that country as belonging to his Britannic Majesty, "and," says Burnaby in his "Travels in Virginia," 1759, "Mr. Washington, a young gentleman of fortune just arrived at age, offered his service on this important occasion. The distance was

more than four hundred miles; two hundred of
which lay through a trackless wilderness, inhabited

George Washington as Major.

by cruel and merciless savages, and the season was
uncommonly severe. Notwithstanding these dis-

couraging circumstances, Mr. Washington, attended by one servant only, set out upon this dangerous enterprise; travelled from Winchester on foot, carrying his provisions on his back, executed his commission; and after incredible hardships, and many providential escapes, returned safe to Williamsburg."

He was in love with action and adventure! He had said to Governor Dinwiddie, "For my own part I can answer that I have a constitution hardy enough to encounter and undergo the most severe trials, and I flatter myself resolution to face what any man dares, — as I shall prove when it comes to the test."

France refused to surrender her claim. The courtly old chevalier abated nothing of his punctilious courtesy when he received the youthful ambassador — doubtless bronzed and travel-soiled. He said, very politely, "I am here by the orders of my General, and I entreat you, Sir, not to doubt one moment but that I am determined to conform myself to them with all exactness and resolution that can be expected from the best officer." So, in 1754, Dinwiddie sent the young major back again — this time at the head of some soldiers. In writing to the other governors for men, he says, "I sent a Gent: to the Place by whom I know the Truth." A large force of the French appearing, "The Gent" (Major Washington) was compelled to surrender and, politely bowed out by the old chevalier, permitted to return to Virginia.

This bitter experience had not the effect of discouraging Washington. It only made him long for another chance, with another result. He had written lightly to Governor Dinwiddie, as if he were arranging a tournament, "We have prepared a charming field for an encounter." It is even said that he added, "I know no music so pleasing as the whistling of Bullets." This was repeated to George the Second. "He would not say so," said the soldier-king, "had he been used to many!" Years afterward Washington was reminded of this incident, and he thoughtfully replied, "If I said so, it was when I was young!"

His mother, foreseeing the tendency of all these events, had bitterly opposed his last disastrous expedition. He was a man of independent fortune, and had declined remuneration for his services as he afterwards declined all pay during the years he served in the war of the Revolution. She wished him to live on his own estate as became a country gentleman. Her opposition to his fighting against the English crown was not one whit greater than her opposition to his fighting for the crown. The word "loyal" was a shifting quantity in her time, meaning one thing to-day and another to-morrow! The peril and the hardship were the same in either case.

The first time that he set forth for the frontier his mother almost succumbed. "Oh, this fighting and killing!" she exclaimed, as she entreated him not to go. When convinced that she must sacrifice herself to his duty to his country she became calm. Laying her hand upon his shoulder, she said, solemnly: "God is our sure trust. To Him I commend you." She thus unconsciously provided him with an unanswerable argument for another time. When General Braddock offered him a place on his staff she drove to Mount Vernon to entreat him not to accept the honor. "The God to whom you commended me, Madam, when

General Braddock.

I set out on a more perilous errand, defended me from all harm, and I trust he will do so now," was the reply.

When the news of Braddock's defeat and the dreadful slaughter of his army reached Fredericksburg the anxious mother was forced to wait twelve days before she could be assured of her son's safety. In a long, calm letter he tells her of all his dangers and his own wonderful escape, with four bullets through his coat and two horses shot under him. He tells her, too, of an illness which confined him in a wagon for more than ten days ; how he was not half recovered at the time of the fight ; how he must halt and rest often upon his way home to Mount Vernon, which he could scarce hope to leave before September ; how he was, " Honored Madam," her most dutiful son.

She drove to Mount Vernon to meet him, and warmly entreated him to leave the service forever, urging the loss of health and fortune should he remain in it.   He had no answer then, but after she was at home she received his final word.

" Honored Madam : If it is in my power to avoid going to Ohio again, I shall ; but if the command is pressed upon me by the general voice of the country, and offered upon such terms as cannot be objected against, it would reflect dishonor upon me to refuse it, and that, I am sure must, or ought, to give you greater uneasiness than my going in an honorable command.   Upon no other terms will I accept it."

The code of manners which ruled Virginia in the eighteenth century forbade familiarity or the discussion of personalities.   Washington's letters to " Honored Madam," as he always addressed his mother, relate mainly to important public events. Nothing is told of his ups and downs, which he seems to have had in common with ordinary mortals ; of the envious slanderers who strove to undermine him in the estimation of the governor ; still less of his repulse by the father of Miss Mary Cary who curtly refused him his daughter's hand for the reason that she was "accustomed to riding in her own carriage" and therefore above Virginia's young major. Bishop Meade says that this lady, afterwards the wife of Edward Ambler, was in the throng of applauding citizens when Washington passed through Williamsburg at the head of the American army. He recognized her, and gallantly waved his sword to her, whereupon she fainted. Nobody knows that she ever wished to accept Major Washington. Had he waited until 1753, her prudent father could have urged no objection to the handsome young lover. In 1752 Lawrence Washington died, directing in his will, in case of the demise of his wife without issue, the estate at Mount Vernon should become the property of his brother George. Within the year the young major received this legacy.

He seems to have been — for him — very faithful to an early dream. If he cherished, as he doubtless did, hopes of winning his "Lowland Beauty," she now put an end to his dream by marrying, in 1753, Henry Lee of Stafford; and it may be remembered that it was in this year, and only one month before her marriage, that he sought the governor's permission to bear a message of remonstrance to the Chevalier de St. Pierre. Like a wise soldier he knew when he was defeated and retreated accordingly.

He did not marry until 1759; but it is not to be

MOUNT VERNON.

supposed that his heart was breaking all these six
years for Miss Mary Cary or for the lovely Lucy
Grymes, the " Lowland Beauty." Do we not know
of Miss Mary Philipse, whose father's manor-house
may still be seen on the Hudson? Washington
Irving thinks she could not have refused him, that
he " rode away " before he had " made sufficient
approaches in his siege of the lady's heart to warrant
a summons of surrender."

However this may be, all went well with the
parties to the drama in Virginia. The " Lowland
Beauty " was the wife of one of Virginia's honored
sons, and the mother of " Light-horse Harry " Lee.
Perfect happiness was only waiting a few necessary
preliminary events to crown the young soldier's life
with joy, in the person of the fascinating widow,
Martha Custis, who, according to old Bishop Meade
(who relished an innocent bit of gossip), resembled
Miss Cary as one twin-sister does another. He
resigned his position as commander-in-chief of the
Virginia forces, and reasonably looked forward to a
life of calm content in his home on the right bank
of the Potomac.

Washington had always, his rebuffs to the contrary nevertheless, flattered himself that he could
" get along " with the ladies. There was never a
moment that some " Faire Mayde " was not well to
the fore, and it is known that he offered his heart
and sword to three, — Mary Cary, Lucy Grymes,

and Mary Philipse. With the latter he acknowledged that he had been too hasty. He thought
things might have resulted differently if he had
"waited until ye ladye was in ye mood."

Two years later he repeated his imprudence. Mr.
Tony Weller had not then been born, and there
was nobody to bid him beware. He paid an afternoon call, fell in love in an hour, and stayed on and
on until he was accepted. In a few days we find
this entry in his cash account, "One Engagement
Ring, £2, 16s., od."

Mrs. Custis felt a little shy in announcing so
hasty an engagement to her friends, "My dear, the
truth is my estate is getting in a bad way, and I
need a man to look after it."

The estate was large. She owned fifteen thousand acres of land, many city lots, two hundred negroes, and money besides,—a great fortune in colonial
days. He had just returned from a brilliant campaign ; was gallant, young, and handsome ; was just
elected member of the House of Burgesses ; and
was master of a fair domain on the right bank of the
Potomac, and so "ye ladye" found herself "in ye
mood."

When he married the beautiful, rich widow, his
mother was exultant. Now he was safe ! All the
killing and fighting were over and done with. He
was to live near her at Mount Vernon. She was
now fifty-two years old, and was going to enjoy

a serene and happy old age at last. She wrote her brother, " I have had a great deal of trouble about George, but it is all over now."

She had a long season of busy home life, happy when she might be in the happiness of her children. Her warrior son was behaving at last as became a dignified country gentleman. But Fate was only preparing him for future greatness. In the administration of his large estate, and in the county and provincial business, he was acquiring the rare skill in reading and managing

St. Peter's Church, in which George Washington was married.

men, for which he became so remarkable. But of this he was totally unconscious. He had small ambitions. He was proposing himself to the electors of Frederick County, having " an easy and creditable Poll," cheerfully paying his self-imposed assessment of thirty-nine pounds and ten shillings besides "cyder and dinner" for his constituency. He was attending the Annapolis races; going down to Williamsburg for the assembly with Mrs. Washington and Miss Custis; loading his wagons to provision his family and Colonel Bassett's on a visit "to try the waters of the warm springs," much exercised lest

Williamsburg.

Jack Custis were premature in winning the affections of Miss Calvert (for Jack was only eighteen, had been "fickle, and might wound the young lady"); nay, he was beating his sword into a ploughshare, his spear into a pruning-hook, planting May-Duke cherries and guelder-roses, and lamenting "Rust in the wheat and Drought in the Corn crop." More-

MARTHA CUSTIS.

over, he was writing letters to England, giving orders for all sorts of foreign elegancies, for his own wear and that of Madam Washington and her children. Let us copy a summer order sent to London in 1761.

For his use the great man wants " a superfine velvet suit with garters for the breeches ; pumps, riding-gloves, worked ruffles at twenty shillings a pair; housings of fine cloth edged with embroidery, plain clothes with gold or silver buttons ! "   For Mrs. Washington he orders "a salmon-colored tabby velvet with satin flowers ; ruffles of Brussels lace or point, to cost twenty pounds ; fine silk hose, white and black satin shoes ; six pairs of mitts ; six pairs of best kid gloves ; one dozen most fashionable pocket-hand-kerchiefs ; one dozen knots and breast-knots ; real miniken (very small) pins and hairpins ; a puckered petticoat ; six pounds of perfumed powder ; handsome breast flowers (*bouquets de corsage*) and some sugar candy."

I have not room for Master Custis's outfit at eight years old, nor that of Master Custis's liveried servant of fourteen years old, but I cannot omit the delightful order for little " Miss Custis, six years old," namely, "A coat of fashionable silk, with bib apron, ruffles and lace tucker ; four fashionable dresses of long lawn ; fine cambric frocks ; a satin capuchin hat and neckatees ; satin shoes and white kid gloves ; silver shoe-buckles ; sleeve-buttons, aigrettes ; six thousand pins, large and short and minikin ; a fashionable dressed doll to cost a guinea ; gingerbread, toys, sugar images and comfits ; a Bible and prayer-book ; and one very good spinet, to be made by Mr. Plinius, harpsichord maker, in South Audley street, Grosvenor square, with a good assortment of spare strings." Not too much, assuredly, for the little beauty, but not Spartan simplicity nevertheless.

Six years later, it is recorded that " the Fair Sex, laying aside the fashionable ornaments of England, exulted, with patriotic pride, in appearing dressed with the produce of their own looms."

CHAPTER XVIII

THE origin of the names of the estates in the Northern Neck can easily be traced. A few were Indian: "Quantico," "Occoquan," "Monacan," "Chappawamsic," "Chotank." Many were English : "Stratford," "Wakefield," "Marl-boro," "Chatham," "Gunston Hall," "Mount Vernon," "Ravensworth," "Blenheim," "Mar-mion,"—the latter, of course, not named for Scott's fictitious hero (seeing that Sir Walter had not yet been born), but, doubtless, by some emigrant of Lincolnshire descent, in honor of Sir Robert de Marmion, who "came over with the Conqueror," and was granted a manor in Lincolnshire. "Chantilly" was thus named by Richard Henry Lee, after the beautiful chateau and grounds of the Prince Condé, near Paris.

Mount Vernon was not too distant to be in Mary Washington's neighborhood. She had but to cross the neck of land to the Potomac, and a pleasant sail would bring her to the little wharf at Mount Vernon —just where we, patriotic pilgrims, so often now land to render our pious homage to the sacred homestead.

Within visiting distance of Mount Vernon was the "Chippawamsic" plantation, at which lived another widow, rich, young, and beautiful, — Ann Mason, the mother of George Mason, the patriot and statesman, author of the Virginia Bill of Rights (the first complete formula of the civil and political rights of man ever promulgated) and author of the Virginia constitution of 1776, the first written constitution of government ever adopted by a free people.

No one who studies the peculiar characteristics of Virginians of this period can doubt that both these young widows were sought by many suitors. The zeal with which men made haste to fill the places of departed wives was something marvellous! Samuel Washington was married five times, and one instance is recorded of a colonial dame in the best society who had six husbands! The early marriage of widows was the more desirable because of the outlying estates which required management. Martha Custis gave this as excuse for her prompt acceptance of Colonel Washington. But Ann Mason and Mary Washington never married again. Each possessed great executive ability, as well as unusual personal and intellectual gifts. Each elected to devote those gifts to her children. Each was the mother of a great patriot. And it is altogether probable that each one was the devoted friend of the other, and that the close friendship between the two Georges was inherited from their parents. Another Ann Mason left letters and records which give us a hint of the belongings of a Virginia house-wife of her day. She enumerates among her daugh-ter's expenses prices paid for shoes with wooden heels, hoop petticoats, and linen. George Mason of "Gunston Hall," the greatest, perhaps, of all the statesmen in an age of great statesmen, remembered the furniture of his mother's bedroom. In it was a large chest of drawers — a veritable high-boy ![1] Three long drawers at the bottom contained chil-dren's garments, in which the children might rum-mage. Above these and the whole length of the case were the gown-drawer, the cap-drawer, the shirt-drawer, the jacket-drawer ; above these a series of drawers always kept locked, containing gauzes, laces, and jewels of value — ten or twelve drawers in all! Then there were two large, deep closets, one on each side of the recess afforded by a spacious stack of chimneys, one for household linen, the other "the mistress's closet," which last contained a well-remembered article, a small green horsewhip, so often successfully applied to unruly children that they dubbed it " the green Doctor." George Mason remembered other things in con-nection with this splendid woman. She gathered her children around her knees morning and evening

[1] "Life of George Mason," by Kate Mason Rowland.

K

to "say their prayers." She was a lovely woman, true to her friends, pious to her Maker, humane, prudent, tender, charming : —

> " Free from her sex's smallest faults,
> And fair as womankind can be."

Both these Ann Masons — the wife of the statesman and her mother-in-law — lived and died near Mary Washington's home before 1773. Both were brilliant women, with personal charm and amiable dispositions.

Near the Masons, at "Marlboro," lived John Mercer, a lawyer of fine talents and attainments, and owner of one of the best private libraries in the colony. Virginia bibliophiles still boast in their collections some of his books containing his heraldic book-plate. There was a George in his family, one year younger than George Washington. Their homes were just sixteen miles apart — a mere nothing of distance, as neighborhoods were reckoned in those days — and both in Overwharton parish. The Mercers were lifelong friends of Mary Washington. General Mercer died in her grandson's arms. Judge James Mercer wrote her will.

Then, not far from John Mercer's, lived one of the largest landed proprietors in Stafford, a prominent burgess and planter of his day, Raleigh Travers — of Sir Walter Raleigh's family — and married to

Mary Washington's half-sister, Hannah Ball. They were founders of one of Virginia's great families, "distinguished in later years for breeding, learning, and eloquence." Two miles from "Marlboro" lived one of their daughters, Sarah, married to Colonel Peter Daniel, of the "Crow's Nest."

Then came "Boscobel," the residence of Thomas Fitzhugh, the father of a family of interesting young people. Susannah Fitzhugh still smiles to us from these pages in her rich robe over a pearl embroidered skirt and bodice of white satin, with a necklace of pearls festooned over her fair bodice.

She was just three years younger than her beautiful cousin Elizabeth, who lived at "Belle-Air" (her mother was Alice Thornton), and whose portrait, painted by Hesselius, presents the fashionable dress of her day. The gown is of fawn color, square corsage, elbow sleeves with lace ruffles (like Susannah's), the hair carried smoothly back from her brows, piled high over a cushion, and dressed with strings of pearls.

The Fitzhughs did not quite "own the earth" in their region, — Lord Fairfax did that, — but they owned a goodly portion of it: "Eagle's Nest" in Stafford County, "Somerset" in King George, "Boscobel," "Belle-Air," and "Chatham" in Stafford, "Ravensworth" in Fairfax. At the latter General Custis Lee, an honored descendant of this honored race, sits to-day under the trees his fathers planted.

In the Fitzhugh pedigree the Thorntons crop up again and again. One may sink a mine in any Virginia genealogy and he will encounter the names of all these neighbors of Mary Washington.

At "Salvington" lived the Seldens, to whom Mary Washington was bound by ties of close kindred. Mary Ball, daughter of Major James Ball of "Bewdley," in whose arms Mary Washington had hastened to place her son George when one month old, had married John Selden. For his second wife he chose her first cousin, Sarah Ball, whose tombstone may be seen to-day in the woods a mile from Lancaster court-house.

Later, a Samuel Selden married Mary Thompson Mason (she of the wooden-heeled shoes and hoop petticoat), famous for her beauty, as was her mother before her. The second wife of Samuel Selden was Ann Mercer. Many of the descendants of these women inherited great beauty. Even a little drop of their blood suffices to endow many a Virginia woman of to-day.

At "Cleve," on the Rappahannock, lived Charles Carter, and thither "Light-horse Harry" Lee went for his sweet wife Anne. Charles Carter's father, Robert, the mighty man of Lancaster, — "King" Carter, — died in the year George Washington was born. He had built Christ Church, where Mary Washington was possibly baptized, for her father lived near the church. King Carter owned

300,000 acres of land, 1000 slaves, £10,000 in money. The cattle on a thousand hills were his.

"Light-horse Harry" Lee.

He left many children, all of whom he was able to enrich, and many of whom distinguished themselves in things better than riches.

"Cleve," with its octagon front, is still in good

preservation, and is a fine example of the early Georgian manor-house, having been built early in the eighteenth century. An excellent portrait of its builder, Charles Carter, looks down to-day upon his descendants who still own and live in the mansion.

Governor Spotswood.

Four miles below Mary Washington's home was "New-post," the ancestral home of John Spots-wood, a son of Governor Spotswood. His two sons, Alexander and John, were destined to serve in the Revolutionary War, one as a general, the other a captain, and to mingle the Spotswood with the Washington blood by marriage with one of Mary Washington's grand-daughters. They came honestly by their dash and spirit through the Spotswoods.

It appears that the *Virginia Gazette* of 1737 lent its columns to an article against Governor Spotswood, written by a Colonel Edwin Conway, upbraiding the governor for delaying to turn over

the arms intended for Brunswick County. The
article was entitled, "A Hint to discover a few of
Colonel Spotswood's Proceedings." A few days
after its appearance the *Gazette* printed the following : —

"An Hint for a Hint

"Mr. Parks,

"I have learnt in my Book, so far as to be able to read
plain English, when printed in your Papers, and finding
in one of them my Papa's name often mentioned by a
scolding man called Edwin Conway, I asked my Papa
whether he did not design to answer him. But he replied : 'No child, this is a better Contest for you that are
a school Boy, for it will not become me to answer every
Fool in his Folly, as the lesson you learned the other day
of the Lion and the Ass may teach you.' This Hint
being given me, I copied out the said Lesson and now
send you the same for my answer to Mr. Conway's Hint
from

"Sir, your Humble Servant
"John Spotswood."

"Feb. 10.   A Lion and an Ass

"An Ass was so hardy once as to fall a mopping and
Braying at a Lion. The Lion began at first to show his
Teeth, and to stomach the Affront. But upon second
Thoughts, Well, says he, Jeer on and be an Ass still, take
notice only by the way that it is the Baseness of your
Character that has saved your Carcass."

There was a famous beauty in the family of
Spotswood who shared, as we shall see hereafter,

in the spirit of her race. This was Kate! She wore, on her high days and holidays, fawn-colored satin, looped over a blue satin petticoat, square bodice and elbow sleeves and ruffles; and her feet, which were extremely small and beautifully formed, were shod in blue satin shoes, with silver buckles. Age did not wither this haughty beauty. Her granddaughter remembered her as she combed a wealth of silver hair, a servant the while holding before her a mirror.

Not far from " Pine Grove " was " Traveller's Rest," the most beautiful and significant of all the ambitious names of stately mansions on the Rappahannock. " It should be called," said Byrd Willis, " Saint's Rest — for only *they* ever go there ! " " Traveller's Rest " was part of the " 200 acres of land on ye freshes of Rappahannock River " bequeathed to Mary Ball by her father, Joseph Ball. The family of Gray long lived at " Traveller's Rest," and thither in after years, Atcheson Gray brought his child-wife Catherine Willis, the great-granddaughter of Mary Washington.

These are only a few of the country gentry among whom Mary Washington lived, and to whom she was related. Time would fail to describe them all — Colonel Thomas Ludwell Lee of " Berry Hill "; " Bellevue " and its occupants; the Brent family at Richland, in Stafford County; " Belle Plaine," the residence of the Waugh family.

All these places were in a space of eight or ten square miles, and from generation to generation the sons looked upon the daughters of their neighbor cousins, and found them fair, until the families were knit together in every conceivable degree of kinship.

In the town of Fredericksburg Mary Washington had near relatives and friends. Roger Gregory, the merry-hearted, had married a woman as merry-hearted as himself, — Mildred Washington, George Washington's aunt and godmother. Foremost at the races, and first on all occasions of mirth, was Roger Gregory. It has been said that Augustine Washington was optimistic in his temperament, and, like his sister Mildred, conspicuous for cheer-fulness — also that from him Betty Washington and her brothers inherited their love for gay, social life — that Mary Washington was always serious, and in her later years almost tragic. She surely had enough, poor lady, to make her so.

Roger Gregory had died just before George Washington was born, and his widow married Henry Willis of " Willis's Hill," Fredericksburg, afterwards " Marye's Heights," where the fierce battle of the Civil War was fought. Mildred's three charming Gregory girls were prominent figures as they trod the streets of old Fredericks-burg — the streets named after the Royal Princes — clad in their long cloaks and gypsy bonnets tied under their chins.   They were soon absorbed by a trio of Thorntons, and their mother Mildred left alone with her one son, Lewis Willis.   " Old Henry Willis," his father, had married three times, boasting that he " had courted his wives as maids and married them as widows."   He was a rich old fellow with a long pedigree and gorgeous coat of arms on his coach panels.   Mildred Gregory had wept so bitterly when the death of his first wife was announced to her, that a friend expressed surprise.   " Mildred Willis," she explained, "was my namesake and cousin, and I grieve to lose her.   But that is not the worst of it! I am perfectly sure old Henry Willis will soon be coming down to see me — and I don't know what in the world I can do with him!"   Would it be sinister to suggest that the lady was already won? It appears she knew her man.   Had he not been her suitor in her girlhood?   His grandson says, " In one little month he sat himself at her door and commenced a regular siege : and in less than two months after his wife's death he married her."

If the shade of this wife was permitted to be a troubled witness of her recent husband's marriage, she could not complain.   She had been herself the widow, Brown, only for one month before she had married Henry Willis.

This Colonel Henry Willis was known as " The Founder of Fredericksburg."   Colonel William Byrd visited him immediately after his marriage with Mildred Gregory, and spoke of him as " the top man of the place." Mildred Washington (Widow Gregory) had one son by her marriage with Henry Willis. She named him for her first husband — her first love — Lewis. He was two years younger than his cousin, George Washington. The boys attended the same school, and were companions and playmates. Lewis Willis often spoke of George Washington's industry and assiduity at school as very remarkable. While his brother Samuel, Lewis Willis, and " the other boys at play-time were at bandy or other games, George was behind a door cyphering. But one day he astonished the school by romping with one of the large girls — a thing so unusual that it excited no little comment among the other lads."

Through the Willis family Mary Washington's descendants became allied to the Bonapartes. The second child of Byrd C. Willis (son of Lewis Willis) was Catherine. Her mother was the daughter of George Lewis, Betty Washington's son. Thus Mary Washington was ancestress of Catherine Willis, who at thirteen years of age married, and at fourteen was a widow, having lost also her child. She accompanied her parents to Pensacola, where she married Achille Murat, ex-prince of Naples and nephew of Napoleon Bonaparte. She was very beautiful — this child — twice married and a mother before she was fifteen.

The Murat and Bonaparte families at first opposed
the marriage, but all opposition vanished when they
learned that she was nearly related to General
Washington.

It is said that she was well received abroad: "In
London she stood up for her country and fought

Prince Murat.

its battles in all companies." She was once accompanied by John Randolph of Roanoke and other
distinguished personages on a visit to the London
art galleries. In one of these the portraits of
Washington and Napoleon hung side by side, and
Randolph (who was always dramatic), pointing to

the pictures, said, "Before us we have Napoleon and Washington, one the founder of a mighty Empire, the other of a great Republic."   Then turning to Catherine with extended hand, "Behold!" he exclaimed, "in the Princess Murat the niece of both — a distinction which she alone can claim."

As the century neared its highest noon Fredericksburg became the home of one and another of the men destined to earn immortal fame in the Revolution.   James Monroe lived there, whose hand, long since mingled with the dust, has yet the power to stay the advance of nations.   Men of wealth secured the pleasant society all around by a residence in the town.   As many as ten coaches were wont to drive out in company when the summer exodus to the springs set in.

There was a famous tailor in Fredericksburg who made the lace-trimmed garments for these gentry, — William Paul, a Scotchman.   Hanging in his shop, was a handsome portrait of "my sailor brother John" as he explained to his customers.   Anon the tailor died, and John came over to administer upon his estate.   He found friends — Colonel Willy Jones and Doctor Brooke — who aided him materially in the first years of his life in Fredericksburg.   In gratitude to the former he assumed the name of "Jones," and the latter he made surgeon of the *Bon Homme Richard* — for this was John Paul Jones the great, the brilliant naval officer of our Revolution.   Congress gave him a commission and a ship, *The Alfred*, and on board that ship he hoisted before Philadelphia, with his own hands, the flag of freedom — the first time it was displayed.   He claimed and received the first salute the flag of the infant Republic received from a foreign power.   He served through the war, and at his death was the senior officer of the United States navy.

CHAPTER XIX

SOCIAL CHARACTERISTICS, MANNERS, AND CUSTOMS

THE essential principles in the drama of human life are ever the same although its outward aspect changes with changing circumstances. But in some ages events develop more rapidly than in others under the urgency of peculiar conditions.

In colonial Virginia the story was told over and over again before the final fall of the curtain. Scenes shifted with wonderful rapidity. The curtain, in mimic drama, is usually rung down at the church door after the early or late wooing and marriage; but in Virginia in the eighteenth century this was only the first in a drama of five or more acts. The early death of the first bride left a vacancy speedily filled by new and successive unions with new associations and combinations. Five times was not an unusual number for men to remarry.

This meant five wooings, five weddings, five "infairs," many births (varying in number from one to twenty-six), five funerals, — all to be included in thirty adult years more or less. Then, too, there were five tombstones to be erected and as many epitaphs to be composed — no two of which to be alike.   One wife (usually the first) almost exhausts the vocabulary of adoring affection, another's piety is emphasized, another "lived peacably with her neighbors"; each one was "as a wife dutiful." "Obedient" was a word dear to the colonial husband.

We have no authority for supposing that the officiating clergyman at a funeral was ever actually retained for the ensuing nuptials of the bereaved. Initial steps in that direction were never taken in Virginia until a husband or wife was well under the sod.   Divorce being unknown, unthinkable indeed, husbands and wives were united in bonds indisso- luble, until death did them part.   But when it did — why, then there was no reasonable cause for delay. It was not at all unusual for the new husband to offer for probate the will of his predecessor.   Man in those days did not believe he was made to mourn, at least not for maid or matron, nor that charming women were created to weep in widow's weeds beyond the decent period of two months.   The little hands were firmly drawn from their pressure upon the tearful eyes, tucked comfortably under a new, strong arm, and the widow's little baronry stitched to a new sleeve.   There were exceptions, of course, but not many.   When one of the husbands of Mary Wash- ington's charming nieces (the Gregory girls) lay mortally ill, he looked up with anguish at the lovely young wife bending over him, and implored her to keep herself for him. She readily promised never again to marry, and kept her promise. Another, left a widow, essayed to follow the sublime example of her sister. One of the masterful Thorntons sued for twenty years, but won at last. The statute of limitations in Cupid's court held for twenty years only in colonial Virginia.

Writers of the period explain these multiplied marriages by the necessity of a protector for every woman owning land to be cultivated by negro slaves and indented servants, and on the other hand the woful state of a large family of young children left motherless at the mercy of those servants. The new master and the new mother became a necessity.

It sometimes happened that the newly contracting parties had already many children from the three or four previous marriages. These must now be brought under one sheltering roof. The little army must be restrained by strict government; hence the necessity for the stern parental discipline of colonial times. " It is gratifying, my dear," said an amiable patriarch, " to find that *your* children, *my* children, and *our* children can live so peacefully together," nobody knowing so well as the patriarch and the children at what price the peace had been purchased.

Thus it can be easily seen how maddening an

L

enterprise is the attempt to trace Virginia relationships, and how we so often lose a woman and give her over as dead to find her resurrected under a new name. We once lost Mary Washington's sister Hannah (Ball) Travers. She turned up at last as Mrs. Pearson! To sort and label and classify Virginia cousins means nervous prostration. In the families of Thornton, Carter, and their kin, it means more! Madness lies that way!

The spinster of uncertain age, known irreverently as an "old maid," was a rare individual in colonial Virginia. We all know Colonel Byrd's "Miss Thekky, mourning her virginity." We really cannot name another.

When a good man, addressing himself to the compilation of family records for his children, was constrained to admit that one was unmarried, he made haste to declare that she "lived single by her own choice." Colonel Byrd Willis says of his daughter Mary, "She is unmarried — but by her own choice. It will be a fine fellow who can tempt her to leave her home. She has not seen him yet!" He goes on to enumerate her social triumphs. There had. been a "Bouquet Ball," of which a certain commodore was made king. He chose Miss Mary Willis, and bestowed upon her the bouquet. A foot-note informs us that she isn't single any more! She has married the commodore!

Stern as was the parental discipline of the time,
the spirit of the young men, who were accounted

Colonel Byrd.

grown and marriageable at nineteen, was in no
wise broken or quenched.   Many of them ran away

from their masters at the schools in England and Scotland, and their fathers' agents had much ado to find and capture them again. The sons of John Spotswood were lost in England for many months, but were back home again in time to be gallant officers in the Revolution. And even the conservative blood of the Washingtons was not strong enough to temper that of the Willises, for Mildred Washington's grandson "Jack" Willis ran away from school and joined a party to explore the wilderness of Kentucky. They were attacked by Indians, and were scattered; Jack escaped in a canoe, and was the *first white man* to descend the Ohio and Mississippi rivers. His father had sewed some doubloons in his jacket, but he gave them to a man in New Orleans to purchase clothing and food, and never again beheld his agent or the doubloons or their equivalent. He worked his way in a sailing vessel to New York, and *walked* from New York to his home in Virginia, arriving, like the Spotswood boys, just in time to enter the army with his father and serve to its close. He was a son of Lewis Willis, Washington's schoolmate.

About 1740 the importation of horses of the English racing stock commenced, also the breeding of horses for racing. Between 1740 and 1775 are recorded the names of fifty imported horses and thirty mares of note : Aristotle, Babraham, Bolton,

Childers, Dabster, Dottrell, Dimple, Fearnaught, Jolly Roger, Juniper, Justice, Merry Tom, Sober John, Vampire, Whittington, Janus, Sterling, Valiant, etc. Owners of these horses among Mary Washington's neighbors were Roger Gregory, Colonel John Mercer of " Marlboro," Mr. Spotswood, William Fitzhugh of " Chatham," all the Thorntons, and *later* Colonel George Washington of Mount Vernon, who was a steward of the Alexandria Jockey Club and ran his own horses there and at Annapolis ! There was a fine race-course at Fredericksburg, and purses were won from ten to a hundred pounds. This, the prime amusement in spring, summer, and autumn, was varied (alas!) by cock-fights, wrestling-matches, and rough games, in which the common people, as in England, participated, while the gentry looked on and awarded prizes. But in the long winter evenings, neighbors gathered for Christmas and other house-parties, indulged in the gentle art of story-telling. Later, old Fredericksburg boasted a notable, peerless raconteur, John Minor, but his stories were built upon Virginia's legends ; his home, " Hazel Hill," was the rendezvous of all the neighbors, young and old, in quest of sympathy or counsel, or advice in the honorable settlement of quarrels, or for a season of genial companionship. Around the fireside at " Hazel Hill " the children would gather for their own story-telling hour " between daylight and dark," and there the immortal

" B'rer Rabbit " appears, but not for the first time, in the annals of colonial history, and her Serene Highness, the " Tar Baby," held her nightly court.

Around the winter fireside in the old colonial houses, the children, and their seniors as well, learned the folk-lore of their native colony, for, young as was the new country, Virginia had already her legends : the mystic light on the lake in the Dismal Swamp, where the lost lovers paddled their ghostly canoe ; the footprints of the Great Spirit on the rocks near Richmond ; the story of Maiden's Adventure on the James River ; the story of the Haunted House — the untenanted mansion at Church Hill — untenanted for eight decades because the unhappy spirit of a maiden tapped with her fan on the doors where wedded couples slept, invoking curses upon love that had failed her ; of sweet Evelyn Byrd, who rested not under her monument at Westover, but glided among the roses, wringing her hands in hopeless grief for the loss of a mortal's love ; and of the legend of the wonderful curative spring just discovered in Greenbrier County (learned from an old Indian of the tribe of the Shawnees) — how one of the great braves had once been missed from the council-fires and been found in a valley, weak and supine, binding the brows of an Indian maid with ferns and flowers : how two arrows had sped by order of the Great Spirit, one destined for the man, one for the maid ; how the recreant warrior had

WESTOVER.

been slain by the one, but the other arrow had buried itself in the earth and when withdrawn a great, white sulphur spring had gushed forth; how the maiden was doomed to wander as long as the stream flowed, and not until it ceased could her spirit be reunited to that of her lover in the happy hunting-grounds; also how the body of the slain warrior was laid towards the setting sun, and the form of the sleeping giant might be clearly discerned despite the trees that grew over it.

And one more Indian legend is so charming that we may be forgiven for perpetuating it on these pages, remembering that these are genuine Indian legends which have never before been printed. This last was the story of the Mocking-bird. How once long ago there were no wars or fightings, or tomahawks or scalpings among the Indians. They were at perfect peace under the smile of the Great Spirit. And in this beautiful time those who watched at night could hear a strange, sweet song sweeping over the hills and filling the valleys, now swelling, now dying away to come again. This was the music of all things; moon, stars, tides, and winds, moving in harmony. But at last Okee, the Evil One, stirred the heart of the red man against his brother, and the nations arrayed themselves in battle. From that moment the song was heard no more. The Great Spirit, Kiwassa, knew that his children bemoaned their loss, and he promised them the song should not be lost forever. It would be found some day by some brave — loftier, better, stronger, than all others.

It fell at last that a chieftain loved the daughter of a hostile chief. Both were captured and burned at the stake. Both died bravely, each comforting the other. After death the chief, because he had been so brave, was given the body of a bird, and sent in quest of the Lost Song. When he found it, and only then, could all be forgiven and the spirits of the lovers be reunited in the happy hunting-grounds. Since then the bird has travelled north, south, east, west, and wherever it goes it learns the songs of all creatures, learns and repeats them. But the hatchet is not yet buried; the Lost Song not yet found. Imagination can supply few pictures fairer than this: firelight playing on the attentive faces of old cavaliers and matrons, young men and lovely maidens, the centre their accomplished host, " the pink of a chivalric gentleman," gallant, cultured, refined, and at his knees, in his arms, and seated on his shoulders, happy children, not only those of his house-party, but others among his neighbors who dropped in especially for the children's hour.

It is evident that Mary Washington's social life must have been an active one. At the weddings and the christenings of her large circle of neighbors and kindred she was certainly present. But I doubt whether she ever attended the races, " Fish Frys, and Barbecues," of which her neighbors were so fond. Not that she ventured to express disapproval of things with which the clergy found no fault, but she was a strict economist of time, never wasting it on trifles. She kept her own accounts, managed her own plantation, and kept a stern watch on the over-seers of her son's estates.

To do this, and at the same time fill her place in her large circle of friends, whose relations with her warranted their coming at will for long visits, re-quired all the method and management of which she was capable.

Besides the householders, with their sons and daughters, who regularly exchanged visits with each other at least once or twice annually, Virginia had also her class of impecunious bachelors, whose prac-tice was to visit from house to house, taking in all the well-to-do families. Until the Revolution — when they had something else to do — they repre-sented the class of hangers-on to wealth, known to-day as " the little brothers of the rich," — very nice, adaptable, agreeable gentlemen, whom every-body likes, and to whom society is willing to give much, exacting little in return. In pre-Revolution-ary Virginia, however, they could and did give some-thing. They gathered the news from house to house, brought letters and the northern papers; were intelligent couriers, in short, who kept the planter well-advised of all political rumors. They possessed certain social accomplishments, could carve fairy baskets out of cherry stones, cut profile portraits to be laid on a black background, and make and mend pens to perfection. " When I was in Stafford County a month ago," says the tutor at "Nomini Hall," "I met[1] Captain John Lee, a Gentleman who seems to copy the character of Addison's Will Wimble. He was then just sallying out on his Winter's Visits, and has got now so far as here; he stays, as I am told, about eight or ten weeks in the yeare at his own House, the remaining part he lives with his Waiting Man on his Friends." Captain Lee, by the way, is further recorded as "a *distant* cousin of the Lees of Westmoreland."

In making these visits to the large country houses, young people would naturally confer together and manage to meet those they knew best and liked best. Thus it would sometimes happen (and who so willing as the hosts?) that a large house-party would assemble unheralded, and the house be filled with a merry company. "The usual retinue," says General Maury, "at my wife's home was fifteen or more well-trained servants when the house was full of company; and as many as thirty or more of the family and friends daily dined there together for weeks and months at a time." This was at Cleveland, near Fredericksburg; and hospitality quite as generous ruled all the homes in Mary Washington's neighborhood.

[1] Fithian's Diary.

It sometimes happened that the capacity of the elastic house reached its limit. On one such rare occasion a belated Presbyterian minister alighted at the front gate and walked in with his baggage, — a pair of well-worn saddle-bags.   He was warmly welcomed, of course, but the lady of the manor was in despair. Where could he sleep?   Every corner was full. One couldn't ask a clergyman to spend the night on a settee in the passageway, nor lie upon a " pallet " of quilts on the parlor floor. The children heard the troubled consultation as to ways and means with their " Mammy," and were full of sympathy for the homeless, unsheltered guest. The situation was still serious when the household was summoned to family prayers. The clergyman — a gaunt specimen with a beaklike nose and mournful voice — launched into the one hundred and second Psalm, pouring out, as the pitying children thought, his own soul in its homeless desolation. When he reached the words, " I am like a pelican in the wilderness : I am like an owl in the desert : I am as a sparrow alone upon the housetop," the exultant voice of the youngest little girl rang out, " *Mamma, he can roost on the tester !* "   One cannot wonder at this advice from a hospitable man who had been literally " eaten out of house and home," " I advise my son to keep out of other people's houses, and keep other people out of his own."

One can hardly imagine the care and labor involved in so much entertaining. Nobody ever passed a house without calling; nobody ever left it without refreshment for man and beast. Horses and servants attended every visitor.

Think of the quantity of food to be provided! And yet, a housewife's *batterie de cuisine* was of the simplest. The kitchen fireplace held the iron pot

The Kitchen of Mount Vernon.

for boiling the indispensable and much-respected gammon of bacon (Virginia ham), and there were lidded ovens, large and small, standing high on four feet, that coals might burn brightly beneath them. There was a "skillet," with its ever ascending incense from frying chickens and batter-cakes, — a long-handled utensil with no feet at all, but resting upon the portable, triangular "trevet," — which, being light, could be thrust into the very heart of the fire or drawn out on the fire-proof dirt floor. There was a " hoe," known as a cooking utensil only in Virginia, slanting before the coals for the thin hoe-cake of Indian meal. In front stood the glory and pride of the kitchen, — the spit, like two tall andirons with deeply serrated sides, on which iron rods holding flesh and fowl could rest and be turned to roast equally. An ample pan beneath caught the basting-butter and juices of the meat. This spit held an exposed position, and has been known to be robbed now and then by some unmannerly hound, or wandering Caleb Balderstone, unable to resist such temptations. What would the modern queen of the kitchen think of " a situation " involving such trials, — her own wood often to be brought by herself, her breakfast, including four or five kinds of bread (waffles, biscuit thick and thin, batter-cakes, loaf bread), her poultry to be killed and plucked by herself, her coffee to be roasted, fish scaled and cleaned, meats cut from a carcass and trimmed, to say nothing of cakes, puddings, and pies?   And all this to be done for a perennial house-party, with its footmen and maids !

True, the negro cook of colonial times had many " kitchen-maids," — her own children. But even with these her achievements were almost supernatural. With her half-dozen utensils she served a dinner that deserved — and *has* — immortality !

" Old Phyllis," the cook at " Blenheim," " Mammy Lucy " at Cleveland, and many others have a high place in an old Virginian's Hall of Fame, — his heart !

There was no lack of service in Mary Washington's day. The negro was docile, affectionate, and quick to learn, at least these were the characteristics of those employed in households. But even as late as in Mary Ball's girlhood the negroes had no language intelligible to their employers. One of the Lancaster clergymen, Mr. Bell, writes that his congregation includes many " negroes, who cannot understand my language nor I theirs." There is something infinitely pathetic in this picture of the homeless savage in a strange land. The African, finding himself not understood, made haste to acquire the language spoken to him. His intimate association was with the indented white men who labored with him, and he then and there created a language distinctively known as his own, to which he still clings and which contains, I believe, no word that can be traced to African origin — at least this is true of the Virginia negro's dialect. " It appears that the indented servants from whom he learned must have come from Warwickshire. The negro dialect can be found in Shakespeare;[1] for instance, ' trash,' afterwards accentuated by 'po' white trash.' ' What trash is Rome, what rubbish, what offal,' says

[1] " Warwickshire Dialect," by Mr. Appleton Morgan.

Cassius. 'They are trash,' says Iago, etc. 'Ter-
rify,' for 'aggravate' or 'destroy,' is Warwickshire; also 'his'n,' 'her'n,' for 'his' and 'hers';
'howsomdever,' for 'however' (*Venus and Adonis*);
'gawm,' for 'soiling hands or face'; 'yarbs,' for
'herbs'; 'make,' for 'kindle' (make the fire);
'like,' for 'likely' (I was like to fall); 'peart,' for
'lively'; 'traipsing,' for 'walking idly about';
'ooman,' for 'woman'; 'sallit,' for 'green stuff';
'yourn,' for "yours.' These and many more negro
words are taken from Warwickshire dialect, and
are to be found in Shakespeare." Upon this root
the negro grafted, without regard to its meaning,
any and every high-sounding word which he
happened to hear, and which seemed to him
magnificent. The meaning signified so little that
he never deemed it necessary to ask it. The result
was, to say the least, picturesque.

The church being his earliest school, he was soon
impressed by the names of certain of the Hebrew
Patriarchs, and the first names with which he endowed his children were Aaron, Moses, Abraham,
Isaac, Jacob, and Isaiah. Why he scorned Jeremiah,
Nahum, Ezekiel, and others, is best known to himself. Later, he caught from the companionship of
the schoolboys the names of the heroes of antiquity,
giving decided preference to Pompey and Cæsar.
There was a Josephus in a Fredericksburg family,
differentiated in the next generation by *Jim*sephus.

Later still his fancy was caught by the shining lights of the Revolution. A goodly crop followed of Washingtons, Jeffersons, and Randolphs. There was even a Rochambeau, unhappily corrupted into " Rushingbow."

While the queen of the nursery was an ebony incarnation of faithful love, tenderness, and patience, she never surrendered her sceptre until her charges were actually married. She never condescended to be taught by those to whom she had herself been teacher. " Mammy," exclaimed a little Fredericks-burg maiden of ten, " what do you think? I have found an ungrammatical error in the Bible." " Kill him, honey! Kill him quick! He'll eat up the pretty book-mark!" exclaimed the old nurse, too proud to acknowledge her ignorance of the beautiful new word.

" Po' white trash" was a term applied to all householders who could not afford style in living and equipage, notably to those (and they were few) who owned no slaves. There was no squalor, no pauperism in Virginia in 1740 and later. Even indented servants prospered sufficiently after a few years to send to England for servants of their own. The convict labor of Virginia was mainly employed in the fields and on the boats; and it is recorded that these convicts were short-lived, the hot sun giving them always a " seasoning fever" which often proved fatal. Of course political convicts were of a different class, and when found to have been educated were employed as teachers.

Entirely distinct from these was the class who were entitled to write " Gent " after their names, as their English fathers had done.   " The term ' Gentleman,' " says Mr. Lyon Tyler, " assumed a very general meaning in the succeeding century, but its signification at this time was perhaps what Sir Edward Coke ascribed to it, *qui gerit arma,* one who bears arms."

It was not the custom then as now to address a man without some prefix.   He was " Squire " if he was a member of the King's Council ; " Gent " if he bore arms, otherwise " Mr. " ; and if in humble life, "Goodman." Women of any degree were " Mistress " — Mistress Evelyn Byrd, Mistress Mary Stagg ; in middle class, " Dame " ; of gentle blood, " Madam " and " Lady." In the *Virginia Gazette* " Lady Washington's " comings and goings are duly chronicled. Even now the Virginian loves to endow his fellows with a title, and risks " Colonel " in default of a better.

The Virginia woman, at the period of which we write, felt keenly the disadvantage of her remoteness from that centre of knowledge and courtly usage, the mother country.   Men who were educated abroad began to accumulate books for ambitious libraries, but these books were largely in the Latin tongue, and the Virginia girl had not the courage of Queen

M

Elizabeth, and did not address herself to the study of the Classics that she might "match the men." She had good, strong sense, and the faculty known as mother-wit, but I am afraid I must confess she had small learning. What time had she — married at fifteen — to read or study? As to Mary Washington, her library, for ought we know to the contrary, seems to have begun and ended with "Sir Matthew Hale." In 1736 Mr. Parks published his *Virginia Gazette* for fifteen shillings a year. Beverley & Stith had published their "Histories," and William Byrd his "Pamphlets." These she may have read; but it is extremely doubtful whether she read the poems and other society doings, records of races and other happenings, which appeared weekly in the *Gazette*, or approved of seeing the names, qualities, and fortunes of the ladies recorded as frankly as at the present day.

These ladies were the daughters, sisters, and wives of men of brilliant genius and attainments. They could hardly sustain such relations with such men without becoming themselves superior women. Dr. Archibald Alexander knew Mrs. Meredith, the sister of Patrick Henry. "She was, in my judgment, as eloquent as her brother; nor have I ever met with a lady who equalled her in powers of conversation."

Something then was said of a woman besides what she wore, whither she went, and whom she entertained at dinner and tea.   There were women of whom the *Gazette* kindly said they possessed "amiable sweetness of disposition, joined with the finest intellectual attainments," but I am constrained to challenge the latter if it presupposes the attainments to have been literary.   How could it be otherwise when Thomas Jefferson prescribed that his daughter's time should be divided between dancing, music, and French? And when Charles Carter, of "Cleve," after ordering that his sons, John and Landon, then in England, should master languages, mathematics, philosophy, dancing, fencing, law, adds, "And whereas the extravagance of the present age, and the flattering hopes of great Fortunes may be a temptation to run into unnecessary Expenses of Living, it is my positive Will and desire that my Daughters may be maintained with great frugality, and *taught to dance*."

The young women whose brothers had tutors at home were fortunate.   They learned to "read and write and cypher."   Then there were men

> "Glad to turn itinerant
> to stroll and teach from town to town"

and from plantation to plantation.   From these the young ladies had their music and dancing lessons. Their letters are very stilted and polite, — poor dears, — but "intellectual attainments" do not appear in many of them.   They usually end with

laying upon a bad pen all the blame for all shortcomings. " Excuse bad spelling and writing, for
I have ane ill pen," said Jeanie Deans. The
colonial ladies made no apology for their pho-
netic spelling. Was not that all right? If
" hir " did not spell " her," pray, what did it
spell? " Bin " was surely more reasonable than
" been " ; " tha " than " they." There were " Dix-
onaries " in the closets along with the Latin books,
but they were troublesome, and not always to be
trusted. Dr. Johnson — if we can imagine him as
such — was in their day a sweet babe in long
clothes!

When the slow-sailing ships arrived from England
one might have the fashions of six months ago.

English cousins sometimes came over, and very
nervous were the Virginia girls lest the Western
ménage should be found to be behind the times.
Among old letters a certain Miss Ambler appears
to have been dreadfully aggrieved by the criticisms
of some English cousins. " Everything we eat,
drink or wear seems to be wrong — the rooms are
too cold or too hot; the wood is not laid *straight*
on the Andirons : — and even poor Aunt Dilsey does
not escape censure, — dear Aunt Dilsey whom we
all so love! Actually, Aunt Dilsey came to me in
tears, and said she had been ordered to pull down
her bandanna so that none of her wool would show
in the back of her poor neck, and to draw cotton

gloves over her hands for they were 'so black and
nasty'!"

Many of the Virginians, at that early day, were
advocates of negro emancipation. James Monroe,

James Monroe.

who lived in Fredericksburg, was the great friend
of emancipation. Monrovia, the capital of Liberia,
was named in his honor. It was a citizen of Fredericksburg, in 1782, who introduced into the body,

which had replaced the House of Burgesses, the first resolution for the emancipation of negroes and for the prohibition of the slave trade ever offered in America. General John Minor, of "Hazel Hill," was the author and advocate of this measure. In 1792 the first-published utterance against slavery in this country appeared in a tract entitled, " Slavery Inconsistent with Justice and Good Policy," by the Rev. David Rice. When estates were settled large numbers of negroes were manumitted by common consent and sent to Liberia.

We have reason to believe that house servants were treated with the affectionate consideration they deserved. Mr. Custis distinctly declares that this was true of Mary Washington, — that she was always kind to her servants, and considerate of their comfort. The man or woman who treated servants with severity was outlawed from the friendship and respect of his neighbors, many of whom at a later day freed their slaves and left them land to live upon.

CHAPTER XX

"THE search-lights of history have unfolded to us nothing of interest touching Mrs. Washington from the time of the French and Indian War until the awakening of the great Revolution. Fortunate is the woman, said the Greek of old, of whom neither good nor ill is spoken. And, curtained away from the world, the matron lived under the great Taskmaster's eye, in the bosom of that home, by whose fruit ye shall know her. Many years had rolled by since she settled at 'Pine Grove,' with her first-born son. And, while she lived in retirement and in silence, how had great events rushed forward; how had the child become the father to the man? Grave tasks were his while yet a boy. Step by step he ascended the ladder of honor and usefulness. A surveyer for Lord Fairfax at sixteen, crossing the Blue Ridge on horseback, traversing the wilderness to the bounds of civilization, getting six pistoles, or something more than $7 a day, for his efficient service, while in leisure hours he read under the guidance of Lord Fairfax, the history of England, the 'Spectator,' and other books of that high order; appointed public surveyor a little later, and then adjutant-general of Virginia troops at nineteen; managing a great plantation and training the Militia of the State; at twenty-one penetrating the Northwest as a negotiator for Governor Dinwiddie, and fighting the French; aide-de-camp to Braddock,

a little later, in his ill-starred expedition, suffering defeat;
with the victor at Fort Duquesne, where Pittsburg now
stands, at twenty-six; member of the Virginia House of
Burgesses at twenty-seven; ever onward, ever upward,
until, as the great Revolution broke out, we find him
journeying to Philadelphia as a delegate to the Continental
Congress, and presently appearing on the field of Boston as
commander-in-chief of the Continental army!"

Thus spoke, out of the fulness of his heart, Senator Daniel at the unveiling of the Mary Washington monument, but the truth is that these years
were marked by many cares and anxieties.   Five
times had Samuel Washington married: Jane
Champe, Mildred Thornton, Lucy. Chapman,
Anne Steptoe, the widow Perrin.   This list sounds
like a chapter from the reign of Henry the Eighth.
Tradition says he was separated from some of his
wives otherwise than by death.   It is certain he was
unfortunate in money matters, having many children and finding it "hard to get along."   His
brother was always helping him.   His children
were much at Mount Vernon, especially Steptoe
Washington and Harriett Washington, whose names
appear frequently upon the general's expense book.
He enters various items against Harriett, — earrings and necklace and many garments.   He be-
moans, "She was not brung up right!   She has no
disposition, and takes no care of her clothes, which
are dabbed about in every corner and the best are

always in use." "In God's name," he writes to his brother, John Augustine, "how has Samuel managed to get himself so enormously in debt?" He found places from time to time for many of Samuel's sons, and was never other than good to all.

John Augustine Washington, the general's favorite brother, married Hannah Bushrod, and settled in Westmoreland. Charles, the youngest, married Mildred Thornton of the Fall-Hill Thorntons, near Fredericksburg. His home was in Charlestown, Jefferson County. Of him the world has known but little. In the presence of a planet of the first magnitude the little stars are not observed.

Mary Washington was now alone at "Pine Grove." Her windows commanded Fredericksburg and the wharf, where the ships from England unloaded rich stuffs to tempt the Virginian, loading again with sweet-scented tobacco for the old country that had so quickly learned to love the luxury from the new. It is doubtful whether she ever bought from these vessels. She certainly never sold to them. In 1760 she writes to her brother Joseph in England, excusing herself for having sent him no letters, "As I don't ship tobacco the Captains never call on me, soe that I never know when tha come and when tha goe." She was a busy woman, minding her own affairs and utterly free from idle curiosity. Her life was full of interest and occupation. The conscientious housewife of her day was burdened with many cares. The large plantation must support itself. Nearer than Annapolis and Williamsburg were no shops or stores from which supplies could be drawn. The large number of servants living on the plantations demanded great quantities of food and clothing, and the farm work many utensils,— all of which were manufactured on the farm itself. The diary of a New Jersey tutor gives us interesting accounts of life in the Westmoreland neighborhood, where lived the Lees, Carters, Washingtons, Tayloes, and other large landholders. Higher up, near Mount Vernon, dwelt George Mason of "Gunston Hall," and his son, John, is our eye-witness-chronicler of the plantation life near Mary Washington.

"It was the practice of gentlemen of landed and slave estates so to organize them as to have resources within themselves. Thus my father had among his slaves carpenters, coopers, sawyers, blacksmiths, tanners, curriers, shoemakers, spinners, weavers and knitters, and even a distiller. His woods furnished timber and plank for the carpenters and coopers, and charcoal for the blacksmith; his cattle, killed for their own consumption, supplied skins for the tanners, curriers and shoemakers; his sheep gave wool, his fields flax and cotton for the weavers; and his orchards fruit for the distiller. His carpenters and sawyers built and kept in repair all the dwelling houses, barns, stables, ploughs, harrows, gates, &c., on his plantation. His coopers made the hogsheads for tobacco and the casks to hold the liquors. The tanners and curriers tanned the skins for leather and

the shoemakers made them into shoes for the negroes.
A Professed shoemaker was hired for three or four months
in the year to come and make up the shoes for the family.
The blacksmiths did all the iron work required on the
plantation. The spinners and knitters made all the clothes
and stockings used by the negroes, and some of finer texture
worn by the ladies and children of the family. The
distiller made apple, peach and persimmon brandy. A
white man, a weaver of fine stuffs, was employed to superintend the black weavers." [1]

To carry on these operations — to cure and preserve meats, fruits, and medicinal herbs, make
vinegar and cordials, and to prepare constantly for
a great deal of company, coming incessantly to stay
at the house — required unceasing attention and
strict method.

This is a large pattern which was repeated on a
smaller scale by Mary Washington. Method became, with her, almost a mania. Her neighbors
set their watches by the ringing of her bells. She
was never the fraction of a minute too late at church.
She was punctiliously exact in her observance of all
appointments and prompt to the minute in meeting
those appointments. By the well-regulated clock
in her entry — the clock which is now preserved at
" Kenmore" — all the movements of her household
were regulated. Her illustrious son had also such
a clock. He graciously allowed, at dinner, five
minutes for the possible variation of timepieces.

[1] "Life of George Mason," by Kate Mason Rowland.

After they expired he would wait for no one. If an apologizing guest arrived after the dinner was advanced, his excuses were met with the simple announcement, " Sir, I have a cook who never asks whether the company has come, but whether the hour has come." His mother had taught him the value of time. Her teaching followed him through life, and was obeyed after he was President of the United States. The chaplain of Congress records that the hour of noon having been fixed for hearing the President's message, he usually crossed the threshold exactly as the clock was striking twelve.

A contemporary observer relates that " Mrs. Washington never failed to receive visitors with a smiling, cordial welcome," but adds quaintly that " they were never asked twice to stay, and she always speeded the parting guest by affording every facility in her power." Perfectly sincere herself, she believed them sincere when they declared themselves unable to remain.

She was said to possess a dignity of manner that was at first somewhat repellent to a stranger, but always commanded thorough respect from her friends and acquaintances. Her voice was sweet, almost musical in its cadences, yet firm and decided, and she was always cheerful in spirit. " In her person she was of the middle size, and finely formed ; her features pleasing, yet strongly marked."

Her young friends and grandchildren often

visited her. Lawrence Washington, her son's cousin and playmate, said : " I was more afraid of her than of my own parents — and even when time had whitened my locks I could not behold that majestic woman without feelings it is impossible to describe. She awed me in the midst of kindness."

" She was," said one of her family, " conspicuous for an awe-inspiring manner, so characteristic in the Father of our Country. All who knew her will remember the dignified matron as she appeared when the presiding genius of her well-ordered home, commanding and being obeyed," never speaking ill of any one, never condescending to gossip herself or encouraging gossip in others.

I have always felt that this Lawrence Washington, the only person who knew Mary Washington many years intimately, and who wrote his impressions of her, was responsible for the universal opinion that she was stern and repelling, — an opinion that has colored all the traditions of all the others who knew her as children. I am persuaded that this Lawrence did the mischief. Somebody sowed tares in the fair field of her reputation. Lawrence, I am sure, was the kind of boy known as " a terror," — a boy who chased chickens, brought hounds and muddy feet on the polished floors, trampled flower-beds, rifled the fruit trees, overturned pans of milk, upset the furniture, and broke the china. Well might he be more afraid of Mrs. Washington even than of his own parents (and what more could he say?), and we may believe he had many a scolding and in his early years an opportunity to test the flavor of the peach tree.

I am so fully assured that his testimony was the beginning of all that Mary Washington has suffered at the hands of her countrymen, that I have diligently looked up his record, hoping to find that he came to no good: but alas! he is mentioned with affectionate respect in George Washington's will as "the acquaintance and friend of my juvenile years." It is some comfort, however, to find he had a wild son, Lawrence, who fought a duel, and gave him no end of trouble!

And as to the traditions! What are they worth? Has the reader never stood in a line when a story whispered from one to the other was told aloud at the end, and in no case ever found to be the story of the beginning? Thomas Fuller tells of the name "Musard," which became, as it passed down the generations from lip to lip "Roper." A popular dramatic reader once took for his text the words "come here," and showed how accent, gesture, and tone could change their meaning from invitation to menace, from tenderness to fury.

The stories told of Mary Washington were always altered to fit the prevailing opinion of her sternness. Let me give an example. "When General Washington sent over the country to impress horses (and pay for them) his officers were attracted by a pair ploughing in a field. The driver was ordered to unhitch them, but an ebony Mercury ran to warn his mistress who appeared in her doorway. 'Madam,' said the officer, 'we bear General Washington's orders to take these horses.' 'Does George need horses?' said Mary Washington. 'Well, he can have mine, but he must wait until my field is finished.' "

Now this is a poor little story, with no point at all save to illustrate Mary Washington's estimation of the relative importance of the sword and the ploughshare. Like all others it is changed as the years pass. A short time ago a revised edition reached me from the West.

This is the amended story: " ' What are you doing there with my horses?' said an irate old woman who appeared just then on the field. ' Leave the place instantly!' ' But — Madam — we have orders from the Commander-in-chief! We must obey.' ' Well, then, you may just obey *me!* Go back and tell your *Commander-in-chief* ' (with great scorn and derision) ' that his mother's horses are not for sale, and he can't borrow 'em till her spring ploughing is done.' It was the part of prudence to leave. The officers left!' "

The story grew to this proportion in a hundred years. Given another hundred, and we will find that Mary Washington laid violent hands on the men who claimed the horses, and chastised the ploughmen who surrendered them.

In 1765 two pair of observant eyes opened upon the world, and were focussed upon the "awe-inspiring" lady, Betty Lewis, little Betty and Dr. Charles Mortimer's little Maria. The children were playmates, schoolmates, and girl friends from a very early age, each intimate at the other's home and both intimate at the home of Mary Washington. They adored her! They found naught to remember but smiles, gentle words, sweet, motherly ways. Betty (afterwards Mrs. Charles Carter) has furnished many of the unimportant traditions quoted in various accounts of her grandmother's home life. They come to us as traditions of traditions, not to be despised, yet not to be accepted as history. The other pair of eyes were keener for the dress and belongings of her venerable friend. To Maria Mortimer, daughter of Mary Washington's physician, we are indebted for the familiar picture of the short skirt and sack, — a sort of cote-hardi, — the mob cap, the table upon which lay "Sir Matthew Hale" and his ally, in the presence of which there was such small hope for the sinner. Freshly gathered from the friendly peach tree, this was used as freely — this much we willingly concede — as circumstances demanded. The two children played happily at her knee despite the menacing tools of the Inquisition, which we would fain believe were never used on them.

To their dying day they talked reverently and most abundantly; for after General Washington became so very great there were always listeners.

Mrs. Charles Carter.

Had they written conscientiously as the New Jersey tutor did instead of talking, we might have known more of the reserved, stately woman who bore and fostered and taught the revered Father of his

N

Country; but we know too well how sentiments can be trimmed and shaped and clothed upon as they pass down the generations from lip to lip, to venture to give them as gospel facts in clear, twentieth-century type. They will surely live without the aid of any present or future historian, for this is the fortune of trifles! Great thoughts, feelings, aspirations, — great unselfish deeds even, — perish and are forgotten, while trifling words, gestures, peculiarities in dress or speech, live with no apparent reasonableness whatever — certainly not because of their dignity or merit. They swarm around the honored men and women of the world like insects around a traveller on a sunny day, living of their own accord, too insignificant to challenge or brush away, gaining dignity at last from their own antiquity. Who cares whether Thomas Carlyle liked his chops tender, objected to vermin, or abhorred the crowing of a cock? Yet, I venture to say, when his name is called, his image is associated oftener with his peculiarities than with the sublime thoughts with which he sought to elevate and inspire the world.

Mary Washington sustained through a long life a lofty character for Christian purity and dignity; trained a son to lead our country through many years of danger and privation to the liberty and prosperity which places it to-day in the front of all the nations of the earth; yielded her life at last, in pain

unspeakable, with no murmur upon her pure lips.
Yet when her name is called, all the ingenuity of
her countrymen is aroused to accentuate her peculiarities — to treat her with a sort of whimsical
indulgence, as an unlettered old woman, conspicuous for eccentricities of temper, of dress, petty
economies — in short, make her ridiculous! Truly,
in all ages there are Greeks who weary of hearing
Aristides called the Just!

In the face of all the testimony I have presented
and will present, the most remarkable statements
regarding Mary Washington are continually printed
in the Historical Sketches published by the best
firms in the country. What can be their authority
for such statements as these? —

" The Washingtons were poor hard-working people.
Mary Washington cooked, weaved, spun, washed and made
the clothes for her family."

" Her children had no outer garments to protect them
from the cold — no cloak, boots or hats except in winter;
no cloaks then. In severe weather the boys simply put
on two or three trousers instead of one."

" Mary Washington quarrelled with her son so that
when he wished to minister to her comfort in her old age
he was forced to do so through some third party. These
things she accepted as her due, showing a grim half-comic
ingratitude that was very fine."

" Washington's mother scolded and grumbled to the day
of her death — seeking solace only by smoking a pipe."

Could this monstrous woman have held an honored place in a social circle of stately, courteous, cultured people? Why assert such things which completely offset an oft-repeated concession that "all the sterling, classic virtues of industry, frugality and truth-telling were inculcated by this excellent mother (!) and her strong common sense made its indelible impress upon the mind of her son."

She has also suffered much at the hands of her own countrywomen! We must remember she never appeared in the full blaze of public scrutiny until she was over seventy years old, and then, impoverished by a long war with an *entourage* the most discouraging and painful. Women then found her parsimonious, ungraceful in dress and manner, sour in temper! Pray what have we, my fastidious sisters, done for our country in our day and generation? Compare our privileges and opportunities with hers! The wealth, the light, the leisure of a happy era, are ours, and yet not enough can this affluent country afford for our adornment, our culture and pleasure. We can — and do — traverse the earth, flitting from land to land as the seasons change, becoming acquainted, if it so please us, with the cloistered wisdom of libraries, the color and beauty of palaces, the priceless treasures of art centres, able to enrich our minds with all the whole world has to offer, from ancient days to this, and with the possible contact

of brilliant minds at home and abroad. Show me
the result! Something, I grant you, is gained in
personal charm, much, alas! in accentuating the
natural heart-break from which the less fortunate
suffer in witnessing the undeserved contrasts and
inequalities of life.

Surely it is not for American women of this day
— sheltered, treasured, adored — to complain that
industry, simplicity in living, ungraceful dress and
manner, mar the portrait of a noble woman whose
lot was cast in a narrow and thorny path, whose life
was necessarily a denied one, and yet who accomplished more for her country than any other woman
ever did or ever can do!

It was her pleasure to live simply — at a time of
almost riotous profusion. It was her pleasure to
busy her own hands with the housewifely work of
her own household, — knitting, sewing, sorting fleeces
for "Virginia cloth," preserving fruits, distilling
herbs for the sick, — "making drudgery divine"
by sharing the tasks she laid upon others, thereby
earning her many gifts to the poor. In an age of
abundant leisure she was industrious; in an age of
dissipation of time and money she was self-denying,
diligent, and frugal; in an age when speech was
free and profanity "genteel" she preserved her
temperate speech, unpolluted by the faintest taint
of coarseness or irreverance. When the church no
longer concerned itself with the care of men's souls,

she kept her own serene, in her simple faith that prayer would prevail in the end, performing every outward religious duty as conscientiously as if the priests and bishops showed, as well as taught, the way.   So did she —

> " .   .   .   travel on life's common way
> In cheerful Godliness ; and yet her heart
> The lowliest duties on herself did lay."

This, the result of many years spent in studying her character, the writer presents as the true Mary Washington, to be honored all the more for her retired, her simple life, her homely industries.

It is proper that her characteristics should be summed up before the weakness of extreme old age had lessened its activity and usefulness, while she was still young enough to catch the enthusiasm of her friends and neighbors for fine houses, fine coaches, rich dress, and much indulgence in pleasure.

She was better able than some of her neighbors to indulge in these things, deemed in her day the essentials of position.   Perhaps she may have heard the specious argument urged by some to warrant such indulgence, — the argument that expenditure in luxuries becomes the duty of the rich in order to stimulate the industries of the poor.   But Mary Washington believed in the wholesome influence of an *example* of self-denial, which can only become

MARY WASHINGTON'S HOUSE IN FREDERICKSBURG.

of any worth when practised by choice and not by necessity. And yet she lived long before Stuart Mill and other political economists had demonstrated that money spent in rich garments, jewels, and luxury in living adds nothing of permanent value to the world.

She never left the plain, four-roomed, dormer-windowed dwelling at "Pine Grove," until for her greater protection she moved into Fredericksburg, choosing a home still plainer and less spacious than the house on her farm. Says Mr. Custis, who saw her in this home: "Her great industry, with the well-regulated economy of all her concerns, enabled her to dispense considerable charities to the poor, although her own circumstances were always far from rich. All manner of domestic economies met her zealous attentions; while everything about her household bore marks of her care and management, and very many things the impress of her own hands. In a very humble dwelling thus lived this mother of the first of men, preserving, unchanged, her peculiar nobleness and independence of character."

This most valuable testimony as to Mary Washington's character, appearance, and manner is contained in the first chapter of "The Recollections and Private Memoirs of Washington," by George Washington Parke Custis, son of "Jack" Custis, who was the only son of Mrs. George Washington. "Jack" Custis died young (he was married at nineteen), and his son, named for General Washington, with his sister, Nelly Custis, were adopted into the Mount Vernon family. Although this son was too young to have fully appreciated Mary Washington, his testimony comes directly from her own sons and daughter and others who knew her intimately. Through them he studied her, and by no one of them was he contradicted. His statements are conclusive — not to be challenged. They need no additional force from the tradition that between the Custis family and Madam Washington "there was never perfect accord" — one of the meaningless traditions originating in the busy brain of some gossip, for which there was no foundation in truth. Although several extracts have already been given from Mr. Custis's book, the fact that the book itself is now out of print, and to be found only in the Congressional Library at Washington, and possibly in some of the older libraries of the country, will perhaps excuse me for having quoted so freely the chapter relating to Mary Washington. It was written only thirty-seven years after her death, and from it has been drawn the relations given by Sparks, Lossing, and others.

"The mother of George Washington," says Mr. Custis, "the hero of the American Revolutionary War, and the first President of the United States, claims the noblest distinction a woman should covet or can gain, that of training a gifted son in the way he should go, and inspiring him by her example to make the way of goodness his path to glory."

But the noblest tribute to this great woman was Washington's own. "All that I am," said he, " I owe to my mother." All that we are as a nation we owe to him. His debt is ours. It is many times multiplied. It is ever growing as the ever growing Republic illustrates in its virtues and in its faults alike the merit of his example and the wisdom of her teachings. We but degrade ourselves when we refuse to recognize this debt. Let us rather discharge it as best we may, in " coin of the highest value — the pure gold of devotion and gratitude."

CHAPTER XXI

NOON IN THE GOLDEN AGE

VIRGINIA, between the years 1760 and 1775, attained her highest prosperity. The growth of the colony in general, and the advance of luxury in living was rapid, marked by an increased taste for amusements of the most costly kind, and great expenditure in living and entertaining.

It was high noon in the Golden Age! Life was far more elegant and luxurious than it was even fifteen years before. The transplanted Englishman had rapidly prospered in the new land. Great wealth had suddenly come to him through his tobacco, and he made haste to use and enjoy it. The four-roomed house — quite good enough for his cavalier grandfather — had stepped aside to give place to a pillared, porticoed, stately mansion. The dormer windows — like heavy-lidded eyes — had been superseded by "five hundred and forty-nine lights" for one dwelling. The planter often built on the site of his old colonial residence, sometimes incorporating the old into the new. An eminence, commanding a wide view of the surrounding country, was a coveted spot in plantation times. It behooved the settler (for reasons similar to those which influenced Captain John Smith) to build his house " on a high hill neere a convenient river, hard to be assalted and easie to be defended." When the perilous days of Indian massacre and treachery had passed away, and the country had entered upon its Saturnian age of peace and plenty, the Virginians clung to the old historic building-sites, and upon them erected ambitious mansions, with flagged colonnades, extended wings, and ample offices ; surmounting the whole with an observatory whence the proprietor with his " spy-glass " could sweep the country — not now for the stealthy approach of an enemy, but to feast his eyes upon a scene of unbroken beauty peacefully lying beneath a summer's sun. The mansion stood apart in solemn grandeur upon some knoll or eminence overlooking the great highway, the river. It was not to be taken casually, in a by-the-way sort of a manner, not to be stumbled upon by accident. It was to be approached with deliberation through a long line of sentinels — an avenue of Lombardy poplars — " the proper tree, let them say what they will, to surround a gentleman's mansion."

This landward approach to the house passed sometimes between columns of trimmed boxwood or stone gate-posts upon which the arms granted the family in England were carved in high relief. Gravelled paths under ornamental trees led to the veranda with its lofty columns. In the rear, the hill sometimes fell sharply to the riverside in terraces, after the English fashion. At a wharf, built out into the bed of the stream, the family often assembled to watch the sailing of their own ships, trading directly with the mother country.

Monticello. The Home of Thomas Jefferson.

On the green, facing the river, there were summer-houses of latticed woodwork, covered with climbing roses, honeysuckle, and jasmine, and haunted by brilliant humming-birds. Other cool retreats from the ardor of the summer sun were made of resinous cedars planted in a close circle, their tops tied together and their walls shaven smoothly until

THE GARDEN AT MOUNT VERNON.

they resembled little mosques of vivid green. A low wall covered with honeysuckle or Virginia creeper bounded the grounds at the water's edge.

But it was in the garden and in the greenhouse that the lady of the manor exulted! No simple flowers, such as violets, lilies, or roses were forced in those days. These would come with the melting of the snows early in February. Only tropical beauties were reared under the glass: century-plant, cacti, gardenias, lemon and orange trees; great, double, glowing pomegranates, and the much-prized snowy globes of Camellia Japonica, sure to be sent packed in cotton as gifts to adorn the dusky tresses of some Virginia beauty, or clasp the folds of her diaphanous kerchief. These camellias were reckoned the most elegant of flowers — so pure and sensitive, resenting the profanation of the slightest touch. Fancy a cavalier of that day presenting nothing rarer than a bouquet of daisies or daffodils!

But the garden! Who can describe a garden in the Virginia of 1770? When the little children of the family were sent forth to breathe the cool air of the morning, what a paradise of sweets met their senses! The squares, crescents, stars, and circles, edged with box, over which an enchanted, glistening veil had been thrown during the night; the tall lilacs, snowballs, myrtles, and syringas, guarding like sentinels the entrance to every avenue; the glowing beds of tulips, pinks, purple iris, and hyacinths; the flowering-almond with its rosy spikes; the globes of golden passion-fruit; the figs, rimy with the early dew and bursting with scarlet sweetness! The whole world filled with bloom and beauty, fragrance and melody.

At a respectful distance from the mansion were smaller houses of brick or stone, far enough removed from "the great house" to secure the master's quiet and privacy. In one, a five-roomed building served for schoolhouse and lodging-rooms for the tutor and boys of the family. Another was "the office" for the transaction of business with agents from the other plantations of the master, or with captains of trading vessels lying at his wharf, laden with outgoing tobacco, or unloading the liquors, books, musical instruments, and fine stuffs for the family. In the rear, hidden by maple or cherry trees, were many houses: wash-house, dairy, bake-house, storehouses, and a kitchen as large as the five-roomed schoolhouse, for the sole use of the great High Priest — the cook — and her family. "All these formed a handsome street," adds Mr. Fithian (the New Jersey Presbyterian tutor, whom nothing escaped), and all were surrounded with little gardens and poultry-yards, and enlivened with swarms of chickens, ducks, pigs, and little negroes. Remote from these were the great stables, well filled and admirably regulated.

The kitchens of these later mansions were always

a long distance away, because that source of comfort, the black cook, had so many satellites revolving around her and drawing sustenance, light, and warmth from her centre, that it was absolutely necessary to give her elbow-room. The satellites, however, had their uses. At dinner-time, each one with shining face, robed in a great apron to supplement various trouser deficiencies, and bearing covered dishes, formed a solemn procession back and forth to the dining room. There the frosty eye of the gray-haired butler awed them into perfect decorum; and in the kitchen the vigorous arm of the cook kept them well within bounds, along with the hounds, and, like them, devouring with hopeful eyes the delicious viands in course of preparation.

The planter felt that the time had come to concern himself with the elegancies of fine living. He went home to England to select books for his library and to have his portrait painted by Sir Joshua Reynolds; perhaps bring over his grandfather's portrait by Sir Peter Lely, or, at least, secure a copy of Sir Peter's portrait of Charles the First. A precious picture now and then found its way to the drawing-rooms of the Northern Neck; and at "Elsing Green," a little lower down in King William County, were hangings of priceless value — a set of Gobelin tapestry presented to the owner's ancestor, Gilbert Burnet, Bishop of Salisbury, by William of Orange. " Race horses, drawn masterly and set in elegant

frames," adorned the dining-room walls of Colonel
John Tayloe of Mount Airy, owner of the great
Yorick, one of the most celebrated horses of the
day; and in the same dining room stood the famous
punch-bowl, since celebrated in verse. The fashion
of adorning the grounds with marble statues is first
mentioned in describing Colonel Tayloe's beautiful
garden, near Mary Washington's girlhood home.

Elsing Green.

Libraries in 1770 had been well chosen, and had
attained respectable proportions. Mr. Robert Carter of Westmoreland, and other men of wealth, had
collected law-books, books on divinity relating to
the Established Church, a large musical library, the
works of Pope, Locke, Addison, Young, Swift, Dryden, " and other works of mighty men," in the Latin
tongue.

MOUNT AIRY.

Mr. Carter had also every musical instrument then known: "An Organ, Spinet, Forte-Piano, Guittar, German Flutes, Harpsichord and Harmonica. The last, the wonderful new instrument invented by one Benjamin Franklin of Philadelphia" (him of the Blackbeard Ballad), " being musical glasses without water, framed into a complete instrument capable of thorough bass and never out of tune." On these the master, his sons, and daughters, and the Presbyterian tutor discoursed learned music, sonatas, etc.

Reading of this age, one is amazed at the activity of these Virginians of the Northern Neck. They were forever in motion, passing up and down the Potomac and Rappahannock — the great canals of their Venice — in barges and batteaux, and across country from one river to the other on horseback, in chaises and chariots.

The Potomac was the theatre of much rivalry and ostentation among the rich planters whose estates bordered the river. Superb barges were made to their order in England; and the negro crew rowing them were clad in showy uniforms. Occasionally a British frigate would appear on the river, when all the country would be thrown into a " paroxysm of festivity." Breakfasts and dinners at Mount Vernon and " Belvoir" (the seat of the Fairfaxes) would be in order, with the return courtesies of afternoon teas on board the frigate.

o

The river was always in order, but the highway on land was about the last thing to which the Virginian turned his attention. He accepted it as it was. If a section became impassable to the family chariot, drawn often by six horses, the outriders simply dismounted, and with axes cleared a passage around it for the vehicle to "turn out." Hence the necessity for these outriders. The family never went abroad unattended. At one dinner, described by our Froissart of the Northern Neck, eight servants accompanied the coach and chaise, namely : coachman, driver, two postillions, two servants for the master, one each to attend the two gentlemen on horseback — the chaise being driven by the master himself.

There were no bridges across the rivers. Logs of wood placed side by side with planks nailed across formed a wide, floating bridge which sank several inches under the weight of the great coach, the horses splashing through the water. When the roads lay through level ground, after rains they were submerged for miles. Struggling through such a watery lane to visit John Augustine Washington, an English traveller lost heart, and called out to the postillion of the coach sent to fetch him, " Here, you fellow ! How far out into the river does your unfortunate master live ? " Nobody ever thought it worth while to drain the roads. When they ran through fields crossed and recrossed by " stake-fences " (stakes set at intervals and woven basket-fashion with " savin " or juniper boughs) the pauses were incessant. Bars had to be let down, gates opened and shut. Our Froissart counted thirteen gates in fifteen miles.

" When the roads were too rough for carriages," says an old writer who remembered them, " the ladies used to ride on ponies, followed by black servants on horseback. In this way ladies, even when advanced in life, used to travel, clad in the scarlet riding-habits procured from England. Nay, in this way, on emergencies, the young ladies used to come to the balls, riding with their hoops arranged ' fore and aft ' like lateen sails, and after dancing all night ride home again in the morning."

A " neighborhood " included everybody within a day's journey, all the way from Westmoreland to Mount Vernon. Dinner-parties were going on as incessantly then in the Northern Neck as now in the metropolis. The nearest neighbors were invited to these every few days, while occasionally, in order to reach the whole community of several counties, balls were given to last five days!

Of course, all this close and familiar intercourse was an important agent in the wonderful unanimity of the entire country when the hour of conflict had come. At these balls and dinners something was done besides dancing and card-playing — some hint or word from eloquent lips to keep alive the spark soon to burst forth in resistless, all-conquering flame. Historians speak of the period as "the lull before the storm." It was not by any means a "lull"—rather a carnival!

CHAPTER XXII

DINNERS, DRESS, DANCES, HORSE-RACES

IF the grave New Jersey Presbyterian tutor — who has given us so faithful a picture of domestic life in the Northern Neck — saw fit to burn his candles at night while he described the dresses, dinners, and dances of his day, surely it is worth our while to pause in our history to consider them.

The planter's daily life began betimes with an early breakfast. The planter was an early riser. He had retired early. The myrtle-berry candle — the costly spermaceti — were not brilliant enough to tempt late hours. Often before daybreak in the winter, when the nights were long, he might be found at his secretary arranging the work of the day. Washington at Mount Vernon would light his own fire and read by candle-light, then breakfast on tea and Indian-meal cakes at eight o'clock. But to all rules he and his mother were exceptions! The usual life of the planter admitted more luxury. His breakfast was a good one! But first, having risen early, he mixed with his own hands the great beaker of crushed ice, peach-brandy, and mint to be sent around to all the rooms as an appetizer. Even the children were admitted to this morning loving-cup. Virginians believed in it!

Luckily the breakfast is not left to a twentieth-century imagination — which would probably suggest an orange, coffee, and roll. The Rev. Andrew Burnaby, Vicar of Greenwich, London, had the pleasure of eating a Virginia breakfast in 1759: "The ancient custom of eating meat for breakfast still continues. At the top of the table where the lady of the house presides, there is constantly tea and coffee, but the rest of the table is garnished out with roasted fowls, ham, venison, game and other dainties. There is scarcely a Virginia lady who breakfasts without ham!"

Dinner at home or abroad was served not later than three, and was preceded by at least one mint julep all around. At one home dinner we read of four kinds of fish, "Sheeps-head, Bass, Perch, Picked Crab: Ham, Mutton, vegetables, pudding, fruits, cheese, old Madeira," which to be presentable must have crossed the ocean more than once. A dinner included three courses, — soup, then the whole dinner placed on the table at once, then dessert. Ducks were served at the fish feasts. The delicious canvasback duck was by no means so highly appreciated as it is now. They were left in comparative peace to feed upon the tender wild celery of the Potomac marshes. The diamond-backed terrapin was much too abundant to be considered a dainty. To save the scarcer and costlier pork, terrapin was fed to the negroes. Laws were enacted in Maryland forbidding the slaves' rations to be exclusively of terrapin !

At one of General Washington's ceremonious dinners there was soup, fish roasted and boiled, "gammon of bacon" and fowl. The middle of the table was decorated with artificial flowers and small images. The dessert was a pudding and apple pie, ice-cream, jellies, melons, apples, peaches, nuts. This dinner was recorded as "a great dinner." To-day it would be considered "a good enough dinner, to be sure, but not a dinner to *ask* a man to !" Some of the receipts for these old Virginia dinners have been preserved in the Randolph family — notably the receipts for English plum pudding, and for the Christmas mince pie.

Tables were richly furnished with burnished pewter and handsome silver. So many articles of silver — bowls, cups, and salvers — were imported from England that the thrifty planter was constrained to import an engraver as well, in order that his arms and crests might be engraved under his personal supervision. The china was, of course, English or of English importation. We manufactured no china, imported none from the East — probably none from France. Mary Washington's china we know was blue and white. Knives were of fine Sheffield steel, and served other uses than cutting. How else did the colonial dames eat their peas? Surely not with the little steel fork with two wide-apart prongs. This is a painful reflection, but we must remember that a good many ladies whom the world has admired — Helen of Troy, the Mother of the Gracchi, all of its earth-born goddesses, in fact, until Queen Elizabeth — had to content themselves at dinner with the utensils God had given them. They had no forks at all — not even a chop-stick! Hence the early need for napkins.

There was no lack of good napery in Mary Washington's time, but the usage of napkins differed somewhat from the usage of to-day, at least at General Washington's dinners.

The destruction of cattle by Tarleton's Red Dragoons caused almost a famine of cream and butter, immediately after the war, so that "trifle" and ice-cream were articles of prime luxury. To obtain sufficient cream for the dish known variously as trifle, syllabub, or floating island, it was sometimes necessary to save it until it soured or grew rancid.

Mrs. Morris tells of such a misfortune at one of Washington's state dinners. She did not hesitate to consign her own unswallowed morsel to her napkin, but records with wicked glee that "poor Lady Washington ate a whole plate-full without wincing."

At dinner much ceremony was observed. " I have

fortunately learned by heart all the ceremonies of the table, and will make no mistakes," says the tutor exultantly, when he finds it necessary to preside in the illness of the mistress and absence of the master. Toasts were regularly drunk at dinner if there were guests — but postponed to the evening bowl of "toddy" or punch when the family was alone. No day passed without these toasts. "To the King and Queen, the Governor of Virginia and his Lady, and success to American Trade and Commerce." After these each person was called upon by the master for his toast. "I gave the Lovely Laura," says our tutor — Laura being the name in Cupid's court for Miss Betty Beatty.

One might trace the changes in political feeling by these toasts. At first, after the royal family and success to Virginia commerce, only the respective favorites among the ladies. Presently we observe that "The Sons of Liberty" have crept into the company to demand a toast. Then an ominous toast follows the king and all the rest, "*Wisdom* and *Unity* to the Conference now assembled." Then the royal family, governor, and his lady are dropped altogether, and the toast, praying for "Wisdom and Unity," takes their places. The Prince de Broglie records the toasts at General Washington's table, — "The United States of America, the King of France, the Queen "; "Success with our Enemies and the Ladies "; "Success in War and Love." After these, the Marquis de Lafayette and the military heroes of the war. General Washington, when President, discontinued this custom, contenting himself with grave bows, and "Your Health, Sir; your Health, Madam," all around the table, until every one was thus honored.

One can hardly repress a shudder at the accounts given by Robert Maclay and others of the deadly dulness and formality of General Washington's state dinners. He kept up this formal coldness to the end. Free and easy manners came in with Mr. Jefferson and long trousers. Fancy this incident occurring at General Washington's table: "Here's to thy Absent Broad-brim Friend Hollingworth," from Dolly Madison. "Here's to thy Absent Kerchief, Friend Dorothy," from the Quaker.

At informal dinners among neighbors the company "sat until sunset," then coffee, and at nine o'clock supper, — artichokes, crabs, oysters, strawberries and cream, the punch-bowl again. Record is made of "Sudden Pains and Sickness at the Stomach at night."

The dancing class was held in succession at all the mansions along the Potomac as far as Mount Vernon. Mr. Christian — stern but elegant — taught minuets and country-dances, first politely requesting each guest "to step a minuet." He does not hesitate to rap two young misses across the shoulder for a fault, and to inform "one young

Fellow" that he has observed him "through the course of the Dance," to be "insolent and wanton," and shall require him to alter his manner or leave the school. Then, when candles are lighted, having danced all day, Mr. Christian winds up with another minuet and country-dance, and at seven is glad to retire. But fun holds awhile longer. They all "play Button to get Pauns for Redemption, and carry it on with sprightliness and Decency." The tutor is in luck. "In the course of redeeming my Pauns I had several Kisses of the Ladies." Then Colonel Philip Ludwell Lee arrives in a travelling chariot from Williamsburg. "Four candles on the table make the room luminous and Splendid." There is a fine supper with four instructed waiters. After supper all gather around the fire and "play 'break the Pope's neck'" until ten o'clock, and then to bed.

"Almost every lady wears a red cloak,"[1] says our tutor; "and when they ride out they tye a red handkerchief over their Head and face, so that when I first came to Virginia I was distressed whenever I saw a Lady, for I thought she had a Tooth-Ach." At a five-days' ball at Squire Lee's "the Ladies were dressed Gay and splendid, and when Dancing their Skirts and Brocades rustled and trailed behind them. For five days and nights they Danced minuets, reels, marches: Giggs (an exaggerated dance resembling the *Trescone*

---

[1] "Journal of Philip Vickens Fithian," edited by John Rogers Williams.

of Italy) and, last of all, Country Dances to the Music of a French Horn and two Violins, for," says the astonished tutor, " Blow high, Blow Low, the Virginians are genuine blood — they will Dance or die ! "

The plantation fiddler belonging, as did the barber, shoemaker, and carpenter, to each establishment, seems to have sufficed for Mr. Christian's class. At this the gentlemen were " drest in black, superfine broadcloth, laced Ruffles, Black silk Stockings, buckles at knee and instep. They wore powder on their Hair, or the short Wig now in fashion."

The ladies, well, the principal ladies, must each sit for her own portrait.

First, Mary Washington's granddaughter, " Miss Jenny Washington,[1] about seventeen, not a handsome face, but neat in her Dress, well-proportioned, and has an easy, winning Behaviour. She is not forward to begin a conversation, yet when spoken to is extremely affable without assuming any girlhood affectation or pretending to be overcharged with Wit. She moves with propriety when she dances a *Minuet*, and without any *Flirts* or vulgar *Capers* when She dances a *Reel* or *Country-Dance*. She plays well on Harpsichord and Spinet, understands the principles of Musick and therefore performs her Tunes in perfect time — a neglect of which always makes music intolerable, but it is a fault almost universal in young Ladies. She sings likewise to

---

[1] Fithian's "Journal."

her instrument, has a strong, full voice and a well-judging Ear.   Most of the Virginia Girls think it labour quite sufficient to thump the Keys of a Harpsichord," etc.   " Her Dress is rich and well-chosen, but not tawdry, nor yet too plain.   She appears to-day " (at the dancing class in the morning) " in a chintz cotton gown with an elegant blue Stamp, a sky-blue silk Quilt " (petticoat over which the gown opens), " a spotted apron.   Her Hair is a light Brown, it was craped up high with two Rolls at each Side, and on the top a small cap of beautiful Gauze and rich lace, with an artificial flower interwoven."

Very satisfactory indeed for Mary Washington's granddaughter, sister of Bushrod Washington, afterwards judge of the Supreme Court.

Next, Miss Betsy Lee : " She is a well-set maid of a proper Height, neither high nor low.   Her Aspect when she is sitting is masculine and Dauntless : she sits very erect ; places her feet with great propriety, her Hands she lays carelessly in her lap and never moves them but when she has occasion to adjust some article of her dress, or to perform some exercise of her Fan.   Her Eyes are exactly such as *Homer* attributes to the Goddess *Minerva* and her arms resemble those which the same Poet allows to *Juno*.   Her Hair which was a dark Brown was craped up very high and in it she had a Ribbon interwoven with an artificial Flower.   At each of

her ears dangled a brilliant jewel.   She was pinched
up rather too near in a long pair of new-fashioned
Stays, which I think are a nuisance both to us and
themselves — For the late importation of Stays, said
to be now most fashionable in London, are produced

Bushrod Washington.

upwards so high that we can have scarce any view
at all of the Ladies' Snowy Bosoms; and on the
contrary they are extended downwards so low that
Walking must, I think, cause a disagreeable friction
of some parts of the Body.   I imputed the Flush
which was visible in her Face to her being swathed

up *Body and Soul and Limbs* together.   She wore a
light chintz gown with a blue stamp elegantly made
which set well upon her.   She wore a blue Silk
Quilt.   Her dress was rich and fashionable and her
behaviour was such as I should expect to find in a
Lady whose education had been constructed with
some care and skill."

So much for Miss Lee.   Now for the country
beauty, Miss Aphia Fauntleroy (afterwards married
to Captain John Champe Carter of the Revolution).

" Is the best dancer of the whole absolutely !—And
the finest Girl !   Her head powdered as white as
snow and craped in the newest taste.   She is the
copy of the Goddess of Modesty — very handsome.
She seemed to be loved by all her Acquaintances
and Admired by every Stranger."

" Miss Priscilla Carter is 16 — small of her
age, has a mild winning Presence, a sweet obliging
Temper, *never swears* which is here a distinguished
virtue, dances finely, plays well on key'd Instruments, is never without what seems to have been a
common Gift of Heaven to the *fair Sex*, the Copia
Verborum, or readiness of Expression."   (This
sweet-tempered fifteen-year-older, a pupil of the
Presbyterian tutor, was a young lady of spirit.)
" Miss Prissy is much offended !   She retains her
anger and seems peculiarly resentful, refusing to
walk over to the school.   Indeed she is much
affronted.   Monday afternoon by chance I tapp'd

her on the Head and wholly in Jest." Five days later the Diary records, "At last Prissy is reconciled," having punished him sufficiently.

Next, Miss Hale, fourteen years old. "She is dressed in a white Holland gown, quilt very fine, a Lawn Apron, has her hair craped high, and upon it a Tuft of Ribbon for a cap. Once I saw her standing. I rose immediately and begged her to accept my Chair. She answered most kindly, ' Sir, I thank you,' and that was all I could extract from this Wonder of her Sex for the two days of the dance, and yet I seemed to have an equal Share in the Favours of her Conversation."

Miss Sally Panton, lately come from England to teach Mr. Turberville's daughters French and English, creates a sensation because she is supposed to have brought with her the latest London fashions. " Her stays are huge, giving her an enormous long *Waist*. These stays are suited to come up to the upper part of her shoulders, almost to her chin ; and are swaithed round her as low as they can possibly be, allowing her no liberty to walk at all. To be sure this is a vastly *Modest* Dress !" The stays are all right, but " her *Head-Dress* not to the liking of the Virginia Ladies " being arranged low on the neck, of which they can, on no account approve. " Nevertheless," quoth the tutor, " if her Principles of Religion and her Moral Manner be unexceptionable *I* shall think her Agreeable."

The last picture thrown on the canvas must be another Miss Lee. "A tall, slim, genteel Girl thirteen years old. She is free from the taciturnity of Miss Hale, yet by no means disagreeably forward. She dances extremely well, and is just beginning to play on the Spinet. She is drest in a neat shell Callico Gown, has very light hair done up high with a feather, and her whole carriage is easy and graceful, and free of formality and Haughtiness, the Common foible here."

For aught we know to the contrary this charming young lady was the beauty who roused an anonymous poet to alliterative verse.

> " May mild meridian moonbeams mantle me
> With laughing, lisping Lucy Lightfoot Lee."

The ingenuous tutor is delightful. Not once does he interpret the freezing manner, the haughtiness and formality of the maidens to any dislike of himself. Perhaps it did not exist; his successor, also a Presbyterian tutor, married one of them. But not so, I fancy, did these ladies treat young Harry Lee — "our Light-horse Harry," the son of the " Lowland Beauty " — when they met him at the Squire's ball; and surely not thus would the young junior from Princeton College have been impressed by them. One peep within the leaves of that Diary, — a thing impossible to the veriest madcap in his school, — and all would have been

P

over for the Presbyterian tutor, albeit he and young
Harry had been college mates.

Two things were absolutely necessary in the
etiquette of the minuet, — the pointed foot must be
so firm, so straight, that not a crease or wrinkle
appeared in the quilted petticoat, and, of course,

Mary Ambler.

this quilt must be of a
strength and richness : so
rich, indeed, that it would
" stand alone," yielding
not in dance and courtesy.

Evidently Miss Hale at
fourteen, and Miss Lee at
thirteen, were already in
society.   In a few years,
doubtless, they were all
married to Revolutionary
officers, two or three,
sometimes five, of them
falling in course of time
to his lot, as was usual in
that day of short-lived women.   As we have seen,
Catherine Willis — afterwards Princess Murat —
married at thirteen.

The wife of Chief Justice Marshall, Mary
Ambler, was only fourteen years old when she
attended the Dunmore ball and captured the
young Captain Marshall, who gave the only guinea
he possessed to a clergyman for marrying him soon
after.

Arthur Lee said, "In Virginia a man is old at thirty and a woman at twenty." A certain little

Chief Justice John Marshall.

Alice Lee, twelve years old, wrote this remarkable letter from Stratford in 1772 to a kinsman in London. (Doubtless Miss Alice was one of the dancers at Squire Lee's ball two years later.)

" So you threaten me if I prove deficient in the deference I owe you as a married man, with the power you have of forwarding or retarding my success in the Matrimonial Way.[1] This would be a tremendous threat indeed were I as fond of Matrimony as my young Mistress, as you call her, but happily I am little more than twelve years old and not so eager to tye a Knot which Death alone can Dissolve. And yet I pretend not to ridicule the holy sacred institution, but have all due reverence for that and the worthy people who have entered into the Society, from good and generous motives. It is only those who chuse to be married at all events that I think deserve raillery. . . . I never saw Westmoreland so dull. I was at Squire Lee's when your letter came. He is the veriest Tramontane in nature ; if ever he gets married, if his wife civilizes him, she deserves to be canonized.

" So you can't forbear a fling at femalities ; believe me Curiosity is as imputable to the Sons as the Daughters of Eve. Think you there was ever a Lady more curious than our Cousin the Squire ? He himself is the greatest of all curiosities, but hang him, how came he to pop twice in my head while I was writing to you !

" The Annapolis Races Commence the 6th of October. The American Comp^y of Players are there and said to be amazingly improved. I

1 "Lee of Virginia," Edited by Dr. Edward Jennings Lee.

should like to see them, as I think Theatrical
Entertainments a rational amusement."

Clever little Mistress Alice! Twelve years old,
and already flirting with the sixty-year-old Squire
Richard Lee Burgess from Westmoreland, member
of the Continental Congress, giver of five-day balls;
who yet found time to gather rosebuds, for he
actually married sixteen-year-old Sally Poythress
after he was sixty-two years old.

It is a great misfortune to us that our observant
tutor was not invited to Mount Vernon. Mr.
Christian's class met at Mount Vernon, also at
" Gunston Hall "—the fine residence of the George
Mason who wrote the famous Declaration of Rights
in 1776. Mrs. Martha Washington's lovely
daughter, Martha Custis, was then just thirteen
years old, and there is no doubt, not the least, that
she wore a blue silk quilt and had her hair
"craped" (*crêpé*) high and interwoven with a
feather. On the 18th of April, 1770, Washington
records, " Patsy Custis and Milly Posey went to
Col. Mason's to the Dancing School."

The discipline of children was stern. Their
duties included the courtesies of life as religiously
as its business. " I have no Stockings and I swear
I won't go to the Dancing School," says fifteen-year-
old Bob, who is at the awkward age and dreads
society. " ' Are Bob and Nancy gone to Mr.
Turberville's?' said the Colonel at Breakfast—

'Nancy is gone, Sir, Bob stays at Home, he has no shoes!' 'Poh—what nonsense,' says the Colonel. He sends the clerk to the Plantation Store for a pair of Shoes. Bob he takes to his Study and floggs severely for not having given seasonable notice, and sends him instantly to the Dance" in a suitable and proper frame of mind to enjoy himself!

Balls, fish feasts, christenings, cock-fights, horse-races and *church-going* filled the time as well as visiting and dancing. Everybody went to church through all weathers. In winter the churches were bitterly cold. No provision of any kind for heating them was ever dreamed of. The church was one of the rallying places for the neighborhood. "There are," says the tutor, "three grand divisions of time at the church on Sundays; Viz: before Service giving and receiving letters of business, reading Advertisements" (affixed to the church-doors) "consulting about the price of Tobacco, Grain, &c, and settling either the lineage, Age or qualities of favourite Horses. 2. In the church at Service, prayers read over in haste, a Sermon, seldom under and never over twenty minutes, but always made up of sound morality, or deep-studied Metaphysicks. 3. After Service is over, three quarters of an hour spent in strolling round the church among the crowd in which time invitations are given by gentlemen to go home with them to dinner."

The christenings were seasons of large family gatherings — the silver christening bowl, like the punch-bowl, descending from generation to generation.

There were no "poor whites" — the helpless, hopeless, anæmic race now numerous in Virginia. There were well-instructed men and women in the industrial classes who filled situations as visiting shoemakers, weavers, or housekeepers. The Virginia woman in "The Golden Age" had need of all the help she could get. She married while yet a child — often less than fifteen years old. Her housekeeper was her tower of strength. She helped generally throughout the family, nursing the sick, caring for the children's comfort, and standing sponsor for them in baptism.[1] A letter from one of these humble retainers, a housekeeper at Stratford, somewhere about 1774, has been preserved by which we perceive she represented the wife of Governor Fauquier at a christening.

(Dated)   "STRATFORD, September 27.

"To MISS MARTHA CORBIN — *Dear Miss*. I gladly embrace this oppertunity of writing to you to put you in mind there is such a being as mySelfe. I did not think you two would have slited me so. Your little cosen matilda was made a cristan the 25th of September. The godmothers was mrs washington miss becy Tayloe Miss Nancy Lawson Stod proxse for Miss Nelly Lee and I for

[1] "Lee of Virginia."

Mrs Fauquer, godfathers was col. Taloe Mr Robert Carter mrs washington Col Frank Lee, the Esq : mr washington and your ant Lee Dessers there Love to you I am your very humble servant Elizabeth Jackson."

It is easy to understand why Miss Jackson should have dignified all the Lees who employed her with large capitals, but why she should thus have honored Miss Nancy Lawson above " mrs. washington" we shall never know in this world, only, as everybody knows, no married lady — even Mrs. John Augustine Washington, our Mary's daughter-in-law — could possibly be as important as that most worshipped of all creatures, a Virginia young lady.

As to the race-horses, we cannot begin to reckon their increased importance. Janus and Yorick are among the immortals ! So also should be General Washington's horses, — Ajax, Blueskin, Valiant, and the royal Arabian Magnolia. Nor should Silver-eye be forgotten, nor the lordly Shakespeare, for whose service a groom was appropriated to sleep near him at night in a specially built recess, that his Lordship's faintest neigh might find response.

The men who settled the Northern Neck of Virginia were cavaliers from " Merry England," with an inherited love of horse-racing, and, indeed, all sporting. There was not a Roundhead among them ! They liked cards and dancing. Nobody could make them believe that the devil hunted with the hounds and ran with the race-horses.

The early Virginia historians wrote at length about the pedigrees and qualities of horses and the skill of their riders. The old court records have many quaint entries of disputes about " faire starts," and citizens' depositions were taken to settle them; for instance, " Richard Blande, aged 21 yeares Deposeth that in the Race run between John Brodnax and Capt. William Soane now in tryall, the horse belonging to Henry Randolph on w'ch Capt. Soane layed, came after the Start *first* between the Poles agreed on for their comeing in," etc. William Randolph's task was more difficult. He " Deposeth in ye race between Wm. Epes and Mr. Stephen Cocke," that the latter " endeavoured to gett the other's path, but he did not gett it at two or three jumps nor many more, upon w'ch he josselled on Mr. Epes' path all most part of ye Race."

People took all these things very seriously, and they formed the subjects of conversation until the time came for horse and rider to distinguish themselves in a sterner field.

The horses bred in Virginia were small, fleet, and enduring, varying little from the early English racers, — the immediate descendants of the Arabian horses. There was a fine race-course at Fredericksburg, and Mary Washington's relatives and friends appear in the contests — her sister-in-law's husband, Roger Gregory, always among the foremost. He

ran a famous mare, Dimple; Mr. Spotswood, Fearnaught, — a name reasonably to be expected from
John Spotswood's horse. Then there were Fashion,
Eclipse, Selima, Ariel, Why Not? (why, indeed?),
and many more. Purses from ten to two hundred
guineas or pounds were the prizes; also "Saddles,
Bridles, Cups and Soop Ladles."

Lewis Willis, General Washington's first cousin,
worked his farm principally with blooded plough-
horses. The dams of Maid of the Oaks and Betsy
Blue were plough-horses. Maid of the Oaks — the
most splendid creature ever seen — sold for £15,000
to pay, alas! a security debt. For this astonishing
statement I have as authority Lewis Willis's son,
Byrd Willis, — father of the Princess Murat and
brother of the Jack Willis so loved by everybody
and by none more than General Washington himself. These were splendid, jovial fellows, full of
anecdote and inexhaustible humor. Colonel Byrd
Willis left a diary of the good times of his day.

But, alas for all the good times, the little cloud
no bigger than a man's hand in 1766 was now
darkening the Northern sky. The *Gazette*, that
had chronicled so many merry days, gave its columns to a warning note (July 21, 1774) from "a
Virginian," recommending that Fredericksburg sus-
pend its races and contribute purses to the people
of Boston; and, indeed, there was no more record
of a race before the Revolution.

The Presbyterian tutor, from whom we must now part, was a candidate for the ministry, but saw much to admire and little to condemn in the social life of the Virginians. He had been warned " that Virginia is sickly — that the people there are profane, and exceeding wicked. That there I shall read no Calvinistic Books, nor hear any Presbyterian Sermons." He finds himself under no more nor stronger temptations to any kind of vice — perhaps not so great — as at home, " unless sometimes when I am solicited to dance I am forced to blush" not because of its wickedness — Oh, no ! — but " because of my Inability ! I Wish it had been a part of my Education to learn an innocent and ornamental qualification for a person to appear even decent in Company ! "

This impartial observer of the times in which Mary Washington lived sums up the Virginians thus : " The people are extremely hospitable and Polite — universal characteristics of a gentleman in Virginia. Some swear bitterly, but the practice seems to be generally disapproved. I have heard that this Country is notorious for Gaming, however this may be I have not seen a Pack of *Cards*, nor a *Die* since I left home, nor gaming nor Betting of any kind except at the Races. The *Northern Neck* is a most delightful country — the best people are remarkable for regularity and economy, civil and polite and of the highest quality in Virginia —

well acquainted with the formality and ceremony which we find commonly in High Life — sensible, judicious, much given to retirement and study," etc., at length, of which the above extract is a fair example.

Another tutor, one John Davis, presumably a Welshman, who spent, and wrote of, " Four and a Half Years in America," described the Virginians of George Washington's time and neighborhood and the church he attended : —

" No people could exceed these men in politeness. On the piazza of Mr. Thornton's tavern I found a party of gentlemen from the neighboring plantations carousing over a bowl of toddy and smoking cigars. On my ascending the steps to the piazza, every countenance seemed to say, ' This man has a double claim to our attention, for he is a stranger in the place.' In a moment room was made for me to sit down ; a new bowl was called for, and every one who addressed me did it with a smile of conciliation. But no man questioned me whence I had come, or whither I was going. A gentleman in every country is the same — and if good breeding consists in sentiment, it was found in the circle I had got into.

" The higher Virginians seem to venerate themselves as men ! I am persuaded there was not one in that company who would have felt embarrassed at being admitted to the presence and conversation

of the greatest monarch on earth.   There is a com-
pound of virtue and vice in every human character.
No man was ever faultless; but whatever may be advanced against Virginians, their good qualities will ever
outweigh their defects ; and when the effervescence
of youth has abated, when reason reasserts her empire,
there is no man on earth who discovers more exalted
sentiments, more contempt of baseness, more love
of justice, more sensibility of feeling, than a Virginian. . . .   I found at the taverns every luxury
that money can purchase ; the richest viands covered the table, and ice cooled the Madeira that had
been thrice across the ocean.   About eight miles
away was *Powheek* (Pohick) church — a name it
claims from a run that flows near its walls.   Hither
I rode on Sundays and joined the congregation of
Parson Weems" [our friend of the hatchet and cherry
tree !] "a minister of the Episcopal persuasion, who
was cheerful in his mien that he might win men to
religion.   A Virginian church-yard on a Sunday,
resembles rather a race-course than a sepulchral
ground.   The ladies come to it in coaches, and the
men, after dismounting from their horses, make
them fast to the trees.   The steeples to Virginia
churches were designed not for utility but ornament ; for the bell is always suspended to a tree
a few yards from the church.   I was confounded on
first entering the church-yard at Powheek to hear
' Steed threaten steed with high and boastful neigh,'

nor was I less stunned with the rattling of wheels, the cracking of whips, and the vociferations of the gentlemen to the negroes who accompanied them. One half the congregation was composed of white people, the other of negroes, and Parson Weems preached the great doctrines of salvation as one who had experienced their power."

The Welsh tutor, Davis, and the American tutor and patriot, Fithian, wrote thus of the Virginians of Mary Washington's day, as they saw and knew them. Their horizon was limited to a few representative families in one or two neighborhoods. But a great and good man of the present generation — wise, truthful, candid — has thus recorded his opinion of the Virginians of that period. Says John Fiske : " On the whole it was a noble type of rural gentry that the Old Dominion had to show. Manly simplicity, love of home and family, breezy activity, disinterested public spirit, thorough wholesomeness and integrity, — such were the features of the society whose consummate flower was George Washington."

This section of Virginia could boast a society, more exclusive, if possible, than that of the James River region. It was free from the mixed and motley crowd which infested Williamsburg. Somewhat remote from the commercial centre, the life was that of the landed gentry in England ; quieter, more conservative, more leisurely and elegant than the society gathered in towns.

Thomson Mason of the Northern Neck, providing in his will for the education of his sons, adds, "but I positively direct that neither of my sons shall reside on the South Side of James River until the age of twenty-one years, lest they should imbibe more exalted notions of their own importance than I could wish any child of mine to possess." Already there was a protest against a certain lofty manner in vogue among the planters. Fashions that had lasted long began to change.

With the passing of the century Virginia's picturesque Golden Age passed, never to return in the history of this country.

Even while Washington lived and held his stately court, — powdered, in full court-dress, sword at side, and no "hand-shake" for the crowd at his levees, — even then the Golden Age, the age dominated by English influence, had passed. England was no longer the authority in manner and dress. The people wished none of her customs, traditions, or principles. Naturally their hearts had turned to the French. The emancipated Englishman cared no more for family trees, still less for armorial bearings. When Bishop Meade travelled through Virginia to cull material for his history of the old families, he found them reluctant to acknowledge the possession of a coat of arms or to confess a descent from English nobility. "They seemed ashamed of it. Everybody became a 'Democrat,' a ' patriot,' and in the abstract at least ' an advocate of the rights of man.' Many families who were properly entitled to arms, lost the evidence of it in the general neglect which blighted the tree of pedigree." The manner in which Jefferson, in the opening of his autobiography, almost sneers at armorial bearings reflects the feeling of Virginia for many years after the Revolution.

Judge N. Beverley Tucker prefaces a family history with these words, "At this day it is deemed arrogant to remember one's ancestors." *Nous avons changé tout cela!* At *this* day it is suicidal to forget them!

In presenting these pictures of social life in Virginia in the eighteenth century, I have been careful to accept the testimony only of those who were actually a part of it. It has become the fashion to idealize that old society as something better than our own. It had its charm of stateliness, of punctilious etiquette, of cordial hospitality; its faults of pompous manner, of excess and vanity, differing as conditions have changed, only in type and expression, from similar blemishes in our own manners of to-day; neither better nor worse, perhaps, as the years have passed. In all that is understood by the word " society " we find many points of resemblance, a family likeness, in fact, to metropolitan society in the nineteenth century.

Has the reader ever sought an intelligent definition of the term " society " ?

"Society," says Noah Webster, "is specifically the more cultivated portion of any community, in its social relations and influence ; those who give and receive formal entertainments mutually." This sounds reasonable enough, but the literary world of to-day, if we may credit some of its shining lights, takes exception at the word " cultivated."

"Society," says Bishop Huntington, in his " Drawing-room Homily," "is something too formless for an institution, too irregular for an organization, too vital for a machine, too heartless for a fraternity, too lawless for a school. It is a state wherein all realism is suppressed as brutal, all natural expression or frank sign of true feeling as distasteful and startling. Its subjects are more prostrate than the slaves of the East before the Padishah ! The individual finds everything decided for him. Provided he imitates copies, and repeats his models, he knows all that he need know, and has entered into salvation."

Evidently, neither now, nor in the Arcadian days of Virginia's Golden Age, has society seen fit to adopt the motto inscribed on the palace gates of the young Alexander Severus, " Let none enter here save the pure in heart." One, than whom none knows it better, has declared it to be to-day " a garden of flowers where ' sweets compacted lie.' But underneath the roses lurks a subtle and venomous serpent whose poison already threatens the fair and beloved of the land."

Q

These eminent satirists are part of the society they condemn. They know it well. And yet we would fain find comfort in the summing up of another who also knew it well. "Society," says Emerson, "is something too good for banning, too bad for blessing. In attempting to settle its character, we are reminded of a tradition in pagan mythology. 'I overheard Jove,' said Silenus, 'talking of destroying the earth. He said he had failed; they were all rogues and vixens going from bad to worse. Minerva said she hoped not; they were only ridiculous little creatures with this odd circumstance, — if you called them bad, they would appear so; if good, they would appear good, — and there was no one person among them which would not puzzle her owl — much more all Olympus — to know whether it was fundamentally good or bad.'"

But whether or no society be fundamentally good or bad, its doings have been in all ages interesting. Max O'Rell declares that the upper ten thousand are alike all over the world; that the million only — as affording original types — are interesting. He is wrong. The world cares more for the fortunate few than for the ordinary mass of mankind. Why do we find in every journal of the day long columns filled with the comings and goings, the uprisings and down-sittings of our wealthy classes? Why do readers never complain of the monotonous round of their travels? People prick up their ears and listen whenever the word "society" is uttered, although fully aware that half we read is invented to meet the hunger of the multitude for society news.

Everybody wants a glimpse of that gallant vessel bearing the elect so gayly down the stream of time, — the stream so full of bitter waters to many. They are more interesting, these voyagers in the painted pleasure boat, than the poor man who shades his eyes with his rough hand to gaze as they pass. They are even more interesting than the crowd running along to cheer, or swimming in the wake for the possible chance of being taken on board. There they go! — the happy hundreds — a "merry chanter" at the prow, a merry crew in the rigging; music, song, the flash of jewels, the perfume of flowers mingling with everyday sights, and sounds of everyday life.

We may assure ourselves that it is possible to be happy on board some other vessel, with a better pilot, and bound for a better port, but life is serious on that vessel. We like to be amused, and are keenly interested in those gayer voyagers.

PART II

CHAPTER I

THE LITTLE CLOUD

IT seems to have been hard for England to take her American colonies seriously. " The gentlemen of the opposition on the other side of the water " were regarded as inferiors, or, at best, troublesome children, to be dealt with accordingly, and taught to know — and keep — their places.

As early as 1766 a " Planter " on the banks of the Potomac addressed a letter to " The Merchants of London," and printed in the London *Public Ledger*, in which he says : " The epithets of ' parent and child ' have been so long applied to Great Britain and her colonies that individuals have adopted them, and we rarely see anything from your side of the water free from the authenticated style of a master to a schoolboy. He seems to say, ' We have, with infinite difficulty and fatigue, got you excused this time; pray be a good boy for the future; do what your papa and mamma bid you, and hasten to return them your most grateful acknowledgments for condescending to let you keep what is your own. If you are a naughty boy, and turn obstinate, and don't mind what your papa and mamma say to you, and pretend to judge for yourself when you are not arrived at years of discretion or capable of distinguishing between good and evil, then everybody will hate you; your parents and masters will be obliged to whip you severely, and their friends will blame *them*.' See what you have brought this child to! If he had been well scourged at first for opposing your absolute will and pleasure and daring to think he had any such thing as property of his own, he would not have had the impudence to repeat the crime."

The first word of resistance to the enforcement of the Stamp Act came from the Northern Neck of Virginia. At Leeds, Richard Henry Lee, born in the same county and same year with George Washington, wrote a set of resolutions which were unanimously adopted by one hundred and fifteen of the most influential of his neighbors. No Virginian could be legally tried but by his peers. No Virginian (for were they not all British subjects?) could be taxed but by consent of a parliament in which he is represented by persons chosen by the people. "Any person using the stamp paper was an abandoned wretch, lost to virtue and public good!" They bound themselves to resist and punish such persons; and at the utmost risk of lives and fortunes to protect any and every citizen who should suffer persecution because of adherence to these resolutions.

This was in 1766. The defiant paper was signed by Mary Washington's three sons,—Samuel, Charles, and John Augustine,—also by Dr. Mortimer, her family physician. The Stamp Act was soon repealed, and the stir and excitement naturally subsided. Several years later a tax on tea, glass, and paper awakened it again. Even then there was no apprehension of danger. Nobody dreamed of final separation from England. The little cloud had been no bigger than a man's hand; it was resting on the distant horizon and would give trouble to nobody.

In 1766 the odious Stamp Act was repealed. In 1767 a new and more oppressive duty was laid on glass, paper, and tea. England, in the next year, drew back again and repealed this later tax, excepting only the tax on tea, "for," said Lord North, "a total repeal cannot be thought of until America lies prostrate at our feet."

Virginia retaliated by her non-importation resolutions, binding herself to import nothing from England until the obnoxious impost should be repealed. Every known article of luxury in living or dress was specified in her proscribed list, except — oh, wise and prudent burgesses!—"women's bonnets and hats, sewing silk and netting silk!"

The resolutions were signed by 170 Virginians, including George Washington, Spencer Ball, Samuel Eskridge, and the Lees, Tayloes, Corbins,

Carters, and others of Mary Washington's family, friends, and neighbors in the Northern Neck. The firmest spirit pervaded the assembly. At its close, the *Gazette* goes on to say, "the whole company walked in procession from the Capitol to the Raleigh Tavern, where loyal and patriotic toasts were drunk — the King, the Queen and Royal family, the Governor of Virginia, the Duke of Richmond, Lord Chatham, Lord Camden, Lord Shelburne, British Liberty in America." Warming up after half a score of glasses, somebody gave, " May the Efforts of Virginia, joined with her Sister Colonies in the Cause of Liberty, be crowned with Success;" and then, warmer still, and jealously fearful of discourtesy to the government it had just defied (for a gentleman must be polite on his own soil) this toast was enthusiastically presented and applauded, " May the Rose flourish, the Thistle grow, and the Harp be tuned to the cause of American Liberty!"

A fine "schoolboy" this, loving liberty, loving fun, too much in love with happiness to bear malice!

It was not long before the schoolboy had a fine chance for a frolic. Ships laden with tea appeared in Boston harbor. A party disguised as American Indians boarded the ships and threw the cargo overboard. This was more than any indulgent parent could be expected to stand. The schoolboy must be shut up in a closet, and the key turned on him.

The port of Boston was ordered by Act of Parliament to be closed!

And now Richard Henry Lee's "Committee of Correspondence and Communication with the Sister Colonies" came into active service. Of course the governor had dissolved the assembly that adopted it. He was too late! From the moment of its adoption expresses were flying from Massachusetts to Virginia, back and forth, with details of every step in the progress of events. William Lee wrote from London that "this inter-colonial consultation had struck a greater panic in the ministers than all that had taken place since the Stamp Act." The expresses travelled fast. Not for nothing had the Virginians bred fleet horses and trained fearless riders! It was said of those riders that "they must almost have flown," so promptly did the pulse in Virginia respond to the heart-throb in Massachusetts.

The news from Boston was overwhelming. Not only was the port to be closed as punishment — the thumb-screw drew still closer. Parliament passed an "Act whereby the People of Boston shall have no power of trying any Soldier or Person for committing any crime: all such offenders to be sent Home for legal Tryal." 14 Geo. III, c. 39.

The Virginia leaders were not surprised. The little cloud, no bigger than a man's hand in 1766, had never disappeared altogether. For ten years the storm had been gathering. The sky was now overcast, the thunder was heard, the tempest was at hand. With a keen realization of all that resistance implied, some of them hesitated. Many of them were descendants of the royalists who had come over after the execution of Charles the First. They knew what revolution meant! The halter and the scaffold were still vivid in their traditions.

When the news came of the Act of Parliament closing the port, the House of Burgesses was in session. They ordained "a day of solemn fasting, humiliation and prayer, devoutly to implore the Divine interposition for averting a heavy calamity which threatens the civil rights of America."

Every man, one would think, has a right to humble himself, abstain from food, and pray God for help in time of trouble. Not so thought his Excellency, Governor Dunmore. Summoning the Honorable — the House of Burgesses — to his Council Chamber, he spoke to them thus: " Mr. Speaker and Gentlemen of the House of Burgesses, I have in my hand a paper published by order of your House conceived in such terms as reflect highly upon his Majesty and the Parliament of Great Britain, which makes it necessary for me to dissolve you, and you are dissolved accordingly.'

So, then, the guardians of the colony were to be sent home to do their fasting and praying in private, and perchance repent or hold their tongues, at least.

But just here the unexpected happened. While the Virginians were growing more and more hostile to Lord Dunmore and treating him with ill-disguised contempt, his family arrived at Williamsburg, — the Right Honorable, the Countess of Dunmore, Lord Fincastle, and the Ladies Catherine, Augusta, and Susan Murray.

Here was a pretty state of things, — distinguished strangers arriving on Virginia soil and Virginia on the eve of a political earthquake. However, there was but one way out of the difficulty,—hospitality and hostility both claiming the hour, hostility must step aside for a while. There was time for all things. There must be

Lord Dunmore.

an illumination of course; and if the ladies smiled as they entered Williamsburg in their chariot drawn by six white horses, they must receive acclamations in return.

They did smile. They made a most agreeable impression. The *Virginia Gazette* declared next day that the arrival of the countess gave inexpressible pleasure, that she was a very elegant woman, that her daughters were "fine, sprightly girls," and that "goodness of heart flashed from them in every look."

Before they turned into the great palace gates they had won all hearts. They were the guests of the colony. Already a herald had published a Court Etiquette, whose leaflets were in the hands of the pretty Jacqueline and Ambler girls. The finishing touch of courtly grace and usage was to be given to the high-born Virginia beauties.

True, there was small time now to study court etiquette, but a little delay could not matter much. Whether it did or no, hospitality was the prime, sacred, delightful duty of the hour.

Accordingly, the gentlemen of the House of Burgesses caused the *Gazette* to announce a "Ball at the Capital to Welcome Lady Dunmore and her Family to Virginia." The Apollo, which still echoed Henry's eloquence and Washington's appeal for Boston, was hastily made ready; and the men who had been most bitter in the morning in their denunciation of the Port Bill bowed low in the evening to the Countess of Dunmore, and led her and her daughters with grave courtesy through the stately figures of the minuet.

Presently it is all over. The last note dies upon the strings, the lights burn low in the coming dawn, parting words are whispered, — " *adieu*," not " *au revoir*," — and the hands that had touched with

refined finger-tips harden themselves for the gauntlet
and the sword.   No matter, now her ladyship has
been suitably welcomed, how soon she runs away
with her pretty daughters from the guns and finds
refuge on the *Fowey!*   The sooner the better, in
fact.

. But before that could happen Lady Dunmore
had time to become immensely popular in Williamsburg.   The *Gazette* was forever printing verses in
her praise.   The burgesses were welcomed to the
handsome " palace " of their governor, — the palace
of which they were so proud, with its " imposing
cupola, lit at night on public occasions, its ample
green lawn in front, its artificial lakes, gardens and
terraces."   Lady Dunmore gave an afternoon reception on Queen Charlotte's birthday when her
youngest child was christened *Virginia* in compli-
ment to the Old Dominion.   Everybody was invited
at night to join the royal party in a splendid ball in
honor of the Queen's birthday.

" The Mimic Court at Williamsburg was exerting
all its powers to please, but the patriots were not
to be turned aside."   They could draw the velvet
glove over the gauntlet to pleasure a lady, but the
gauntlet was there, nevertheless, and the gauntlet
was of steel.

We are impressed in reading of all this, with the
punctilious etiquette of Williamsburg society which
forbade the intrusion of politics into the social life.

Lord Dunmore had been regarded with suspicion and distrust from the moment of his arrival in 1772. He was perfectly aware of the feeling of the First Assembly which met under his administration. Colonel Washington was a member of that assembly, and had been present — and active — at the consultations on public affairs held in the old Raleigh tavern. Yet, but for the death of Miss Custis, he would have been Dunmore's companion when he journeyed to Western Virginia to purchase land.

He dined with Lord Dunmore a few days before the couriers brought news of the Act of Parliament closing the port at Boston. Nobody was more resolute than he in denunciation of that act, and in support of the resolutions of "sympathy for our distressed fellow-subjects of Boston." At that moment his pocket held an accepted invitation to dine with the governor. He did so dine, spent the evening with him, probably the night, too, for he breakfasted with him the next day at his farm. Two of Lord Dunmore's sons were students at William and Mary College. To all outward appearance everything was going well and smoothly among good friends and neighbors.

The fast was appointed for the first day of June, 1774. The port was to be closed on the fourth. On that day Washington wrote in his diary, " Fasted all day and went to Church." George Mason, of

"Gunston Hall," in the Northern Neck wrote
home, "Please tell my dear little family that I

Robert Carter of Nomini Hall.

desire my three eldest sons and my two eldest
daughters may attend church in mourning."
His friend and neighbor, Robert Carter, ordered

R

differently.   "No one must go from hence to church or observe this fast at all."   Not yet were all the colonists prepared to follow Washington, Jefferson, Henry, Mason, and Lee in defiance to the British Crown!

The fast was generally observed.   The governor, it appears, had no power to prevent it.   The time had not yet come when Virginia patriots, to avoid his interference, must hold their conferences in old St. John's Church at Richmond.   At Williamsburg a sermon was preached from the text, "Help, Lord! for the godly man ceaseth, for the faithful fail from among the children of men."

The tea was sealed up and destroyed, and money and provisions ordered to be sent to Boston.   The counties were canvassed for these, and they were immediately forwarded.

The Virginia women entered with enthusiasm into all schemes for sending help to their "distressed fellow-subjects in Boston," and applauded Colonel Washington when he declared that "he was ready to raise one thousand men, subsist them at his own expense and march at their head to Massachusetts."

The colonial dames packed away in lavender-scented chests all their imported finery, their "quilts" and brocades, and clothed themselves in homespun or in mourning, destroying or sealing up their precious stock of tea, and regarding with unfriendly eyes a certain dame who continued to indulge in the proscribed luxury. It seems hard, poor lady, that she should come down in history as the only one who thus transgressed, "who continued to sip her tea in her closet after it was banished from every table," and that even her name and lineage should be given by an irreverent historian! This was no other than Kate Spotswood, she of the fawn and blue satin gown and the silver hair, now Mrs. Bernard Moore!

Even the master of "Nomini Hall" proscribed the tea long before he ceased, for he *did* cease at last, to toast "his Gracious Majesty, the King." "Something," says our old friend, the tutor, "in our palace this Evening very merry happened. Mrs. Carter made a dish of Tea! At Coffee she sent me a dish— I and the Colonel both ignorant. He smelt, sipt, look'd! At last with great gravity he asks, '*What's this?*' 'Do you ask, Sir?' 'Poh!' and out he throws it, *splash!* a sacrifice to Vulcan."

It seems the tea was restored to favor, at least in the army, only three years later. The colonists were then expressing themselves in sterner language! An island was found somewhere near headquarters in June, 1778. Here the officers invited their friends in the afternoon to drink tea, and because the island was so beautiful and enchanting they honored it with the name of "Paphos." There "Lady Stirling, Lady Kilty, and Miss Brown, met his Excellency's lady, an agreeable, well-disposed, excellent woman. The prospect of an alliance in Europe had cheered every heart, and cheerfulness enlightened every countenance." Was it the "alliance" or the dearly loved beverage of which they had been so long deprived? Thenceforward and until to-day the afternoon tea has been an institution, linked with the history of our country. It came back on the island of Paphos, and it came to stay! We hear of it once again in the annals of the Revolution. The Marquis de Chastellux tells us of another afternoon tea! "I left Mr. Samuel Adams with regret, and terminated my day by a visit to Colonel Bland. He is a tall, handsome man who has been a good soldier, but at present serves his country and serves it well in Congress. I was invited to drink tea, that is, attend a sort of Assembly: pretty much like the *conversazioni* of Italy; for tea here is the substitute for the *rinfresca*. Mr. Arthur Lee, M. de La Fayette, M. de Noualles, M. de Dames, etc: were of the party." In those days men could be found at an afternoon tea!

CHAPTER II

THE stirring events which marked every month in the next two years are known to every reader of American history: the steady injustice and oppression of the governor, his attempt to disarm the colonists by removing the powder of the colony from "The old Powder-horn," the quaint old building at Williamsburg, now cherished by the association for the preservation of Virginia antiquities, the arming of the Virginians headed by Patrick Henry to reclaim it, the flight of poor Lady Dunmore and her pretty daughters to the protecting guns of the *Fowey*, finally, the flight of the governor himself, followed by the curses of the people, — how he trained his guns on Norfolk, giving Virginia her first experience of the horrors of war, how he hung about the coast to the terror of the country people, and finally announced his intention of sailing up the Potomac and capturing Mrs. Washington!

When the powder was stolen by Governor Dunmore, seven hundred citizens, calling themselves the Friends of Liberty, armed and met in Fredericksburg, ready to march to Williamsburg, and reclaim it by force. They were led by Hugh Mercer, Mary Washington's friend and neighbor. George Washington and George Mason prevailed upon them to wait until Dunmore made restitution.

These were days of fearful trial to Mary Washington. Hitherto, on her quiet farm on the banks of the Rappahannock, she had known little of all the stir and excitement. Of the little that she heard she disapproved. She was a loyal subject of the king and a devoted churchwoman. All her early prejudices, traditions, ideas of duty, close ties of kindred, bound her to the mother country and the Church of England. That these should be resisted by her own family, her four sons, and the Mercers, Travers, and Gregorys, was an overwhelming disaster, to which she found it hard to be resigned.

When war was declared and she learned that her son was to lead the rebellious army, her anguish was expressed in the most vehement language. " Grandma Knox " strove in vain to console her. " Oh, is there to be more fighting, more bloodshed? Surely it will all end in the halter," exclaimed the devoted mother. So bitter were her feelings at this moment, that when General Washington rode to Fredericksburg to induce her to remove into the town, he was doubtful in what manner she would receive him. He thought it prudent to pause at the little inn, " The Indian Queen," and reconnoitre.

That a member of the family should " put up at a tavern " was so tremendous an event that no one dared mention it to his mother. Observing an air of mystery in the faces of her servants, she demanded an explanation. " Tell George to come home instantly — instantly ! " she exclaimed ; and straining him to her bosom, she again commended him to God, and again gave him, with her blessing, to his country.

On the 15th of June, 1775, he was elected commander-in-chief of the American forces, and crossed the threshold of his mother's home, and his own beloved Mount Vernon, on the right bank of the Potomac, to return no more until the war should end. He was in his saddle, on his way to Boston on horseback, when he was met by the news of the battle of Bunker Hill. On the second of July he entered Boston amid the acclamations of the people and the thunder of cannon, and the next day assumed command of the American forces.

The anguish of his mother was shared by the wife, left alone at Mount Vernon. She wrote to a relative who censured the folly of Washington's position : " I foresee consequences, dark days, domestic happiness suspended, eternal separation on earth possible. But my mind is made up. My heart is in the cause. George is right ; he is always right ! "

" Escorted," says Washington Irving, " by a troop of light-horse, and a cavalcade of citizens, he proceeded to the headquarters provided for him at Cambridge, three miles distant. As he entered the confines of his camp, the shouts of the multitude and the thundering of artillery, gave note to the enemy beleaguered in Boston of his arrival."

Abigail Adams.

He was already the idol of the hour ! As he rode along the lines, all travel-soiled and dusty, he found favor in every heart. The soldiers adored him — the women as well. The elegant and accomplished wife of John Adams, destined to be the first American lady to make her courtesy to King George after it was all over, wrote to her husband: "Dignity, ease and complacency, the gentleman and the soldier, look agreeably blended in him. Modesty marks every line and feature of his face. Those lines of Dryden instantly occurred to me: —

> " ' Mark his majestic fabric ! He's a temple
> Sacred by birth and built by hands divine;
> His soul's the Deity that lodges there;
> Nor is the pile unworthy of the God!' "

What said the "Godlike" hero to all this? Simply that he trusted that Divine Providence, which wisely orders the affairs of men, would enable him to discharge his duty with fidelity and success. A year later he wrote, "When I took command of the army I abhorred the idea of independence, but I am now fully satisfied that nothing else will save us."

Dunmore was still in the Virginia waters. He did not leave until the following year, in fact, his burning of Norfolk occurred six months after General Washington left Virginia. It was constantly expected that he would appear upon the Rappahannock and Potomac rivers; and Colonel George Mason, having moved his own family to a place of safety, recommended to Mrs. Martha Washington, who was at Mount Vernon, to leave the neighborhood also. He wrote to General Washington a little later: "Dunmore has come and gone, and left us untouched except by some alarms. I sent my family many miles back into the country, and advised Mrs. Washington to do likewise as a prudential movement. At first she said, ' No, I will not desert my post,' but she finally did so with reluctance, rode only a few miles, and, plucky little woman as she is, stayed away only one night."

During the summer of 1776, Dunmore started again to ascend the Potomac to lay waste " Gunston Hall " and Mount Vernon and capture Mrs. Washington. The county militia harassed him on his way, but he probably would have achieved his purpose but for a dreadful storm that threatened the safety of the ship. But when thunder and storm reached him through the cannon-balls of Andrew Lewis, one of which passed through his flag-ship and smashed his china, " Good God ! " said Lord Dunmore, " has it come to this ? " and weighing anchor, he betook himself to England, having injured as far as possible the colony he was commissioned to protect.

CHAPTER III

MARY WASHINGTON was kept in a state of perpetual anxiety and alarm. She was left unprotected by her nearest friends and relatives. Her son was gone, returning for no brief visits to his old home. Her grandson, George Lewis, was on his uncle's staff. Her sons were enlisted, all her grandsons. The Spotswood boys were at the front. Her good neighbor, Hugh Mercer, was a general in the army; her near relative, Colonel Burgess Ball, had raised and equipped a regiment, and was maintaining it at his own expense. "All Europe was amazed when out of the forests and fields of the remote colonies of the Atlantic coast, from north to south, there stepped forth at the drum beat of Revolution heroes, scholars, statesmen, soldiers, and chieftains who overcame its master spirits in debate and foiled its ablest commanders in the field of combat."

Others of her neighbors and relations were already at the front. In many houses father and sons had gone; in almost every home the first-born was a soldier. She had only with her the women of her kindred and the good and faithful Dr. Charles Mortimer, — the loyal American though English born, — the able, generous physician. At his own expense he equipped and maintained a hospital in which Mary Washington and his little Maria probably felt a deep and common interest.

Her old age was not to be the ideal age so passionately desired by the old, of quiet serenity, " honor, obedience, and troops of friends." The latter she had, with the added pang of keen anxiety for their safety and welfare. She was called upon to surrender all she held sacred or dear, — her king, her church, her glorious son, her kindred, her loved country home. She gave up all resignedly, uncomplainingly.

It was after this triumph over her prejudices, this complete surrender to conviction of duty that her character blossomed into perfect beauty. A great calmness possessed her soul and shone in her face, a dignified resignation differing altogether from dumb despair.

While her son was leading the troops of his country she was busily engaged in the industries of domestic life, — sorting the fleece and mingling it with shredded silk to make long hose for her son, the general; weaving substantial fabrics in the great cumbrous looms; learning cunning secrets of herbs and leaves to dye the cloth for garments; preparing balsams and lotions for the sick and needy. Her hands were never idle. Gathering her apron into a spacious pocket, she walked about with the woollen knitting for her son's soldiers. She became, it is true, somewhat more silent, more reserved. The lines of the face lost all hint of humor. She was too sad for that, but never peevish or complaining. Descendants of her old neighbors acknowledged that " Mrs. Washington was somewhat stern," but add that she and her daughter, Mrs. Lewis, possessed withal a lofty graciousness of manner peculiarly their own. General Washington had this manner, commanding deference and confidence, and forbidding familiarity or the smallest liberty ; although it is certain that neither he nor his mother were conscious of the impression made upon others.

Her daughter, Betty Lewis, lived at " Kenmore," the elegant mansion near Fredericksburg, and entreated her to come to her " to be taken care of," but she said, " My wants are few in this life, and I feel perfectly competent to take care of myself." She elected a home of her own very near " Kenmore," preferring to be independent. Thence she was driven every day by " old Stephen " in her phaeton to her farm across the river, whence she brought seeds and cuttings for her town garden and a jug of water from the spring out of which her husband and children had drunk. Old Stephen witnessed with glee her method of dealing with her overseer. The latter ventured one day to depart from her instructions, and she called him to account.

"Madam," said the agent, "in my judgment the work has been done to better advantage than if I had followed your instructions."

"And pray, sir, who gave you the right to exercise any judgment in the matter?" she asked; "I command you, sir! There is nothing left for you but to obey."

Fredericksburg was in the direct line of communication between Williamsburg and the headquarters of the army. Couriers were perpetually passing to and fro, and many were the respectful letters "honored madam" received from the great commander.

With the coming of these couriers came repeated tidings of loss and defeat. She heard about the battle of Long Island, the long days and nights in the saddle; of the defeat at White Plains; of how the militia quitted and went home; of the Princeton victory, where her loved neighbor, Hugh Mercer, died in her grandson's arms; of the heavy loss at Brandywine and Germantown, where her near neighbor, the son of plucky John Spotswood, fell dangerously wounded into the hands of the enemy; of the misery at Valley Forge; of Howe's occupation of Philadelphia; of General Gates's great victory at Saratoga — perhaps of the cabal against her son, when the victorious general was preferred by some to him. Perhaps her son may have written, or some of Morgan's borderers written to their friends, of their march from the Shenandoah to Boston with

"Liberty or Death" embroidered in white letters on their hunting-shirts; how General Washington had met them as he was riding along his lines; how Morgan had saluted with the words, "*From the right bank of the Potomac, General!*" how the great commander had leaped from his horse, and with tears in his eyes shook hands with each one of them.

"The night was dark and he was far from home!"

Or, perhaps, those watching, waiting women on the Rappahannock heard of how the Virginian, George Rogers Clarke, had begged powder and men, and gone out to shut and guard the back door of the country; how they had waded in freezing water, fasting five days and nights, holding their muskets above their heads as they struggled on; how, finally, ready as they were to give up, a little drummer-boy had mounted the shoulders of a tall soldier, and beat the vigorous "Charge," rallying and inspiring their fainting spirits.   Or, it may be, that some messenger among the fleet couriers had come from Wheeling, Virginia, and could tell of Elizabeth Zane, the brave young girl, who volunteered to cross a plain under Indian fire, and bring a keg of powder from a house in town to save the stockade in which her people were hiding; how she ran across the plain, found and fetched the powder, and saved the day.

"These noble legends," says Esten Cooke, "are

the true glories of American history; the race lives in them and is best illustrated by them. It was a very great race, and faced peril without shrinking, down to the very boys and girls; and what the long years of the future will remember is this heroic phase, not the treaties and protocols of American history." It was the *spirit* behind our little army that compelled events and carried it triumphantly to the glorious result.

It is said that Mary Washington never tolerated an expression of complaint or despair during these trying times. She would rebuke it by saying, "The mothers and wives of brave men must be brave women." Mr. Custis says that, "Directly in the way of the news, as it passed from North to South, one courier would bring intelligence of success to our arms; another, 'swiftly coursing at his heels,' the saddening reverse of disaster and defeat. While thus ebbed and flowed the fortunes of our cause, the mother, trusting to the wisdom and protection of Divine Providence, preserved the even tenor of her life, affording an example to those matrons whose sons were alike engaged in the arduous contest; and showing that unavailing anxieties, however belonging to nature, were unworthy of mothers whose sons were combating for the inestimable rights of man and the freedom and happiness of the world.

"During the war the mother set a most valuable example in the management of her domestic concerns, carrying her own keys, bustling in her household affairs, providing for her family, and living and moving in all the pride of independence. She was not actuated by that ambition for show which pervades lesser minds; and the peculiar plainness and dignity of her manners became in no wise altered, when the sun of glory arose upon her house. There are some of the aged inhabitants of Fredericksburg who well remember the matron as seated in an old-fashioned open chaise; she was in the habit of visiting, almost daily, her little farm in the vicinity of the town. When there she would ride about her fields, giving her orders, and seeing that they were obeyed.

" Hers was a familiar form in Fredericksburg during the Revolution, and its people showed her every respect as she walked the streets leaning on her cane. Devout and worshipful she appeared every Sabbath at church at the appointed hour; and while the armies under her son were struggling for our freedom, the knitting needles were busily plied, and from her home went forth her modest contributions of supplies for him and his soldiers."

Her biographers love to dwell upon her preternatural serenity. This serenity did not serve for dark hours only. She was not surprised when the tide turned, and the waves of triumph were borne to her feet. When her neighbors thronged her with plaudits and praise of her noble son — their idol

s

and hers — she restrained their extravagant words, saying quietly: "George seems to have deserved well of his country, but we must not praise him too much. George has not forgotten his duty!"

When the news reached Fredericksburg of the victories of Trenton and Princeton (in that ten days' campaign which Frederick the Great called the most brilliant in the annals of war) friends gathered around her with congratulations upon the great achievements of her son. She received them with calmness, observed that it was most pleasurable news, and that George appeared to have deserved well of his country for such signal services, and continued, in reply to the congratulating patriots (most of whom held letters in their hands, from which they read extracts), "but, my good sirs, here is too much flattery — still George will not forget the lessons I early taught him; he will not forget himself, though he is the subject of so much praise."

Among the traditions which still linger around Fredericksburg is one illustrating her perfect calmness, trust, and self-control. George Kiger, the courier, having at a time of great anxiety ridden hard to deliver a packet to her from headquarters, was dismayed to see her drop it unread into one of her unfathomable pockets, simply remarking, "It is all right — I am well assured of that." Bursting with curiosity, and mindful of the crowd which had assembled at her gate to hear the news, Kiger sug-

gested : " There may have been a battle.   The
neighbors would like to know."   Thereupon she
fished up the packet, glanced over it, and announced,
" There has been a victory !" adding, in the fulness
of her heart, " George generally carries through
whatever he undertakes."

In relating this we are reminded of the despatch
once handed to General Washington while he was
sitting for his portrait.   He read it apparently un-
moved and in silence.   It announced the surrender
of Burgoyne's army !

As the long years passed heavily away she had
need of more than her own strong nature to sustain
her.   She must seek for strength not her own.   " She
was always pious," says Mr. Custis, " but in her
latter days her devotions were performed in private.
She was in the habit of repairing every day to a
secluded spot, formed by rocks and trees, near her
dwelling, where, abstracted from the world and
worldly things, she communed with her Creator, in
humiliation and prayer."

This favorite resort of hers, sometimes called
" Oratory Rock," was a spot on Colonel Lewis's
estate, sheltered by climbing vines from observation.
Oratory Rock was a knoll on the " Kenmore "
grounds which during her life overlooked the Rappahannock.   The river has since forsaken its bed there,
and flows in another channel.   It was to this spot,
made lovely by shade trees and flowing vines, that

she repaired daily for meditation and prayer, returning home soothed and strengthened. She often expressed her gratitude for these serene hours, and
desired that she might be buried upon the spot,
where she had received such consolation.

And who can tell what heavenly messengers

Oratory Rock.

visited this great spirit and ministered unto her?
At her feet flowed the Rappahannock, over which
her son when a lad had thrown a stone. She could
remember how his heart had swelled with pride, —
that heart now breaking at the falling away of friends,
the desertion of soldiers, the disasters on the Hudson

and Long Island. Who can doubt that the tears of the great commander fell upon his mother's heart! Her life had been one of anxiety, trouble, and strife. It was now almost over! She knew of the end, only that for her it was near! It was then that whispered words may have floated on the mists of the gathering twilight: "In the world ye shall have tribulations! Fear not! I have overcome the world."

CHAPTER IV

OLD REVOLUTIONARY LETTERS

WHENEVER the women of the Revolution appear upon the pages of history or romance they are invested with extraordinary virtues. Our traditions are only of maidens who forsook morning lessons on the harpsichord, and afternoon tea, and embroidery, to knit stockings and make plain garments; of Abigail Adams, who "sought wool and flax and worked willingly with her own hands," of Lady Washington, dignified and domestic, presenting gloves of her own knitting, finished and unfinished, as souvenirs of morning visits, of the angelic ministrations of the women of Massachusetts and New Jersey. "Fairer always are the old moons of Villon, than the moons of to-day!" Chesterfield says human nature is the same all the world over. Woman nature assuredly is!

Letter-writing in the eighteenth century was difficult; the transmission of letters after they were written uncertain. One letter received from London was addressed in the fullest faith of finding its destination to "Major George Washington, At the Falls of the Rappahannock *or elsewhere in Virginia*." Of course, the fate of these letters was doubtful. They were liable to be lost or forgotten. They might be intercepted by the enemy. Hence the stilted style of many of the Revolutionary letters, the liberal use of initials to indicate proper names, the guarded hints, obscure innuendoes and vague allusions which characterize them. Letters were written on coarse paper, the sheet folded over to leave space for the address, tied across with a string, and sealed with wax or a small red wafer. There were no envelopes, no blotting-paper, no pens except those of home manufacture from the goose-quill. Two months was a reasonable length of time to allow for the delivery of letters. To the captain of some passing sloop they were generally confided, or to the pocket of some friend journeying at leisure from neighborhood to neighborhood. When received they were treasured, and packed away in old chests or the secret drawers of old secretaries, thence to arise to accuse or defend, or entertain the curious in future generations.

A New York paper, published about seventy years ago, tells the history of some of these old letters, as follows:[1] " In one of the thirty apartments of the old colonial home of the Bland family, ' Cawsons,' a large party were assembled at dinner with the master of the house, a bachelor, and not a mem-

[1] " Bland Papers," edited by Charles Campbell.

ber of the Bland family, when a servant entered and informed him that the house was on fire !

" He received the information with great coolness and composure, ordered that the fire should be extinguished, and requested his guests not to disturb themselves, that ' the servants would attend to it.'

" For a time the wine continued to circulate, and it appears that the fire did also, for with less ceremony than their host it soon drove the party out of doors.   In the confusion books and papers were thrust into boxes and barrels, or into anything that presented itself, and carried off into a neighboring barn.

" The person who owned the place at the time of the fire has been dead many years, and the accidental discovery, very recently, of the papers was made in the following manner.   A gentleman who had lived on an adjoining farm was called upon one morning by a poor negro who requested him to purchase a basket of eggs.   The basket was lined with manuscripts which proved upon closer inspection to be original letters of importance from General Washington, the Marquis La Fayette and others, addressed to Colonel Theodoric Bland, and written during the Revolution."

There was one letter, alas ! written to the wife of a Virginia officer whom we should be loth to judge by her friends.   It throws a sinister light upon one phase of the social life in the time of Mary Washington, and shows us women who could trifle, dress, dance, and flirt with the enemies of their country in the darkest hour of their country's peril, fiddling when Rome was burning.

Sir William Howe.

Sir William Howe entered Philadelphia in the autumn of 1777, and found "many to welcome him." [1] Philadelphia was a charming old town with substantial colonial mansions surrounded by grounds of great beauty. September roses were blooming

[1] Irving's "Life of Washington."

in those old-fashioned yards and gardens, and the gracious young beauties were quite willing to gather them for the British officers. The officers, when winter set in, were glad to give them all back in ball and concert, play and assembly. It was a light-hearted, happy time! Why should they not enjoy it? Why, indeed! Nobody would bleed the more freely or starve or freeze to death the sooner!

One of the letters in the egg-basket was written by a lady who elected to live in Philadelphia during the occupation of that city by Sir William Howe. It was addressed to the wife of an officer at the front. We cannot profane our fair, patriotic pages, but the original is accentuated by oaths quite worthy of Queen Bess. The ladies mentioned in the letter were wives and daughters of officers in the field. The writer tells some very, very questionable gossip to her " dear Patsy," and then proceeds:
. . . "You see I am obeying your commands and writing a folio — My God! If this should fall into your husband's hands I should die! for heaven's sake, my dear Patsy, don't expose me to him. Your own saucy epistle leads me into this scrape. Mrs. Beekman is still in the City. They were very un-genteelly treated, being turned out of their house to accommodate Lord Howe; they were then moved into the street where my mother lives. Mr. & Mrs. G. are at their house in Chestnut Street. Notwithstanding the gratification of their wishes

was completed in the arrival of the British Army, they received the usual disappointment. Miss Roche did not marry 'S' — by all accounts he is a vile fellow — so tell M. he may have hopes. Miss —— is not shackled, tho' she has many bleeding hearts at her feet." (The owners of the bleeding hearts were British officers.) "Her vivacity makes her admired, though saucy! One of her saucy *bon mots* I cannot omit. Sir William Howe, in a large company one evening, snatched a piece of narrow riband from her the moment she entered the ball room." (Here, alas, a covetous rat made a *bonne bouche* of the *bon mot* — perhaps it is as well!) "Little Poll Redmond still continues as violent a patriot as ever, and sings 'War and Washington' and 'Burgoyne's Defeat' for the British officers, and with a particular emphasis and saucy countenance warbles forth 'Cooped up in a Town.' You have no idea of the gay winter here; and likewise the censure thrown on the poor girls for not scorning these pleasures. You, my friend, have liberality of sentiment and can make proper allowance for young people deprived of the gaieties and amusements of life; with Plays, concerts, Balls, Assemblies in rotation courting their presence. Politics is never introduced. The Whig ladies are treated with the same politeness as the Tory ladies. I myself have been prevailed on to partake of the amusements, and I am, in raillery, styled 'rebel,' and all

the Whig news is kept from me.   I had the 'draught
of the bill' and Lord North's letter.   I have met
a great Hessian Yager Colonel," etc., through end-
less gossip of which the above is the only admissi-
ble sample !

It is unpleasant to observe that this letter was
written in the winter of 1777–1778 — the winter that
young Bartholomew Yates, a lieutenant in a Virginia
regiment, fell into the hands of the enemy, and died
in captivity from wounds *inflicted, after his surrender,
by the Hessians* — possibly at the order of my lady's
"great Hessian Yager Colonel," who was, according
to her narrative, admitted to her society and confid-
ing to her the secrets of the enemy.   At that moment many American prisoners, — among them
young John Spotswood, — desperately wounded,
were in Philadelphia inhumanly treated, dying from
wanton neglect ; and General Washington indignantly threatening retaliation in his letters to Sir
William Howe.   " The English officers were received in the best society with more than toleration,
and they soon became extremely popular.   The
winter was long remembered in Philadelphia for
its gayety and its charm.   There were no signs of
that genuine dislike which had been abundantly
displayed in Boston."   It appears the ladies of
Philadelphia ignored the well-known character of
Sir William Howe.   Also that the courtly Sir
William, when he found a house that suited him,

knew how to make the terms for it.[1] He took
the mansion of a rich old loyalist Quaker, John
Pemberton (in the absence of the latter), and used
also the elegant carriage of the Quaker for his
parties of pleasure. When the latter returned home
he found his property much injured, and claimed
indemnity. Sir William curtly refused. " Thee
had better take care ! " said John Pemberton. " Thee
has done great damage to my house, and thee has
suffered thy wicked women to ride in my carriage,
and my wife will not use it since. Thee must pay
me for the injury or I will go to thy master" (the
King) " and lay my complaint before him."

Sir William did take care ! He paid the money.

That most unfortunate of men, Major André, devised in honor of Sir William Howe the splendid
festival of the Mischianza during the occupation of
Philadelphia. Our gay correspondent received an
invitation with " the Howe arms and motto *vive
vale*. The device was a setting sun with ' He shines
as he sets, to rise again.' We went to Pool's
bridge in carriages — thence boats, barges and galleys bore us to ships of the fleet — all gay with the
colors of all nations and every country, and amid
them, waving with grace and elegance, our own
Stars and Stripes ! " " The entertainment comprised
a regatta, a ball, and a great display of fireworks,
with innumerable emblems and exhibitions of loyalty

[1] " History of the Valley of Virginia," Kercheval, p. 128.

to England.   It brought together one of the most brilliant assemblages of the youth, beauty and fashion of Philadelphia, and it was long remembered that Major André was most prominent in organizing the entertainment, and that the most prominent of the Philadelphia beauties who adorned it was Miss Shippen, soon after to become the wife of Benedict Arnold."

Major André.

The tournament was between the "Knights of the Ladies of the Blended Rose and the Ladies of the Burning Mountain," the latter presumably the daughters of the country about to be consumed !

The gayety was at its height when the army was encamped just across the Schuylkill at Valley Forge — when the winter was one of extraordinary rigor.   During that winter the army was often without bread, often entirely without meat. "Few men" had "more than one shirt, many only the moiety of one, and some none at all."   Men were confined in hospitals or farmers' houses for want of shoes. In camp there were on a single day 2,898 men unfit for duty because they were "barefoot and otherwise naked." In December the men built fires and sat up all night because there were no blankets to cover them. When a march was necessary their way could be traced by their bleeding feet. In three weeks of this time the army at Valley Forge lost, in its overflowing hospitals, hundreds, some say thousands, of men. Just across the river American women were bandying idle compliments with the British and Hessian officers, living on delicacies of their providing, dancing at midnight routs and noonday festivals. Here, at Valley Forge, Martha Washington was passing among the sick with deeds and words of cheer, and the aged mother praying in solitude on the banks of the Rappahannock!

Of the lady, to whom the Philadelphia letter was addressed, we must, perforce, form doubtful conclusions. That she possessed a personality which found immediate favor in the eyes of men, there is not the least doubt. No man could send her an ordinary message of courtesy unadorned by expressions of gallantry. Alexander Hamilton writes of Mrs. Bland to her husband so warmly that he is constrained to explain, "I write in the style *d'amitie*," not *d'amour*, as might have been imagined. Says Arthur Lee, "Lay me at the feet of Mrs. Bland," prudently adding, "and in the bosom of your friendship."

Stephen Higginson of Boston eclipses them all, and dilates upon "the rapturous delight of *one fond kiss* from sun to sun," which it appears she had promised him; doubting, however, his "capacity for enjoyments so excessive and for so long a time." Her own colonel shows himself to be very tender and gentle to his wife. He preserved all her letters. The poor lady had the smallpox, that dreadful scourge of the time, but she had not the greatness of soul to keep from the soldier in the field the knowledge of her disaster. She drives him wild with her indefinite complainings, her vague hints. He begs her to spare him this torture. "You say you have been too ill until to-day to see yourself in the glass. You cannot know what doubts I have had, what altercations in my own mind whether you went to the glass or the glass came to you!" She pines for the stir and excitement of the camp. He entreats her to feel benevolence and interest in the stay-at-home people. But my lady is subtle; all her trouble is forsooth for his sake — and he believes her. He entreats her to spare him her repining *at his absence*, and says, "Remember 'tis for you, for my country, for my honor, that I endure this separation, the dangers and the hardships of war; remember that America cannot be free, and therefore cannot be happy, without the virtue of her sons and the heroism of her daughters."

We observe the lady gains her point. She joins

the Court of Madam Washington in camp. We observe further, as confirmation of our estimate of her charms, that she did not long remain a widow after her husband's early death. She became Mrs. Blodgett, and again Mrs. Curran. Having refused to give John Randolph of Roanoke the papers and family portraits belonging to her first husband, he wrote bitterly of her, always as "the romantic Mrs. Bland-Blodgett-Curran."

With these volatile letters were others lining the ample egg-basket, — the originals of some of the most celebrated letters of Washington, Jefferson, Patrick Henry, Randolph, Richard Henry Lee, on the grave issues of the hour, and all addressed to Colonel Bland. A very important letter was from Arthur Lee, a pure, incorruptible patriot, who could not understand how a public servant living on a small salary could grow rich.

He was ambassador at the French court with Franklin. He left his countrymen in great straits for money, clothing, and provisions. He found their representatives abroad living in affluence. He wrote home, Dec. 13, 1778, "they have made immense private fortunes for themselves and their dependents. Mr. D. (Silas Deane) is generally understood to have made £60,000 sterling while he was commissioner; his clerk, from being penniless, keeps his house and carriage. Dr. Franklin's nephew, Mr. Williams, from being clerk in a sugar bakehouse in London,

T

is become a capital merchant here, loading a number of ships on his own account, while gentlemen of the first fortunes in America cannot get remittances or credit for their subsistence.

Arthur Lee.

"These things are notorious, and there are no visible sources of this property but the public money and State secrets to trade upon.

"They will force me one day or other to bring the proof of these things before Congress and the public; when I am sure they will shed some of their borrowed plumes."

Letters from the French officers, Lafayette, Fleury,

De Francey, speak of "*des lauriers que vous avez gagné à la defense de votre patrie,*" etc.   One from Lafayette's own hand illustrates the excellence of the marquis's English, perhaps quite as good as the American colonel's French : —

"DEAR SIR: I make myself the pleasure of writing to you ; and wishing you an agreeable sejour at home.   If you find there a horse distinguished by his figure as well as his qualities for what you think I can desire of him, I shall be obliged to you to send him to me; Provided he would not be wicked for others or troublesome to me ; as otherwise they are not so dear at equal beauties and qualities.   Being so fine as I wish him, he must be verry dear.   I beg your pardon for this commission and I am, with great affection

"Your most obedient servant,
"LA FAYETTE.

"P.S. We have not any other interesting news in camp but that a vessel is arrived in Portsmouth from France with fifty pieces of cannon and five thousand arms."

Rather an important item to follow an order for a horse.

How "verry dear" the marquis's fine horse was likely to be we can gather from a letter written by the good old gentleman at "Cawsons," from which we have news of some old friends among the race-horses : "I have a new coach which stands me in fourteen thousand and odd pounds of the present money.   I have sold the horse 'Aristotle' at a profit and bought for your use the high-bred horse,

' Janus-and-Silver-eye,' which cost me one hundred and twenty pounds."

Another French officer who preferred his own English to Colonel Bland's French was Colonel Armand. He complains that " Congress have passed a resolve that have *hurted me in my hart and reputation*. I have not practise the way of making friend to me in congress, for I thought such way below the charactere of an honest man, and now God know but I shall trayed to justify myself by myself." Another letter exhibits Washington's stern ideas of honorable warfare, contrasting sharply with some well-remembered methods in later days.

" I am informed that the liberty I granted the light dragoons to impress horses has been horridly abused and perverted into a plundering scheme. I intended nothing more than that the horses belonging to the disaffected, in the neighborhood of the British Army, should be taken for the use of the dismounted dragoons and regularly reported to the quarter-master general that an account might be kept of the number of persons from whom they were taken in order to future settlement. You are to make known to your whole corps that they are not to meddle with the horses or other property of any inhabitants whatever ; for they may be assured, as far as it depends upon me, that *military execution* will attend all caught in the like practice hereafter."

Other letters relate to General Washington's famous order against gaming, he being certain that "gentlemen" — that word so dear to the colonial Virginian — "can find amusement without application to this vile resource attended with so many evil consequences." In vain did one John Hawkins complain of loss because of his erection "for the amusement of gentlemen," of four large houses of entertainment with billiard-tables. It was decided that billiards, as "a game where wagers were laid" were included in the order.

These letters were written in times "well fitted to winnow the chaff from the grain." While Washington wrote of the falling away of the officers, and the desertion of thousands of men, he also paid more than one noble tribute to the brave and true men who remained with him. "Naked and starving as they are," he said, "we cannot enough admire their incomparable patience and fidelity."

Upon Colonel Bland's election to the First Congress, General Washington wrote him a most eloquent letter in behalf of an appropriation for the payment of the army. The original of this grand letter was found in the egg-basket collection.

"This army is of near eight years standing, six of which they have spent in the field, without any other shelter from the inclemency of the seasons than tents or such houses as they could build for themselves without expense to the public. They have encountered cold, hunger and nakedness. They have fought many battles and bled freely. They have done this without pay." This superb tribute to the men whose blood flows in the veins of the Sons and Daughters of the American Revolution, concludes with an earnest appeal to Congress for harmony. The jealousies already evident between the states filled his heart with anguish. He continues, "Unless our Union can be fixed upon this basis — the removal of the local prejudices which intrude upon and embarrass that great line of policy which alone can make us a free, happy and powerful people — unless our Union can be fixed on such a basis as to accomplish these, certain am I *that we have toiled, bled and spent our treasure to very little purpose.*"

With this eloquent utterance we conclude our extracts from the half-burned letters, with which the poor negro's egg-basket was lined.

CHAPTER V

IN Virginia, about to become the battle-ground of the Revolution, the condition of affairs was gloomy, humiliating, apparently almost desperate. After a war of five years the state was still unfortified, unarmed, unprepared. Her strength, her money, her sons had been sent to fight her battles in the North. She had entered the war already loaded with debt from the Indian and French wars, and further depleted through her patriotic non-importation policy. Navigable rivers ran, at intervals of a few miles, from her interior to the coast. An invading fleet had but to sail up these rivers, to lay waste the entire country, and end all by a single, well-directed blow.

Virginia was slow to appreciate the necessity of an armed naval force. She never desired to meet her enemy at sea. One of her sons declared in Congress, " I deem it no sacrifice of dignity to say to the Leviathan of the deep, ' We cannot contend with you in your own element, but if you come within our limits we will shed our last drop of blood in their defence,' " adding " What ! Shall the great mammoth of the American forests leave his native element, and plunge into the water in a mad contest with a shark? Let him stay on shore and not be excited by the muscles and periwinkles on the strand to venture on the perils of the deep. Why take to water where he can neither fight or swim?"

But in 1775 the Convention of Virginia directed the Committee of Safety to procure armed vessels for the better defence of the colony.[1] About seventy vessels were placed in service, built at the Chicka-hominy Navy-yard, South Quay, and Hampton near Norfolk. George Mason, for the Committee of Safety, built two galleys and a fine battle ship, *The American Congress*, to carry fourteen guns and ninety-six marines. The vessels were to serve sep-arately for the defence of the coast, but there was great difficulty in obtaining sailors to man them. Among the seamen were faithful negroes who pur-chased their freedom by serving through the war. These ships sometimes captured sloops laden with supplies for the officers of the invading army. Luxuries intended for British officers found their way to rebel tables. The planters lacked many es-sential articles, — food, clothing, medicines, — but they had a pineapple now and then. They sent out their own tobacco in ships which often never returned, and in time most of the Virginia ships were either destroyed or captured. Then it was that John Paul Jones obtained a commission from

[1] Campbell's "History of Virginia."

Congress to "harass the enemies of the Commonwealth," and swept the seas.

In January, 1781, Virginia was invaded by the
enemy. Tarleton's cavalry carried the torch and
sword throughout the whole James River region,
burned houses, carried off horses, cutting the throats
of those too young for service. They made a
dash to the mountains and captured seven members
of the assembly, then in session at Charlottesville,
announcing an intention to go as far as Fredericksburg and Mount Vernon. In May, Tarleton
was confidently expected at Fredericksburg. The
planters abandoned their homes and removed their
families from place to place for safety. The homestead was totally destroyed or pillaged, china
pounded up, servants carried off, and every
animal stolen or slaughtered. "Were it possible,"
said one old citizen, "I should remove my family
to some other country, for nothing can compensate
for the sufferings and alarms they daily experience.
Scarce do they remain one week in a place, before
they are obliged to abandon their shelter and seek
an asylum from the bounty of others." The state
was swept as by a tornado — growing crops destroyed, plantations laid waste. The destruction of
property was estimated at thirteen million sterling.
So dearly did the peaceful citizens of Virginia purchase freedom for their descendants!

Among the stories of this prince of raiders still

told at Virginia firesides, is one of a day when he made a clean sweep of everything portable on an old lady's plantation. Standing calmly in her doorway, she watched the rifling of her poultry-yard. One cowardly and aged Muscovy drake basely abandoned his harem and hid in a hedge. The old dame espied him just as Tarleton and his staff rode off. " Here, you Jim," she called to a negro lad; "catch that old duck and ride for your life after that general. Tell him he forgot one lean old duck, and I send it to him with my compliments." " What did he say?" she asked the boy on his return. " He jes put dat old Muscovy in he wallet, an' he say he much obliged."

The raids of the enemy along the navigable waters of Virginia became incessant. Gunboats would ascend the rivers, to the terror of all who dwelt on their banks. One of these went up the Pamunkey at night, and was kept from landing by a handful of men who fired, ran on ahead and fired again, and so on until the captain, believing himself to be in the midst of a large force on shore, and uncertain as to the possibility of return, hoisted a white flag in the moonlight and surrendered! Then the captain on shore (John Otey, with only twenty men) was, indeed, in a dilemma! Waiting until the moon went down, he ordered the crew ashore, forbade any to speak, took their arms and marched them through the darkness to headquarters!

A schooner on April 9, 1781, ascended the Potomac as far as Alexandria, landing at every house on the way, burning, destroying, stealing, loudly declaring their errand to "burn out the traitors, George Washington and George Mason."

On the 12th six armed vessels ascended the river, and the counties of Stafford, Prince William, and Fairfax became the "scene of war." Fifty miles from Fredericksburg, Cornwallis was encamped with his main body of the British army. Twenty miles from Fredericksburg, Lafayette was protecting, with his small force, the homes of the mother, wife, and sister of the commander-in-chief. "Before this letter reaches you," warned Colonel Bannister, "the enemy will have penetrated to Fredericksburg."

To be brave and serene became the high duty of the commander's family. They must present an example of fortitude and courage. This was the obligation laid upon them by their position. Nor did they demand, because of this position, anything more than the protection accorded to all. No sentries or guards were posted around their dwellings, no force detailed for their special protection. When Mary Washington's daughter expressed alarm, her mother reminded her that "the sister of the commanding General must be an example of fortitude and faith." Even the general himself could not repress a cry of anguish when he heard of the desolation of his native state. "Would to God," he said, "would to God the country could rise as one man and extirpate Cornwallis and his whole band!"

The general's family held their posts in calm silence, expressing no excitement or alarm. Tarleton's cavalry — mounted on Virginia's race-horses — were dashing all over the country, and liable at any moment to appear wherever it pleased him. For Mary Washington there was no security, no peace, save in the sanctuary of her own bosom. Virginia was the battle-ground, convulsed through her borders with alarms! Finally, General Washington could bear it no longer. Despite her remonstrance he removed his mother to the county of Frederick, in the interior of the state, where she remained for a short time to escape the Red Dragoons of the dreaded Tarleton.

"As for our present distresses," he wrote to George Mason, " they are so great and complicated that it is scarcely within the powers of description to give an adequate idea of them. We are without money and have been so for a long time; without provision and forage, without clothing, and shortly shall be (in a manner) without men. In a word, we have lived upon expedients till we can live no longer."

The eventful year of 1781 — destined to bring so great a deliverance to the country — brought infinite sorrow to Mary Washington and her daughter.

The good man and pure patriot, Fielding Lewis, died in January. Always too frail in health to bear arms, he had sent his sons to the front, advanced £7000 for the manufacture of arms, and so impoverished himself by advances of money to the colony that he was unable to pay his taxes (Calendar State Papers, Vol. i, p. 503; Henings Statutes, Vol. ix, p. 71).

In the same year Samuel Washington died at his home, "Harewood," in Jefferson County. The family bond was close in Mary Washington's household and no one was dearer than her son Samuel!

Washington's letters in 1780 repeat the story of Valley Forge. "The present situation of the army" (Jan. 8, 1780) "is the most distressing of any we have experienced since the beginning of the war. For a fortnight past the troops, both officers and men, have been almost perishing from want. The troops are half starved, imperfectly clothed, riotous, and robbing the country people of their subsistence from sheer necessity." In April things had not improved. "We are on the point of starving," he wrote to Reed of Pennsylvania. "I have almost ceased to hope. The country in general is in such a state of insensibility and indifference to its interests that I dare not flatter myself with any change for the better." And he adds, like a sigh of hopeless anguish, "In modern wars the longest purse must chiefly determine the event."

The English were fully cognizant of this state of affairs. "We look on America as at our feet," wrote Horace Walpole, in 1780, to Mann.

"Poorly clothed, badly fed, and worse paid," said General Wayne in 1780, "some of them not having had a paper dollar for nearly twelve months; exposed to winter's piercing cold, to drifting snows and chilling blasts, with no protection but old worn-out coats, tattered linen overalls, and but one blanket between three men! In this situation, the enemy begin to work upon their passions, and have found means to circulate proclamations among them. The officers in general, as well as myself, stand for hours every day exposed to wind and weather among the poor naked fellows while they are working at their huts, assisting with our own hands, sharing every vicissitude in common with them, participating in their ration of bread and water. The delicate mind and eye of humanity are hurt — very much hurt — at their distress."

These were the trials to which the soldiers of the American Revolution were subjected, and which those who endured to the end bore without murmuring; for no stress of suffering could wring from their brave hearts a word of injury to the cause for which they suffered!

May the honors now so gladly awarded to those brave men, by those descended from them, never be given by inadvertence or mistake to the caitiff host that forsook their commander in his dark hour!

The army that bore the sufferings of which so many have written was a small one. Few armies have ever shown a nobler self-devotion than that which remained with Washington through the dreary winter at Valley Forge, but the conscientious historian must not give honor equally to them and the mighty host of the American people who had no sympathy with the movement. Washington himself wrote, Dec. 30, 1778, "If I were called upon to draw a picture of the times and of the men from what I have seen, heard, and part know, I should in one word say that idleness, dissipation, and extravagance seem to have laid fast hold upon them; that speculation, peculation and an insatiable thirst for riches seem to have got the better of every other consideration — that party disputes and quarrels are the great business of the day; whilst the momentous concerns of an empire, a great and accumulating debt, ruined finances, depreciated money, and want of credit — which in its consequence is want of everything — are but of secondary consideration."

Under these circumstances the nobility and beauty of the character of Washington can indeed hardly be surpassed. "He commanded," says Lecky, "a perpetually fluctuating army, almost wholly destitute of discipline and respect for authority, torn by the most violent personal and provincial jealousies, wretchedly armed, wretchedly clothed, and sometimes in danger of starvation. Unsupported for the most part by the population among whom he was quartered, and incessantly thwarted by Congress, he kept his army together by a combination of skill, firmness, patience, and judgment which has rarely been surpassed, and he led it at last to a signal triumph."

But while he thus held his army discontent, distrust, suspicion, — the train which inevitably follows failure, — possessed the minds of the people and embittered the hearts of those who were striving to serve them. The leaders were blamed for the misfortunes of the time, their ability doubted, their patriotism suspected.

Thus hampered and trammelled, weak, sick at heart, America stretched out appealing hands to France.

CHAPTER VI

FRANCE IN THE REVOLUTION

THE rebellion of the colonies had been long expected in France. As early as 1750, Turgot, before the Sorbonne, had compared colonies to fruits which only remain on the stem until they reach maturity, and then drop off.

Vergennes, in conversation with an English traveller, had predicted: "England will soon repent of having removed the only check that can keep her colonies in awe. They stand no longer in need of her protection. She

Vergennes.

will call upon them to contribute towards supporting the burdens they have helped to bring on her. They will answer by striking off all dependence."

France had excellent reasons for hating England. Her lilies had gone down again and again before the British flag. Despoiled by England of her American and Canadian possessions, dislodged from her foothold in India, subjected to the espionage, and stung by the arrogance of her enemy, her policy was directed toward one object, the rehabilitation of her former glory at the expense of her greatest rival.[1]

Beaumarchais.

Louis the Sixteenth, young and pleasure-loving, was glad to shift all responsibility upon his able advisers, — Maurepas, whom he tolerated, Vergennes, whom he feared and respected, and Beaumarchais, the son of a watchmaker, author of "Le Mariage de Figaro" and "Le Barbier de Seville," — whom he cordially admired and loved, and who had probably more influence at court than all the

[1] Edwardes's " Translations of Lemonie," p. 259.

rest put together. These were the men with whom Deane and Franklin labored, with varying result, for many years — sometimes thwarted and discouraged, at others cheered by promises, and sustained by substantial favors. Presents of money were given by

Silas Deane.

France to America, and her ports were open to American trading-vessels. But England had a vigilant ambassador at the French court, watching like a cat lest the plucky little mouse should venture too far. It behooved the mouse to keep well in hiding. He could hope to gain an advantage over his enemy by stealthy diplomacy only.

France had, early in September, 1776, sent secret messengers to America to ascertain the state of affairs and report to the court of Versailles. Congress

Benjamin Franklin.

sent Silas Deane, Benjamin Franklin, and Arthur Lee to plead the cause of the colonists at the French court, and negotiate treaties with foreign powers.[1]

Franklin, on being selected, had said to Dr. Rush, "I am old and good for nothing, but, as

[1] Sparks's "Diplomatic Correspondence," Vol. I, p. 5.

store keepers say of their remnants of cloth, I am
but a fag-end, and you may have me for what you
please;"[1] but Franklin had strong personal reasons
for hating England. Accused once by the solicitor-
general (Wedderburn, Lord Loughborough) of
stealing political letters, the latter had arraigned
him and poured upon his head all the vials of min-
isterial wrath, branding him as a thief in the most
fearful philippic ever pronounced against man.[2]
" Franklin stood," says Dr. Priestly, "conspicu-
ously erect during the harangue, and kept his countenance as immovable as wood." He was dressed
in a suit of Manchester velvet, which he laid aside
and never wore after the terrible lashing of Lord
Loughborough ; but, " Seven years afterwards, on
the termination of the war, so triumphant to his
own country, and so humiliating to Britain, he
signed the articles of Peace, being then Ambassador
at Paris, *dressed in the Manchester velvet*," — once
the garment of heaviness and humiliation, now
the royal robe of triumph !

He became, fortunately, a toast at the French
court. The statesman who could write ballads and
invent musical instruments possessed a charming
versatility which attracted the French. How ver-
satile he still could be, even in old age, is attested

---

1 Parton's " Franklin," Vol. II, p. 166.
2 " Lives of the Lord Chancellors of England," by Lord Campbell, Vol. VI,
pp. 110–111.

by the fact that poets, philosophers, and men of fashion, — Vergennes, Voltaire, Turgot, — nay, the queen herself, admired and sought him. Turgot described him in a line which afterwards adorned the snuff-boxes, medallions, and rings of the court. On these Franklin's head appeared, with this legend, *Eripuit fulmen sceptrumque tyrannus*, the dignified, old, unpowdered head, its thin hair concealed by a fur cap, which yet had wisdom to guide the hand that "tore the lightning from heaven and the sceptre from the tyrant!"

It was not designed by Providence that America should fail in her contest. Rough-hewn as her methods must perforce be, they were given shape by the hand that guides our ends. Every event here, every move on the chess-board in France, tended to the same result. One of the fifteen decisive battles of the world was fought at Saratoga. "The Capitulation of General Burgoyne to Mr. Gates" (as the English in their wrath expressed it) turned the tide of affairs. It resulted immediately in the alliance with France, so long and ardently desired, without which this country might not have won independence.

Of course, we sent post-haste to tell the good news of this victory to our long-suffering envoy at the French court. The "Capitulation to Mr. Gates" occurred Oct. 17, 1777; the news reached Franklin Dec. 4, of the same year — nearly two

months afterward.   But we are the last people
who should ever lament the want of telegraphic
service in our early history.   Had such existed
during the Revolution, we would surely this day

General Burgoyne.

be sending our humble duty, with many gifts,
to our Gracious Sovereign, his Most Sacred Majesty, Edward VII, upon his coronation.   A polite
ambassador would not be nearly sufficient.

When Benjamin Franklin received the news he
was quietly dining, not dreaming of any better for-

tune than that we should be able to hold Philadelphia.[1]   No more dramatic scene can be imagined than that which took place on the evening of Dec. 4, 1777, when Jonathan Austin's chaise rapidly drove into the courtyard at Passy and

General Gates.

rudely interrupted Dr. Franklin's dinner-party. The guests, among whom were Beaumarchais, rushed out.   "Sir," exclaimed Franklin, "is Philadelphia taken?"   "Yes, Sir," replied Austin; and Franklin clasped his hands and turned to reënter the house.   Austin cried, "I have better and

[1] Morse's "Franklin," p. 267.

greater news; General Burgoyne and his whole
army are prisoners of war." Beaumarchais set out
with all speed to notify Vergennes, and he drove
with such haste that his coach upset, and he dis-
located his arm.

Rochambeau.

It was not, however, until July 10, 1780, that
Rochambeau wrote from Newport to Washington:
"We are now at your command. It is hardly
necessary for me to tell your Excellency that I
bring sufficient cash for whatever is needed by the
King's army."

Lafayette was holding Cornwallis at Yorktown, having orders from Washington that he was on no account to be permitted to escape. In order to prevent this it was necessary to have the assistance of the French fleet. To this end he despatched a frigate to Cape Henry, where De Grasse was

De Grasse.

expected to touch, urging him to come up Chesapeake Bay as soon as possible to clear the James River and blockade the York. This word was received by De Grasse, who arrived with his fleet of twenty-eight ships of the line in Chesapeake Bay on Aug. 30, 1781.

The French forces then joined Washington in a

rapid march to Virginia, having made a feint of attacking New York, and thus deceived Sir Henry Clinton. Well for us there were no railroads or telegraph wires in those days! Washington and his allies were not discovered until they were almost in front of Cornwallis.

The march through Philadelphia was a species of triumph. And now who more ready than the Tory ladies to welcome and applaud! "The windows were filled with ladies waving handkerchiefs and uttering exclamations of joy. The ragged Continentals came first with their torn battle-flags and cannon; and the French followed in gay white uniforms faced with green to the sound of martial music. A long time had passed since Philadelphia had seen such a pageant; the last resembling it had been the splendid Mischianza festival, devised by poor André in the days of the British occupation,"[1] and enjoyed, alas, by these same ladies, while these same Continentals were starving and perishing with cold!

They were equal to any situation, these Philadelphia ladies! The first duty of woman, according to them, was to make herself agreeable to the powers that be — the heroes of the hour. Said Washington Irving, "The beauties who had crowned the British Knights in the chivalrous time of the Mischianza, were now ready to bestow wreaths and smiles on their Gallic rivals."

[1] Irving's "Life of Washington."

Fifteen days after the arrival of the allied forces successful assaults were made upon the enemy's redoubts, Washington putting the match to the first gun; and on Oct. 17, Cornwallis, after having made unsuccessful efforts to relieve his position and to escape by water, proposed a cessation of hostilities

Lord Cornwallis.

and the appointment of commissioners to settle terms of surrender. On Oct. 19, in pursuance of articles of capitulation, drawn by Vicomte de Noualles and Colonel Laurens, representing the allies, and Colonel Dundas and Major Ross, representing the British, Lord Cornwallis surrendered; the English marching out to the tune, "The World's Turned Upside Down," — a fact which was, no doubt, accepted by the brave Cornwallis as the only solution to the turn events had taken.

"The work is done and well done," said Washington as he heard the long shout of the French and the Americans.

To Maurepas, in France, Lafayette wrote: —

"The play is over, Monsieur le Compte, the fifth act has just come to an end." [1]

"It's all over now," said our old friend Lord North,[2] heartily relieved, we may well believe, to be rid of all the bother.

At midnight on Oct. 23, 1781, Philadelphia was startled by the cry, "Cornwallis is taken." And on Oct. 24, on motion of Mr. Randolph, it was resolved, "That Congress at 2 o'clock this day go in procession to the Dutch Lutheran Church and return thanks to Almighty God for crowning the allied arms of the United States and France with success by the surrender of the whole British Army under the command of the Earl of Cornwallis."[3]

But not with joy and gratitude was the news received by old Lord Fairfax, who had given Washington his first opportunity in life. He had liked the fifteen-year-old lad, had taught him to follow the hounds, and been his cordial friend as long as he fought for the Crown. Lord Fairfax, "the Nimrod of Greenway Court," was now ninety-two years old. "When he heard," says the irrepressible Parson Weems, "that Washington had captured Cornwallis and all his army, he called to his black waiter: 'Come, Joe! Carry me to bed, for it is high time for me to die.'"

> "Then up rose Joe, all at the word
>   And took his master's arm.
> And thus to bed he softly laid
>   The Lord of Greenway farm.
>
> "There oft he called on Britain's name
>   And oft he wept full sore.
> Then sighed, 'Thy will, O Lord, be done,'
>   And word spake never more."

The old Royalist's heart had broken with grief and disappointment.

But how was the aged mother to hear the news? Would her heart break with the sudden access of joy?

Washington himself despatched a courier to her with the news of the surrender. She raised her hands to heaven and exclaimed with the deepest fervor:—

"Thank God! Thank God! All the fighting and killing is over. The war is ended and now we shall have peace and happiness."

Mindful of her age her son would not come to her suddenly and unheralded. He could not come

GREENWAY COURT.

immediately. He had to attend to the distribution of ordnance and stores, the departure of prisoners, the embarkation of troops, to say nothing of the courtesies of the hour — such as the selection of two beautiful horses as a present to De Grasse, who did not sail until Nov. 4. He was then summoned in haste to Eltham, the seat of his old friend Colonel Bassett, there to fold his tender arms around the dying form of Parke Custis and receive his last breath. Years before, he had thus comforted the sweet young sister, " Patsy Custis," in her last hour.

Martha Washington, the mother, and the wife and four children of Parke Custis (who was only twenty-eight years old) were all at Eltham, and with them Washington remained until the last tribute of respect was paid to the deceased. And that he might comfort his wife and help the young widow, he then and there adopted George Washington Parke Custis and Nellie Custis into his family.

From Eltham he proceeded immediately on pressing business with Congress at Philadelphia, and not until Nov. 11 did he reach Fredericksburg.

CHAPTER VII

THAT was a great day when the news came
to Fredericksburg — " Cornwallis has surrendered." "With red spurs" rode the
couriers that carried the glad tidings, and the hearts
of the people leaped with joy. Twenty-eight British
captains had stepped forth from the lines and surrendered as many colors to the ragged Continentals.
With instinctive magnanimity the conquerors had
given a banquet to their captive officers, and Washington had saluted Cornwallis with a toast to the
British army. Thus the brave honor the brave.
And now — courtesies all rendered, the sword
sheathed, the guns stacked — the great commander
was coming home, first to his mother, attended by
a brilliant retinue of French and American officers.
When the soldier of his people laid his country's
freedom at his mother's feet, if ever in this world a
foretaste of heavenly joy be given to human beings,
to Mary and George Washington alike this was the
hour. Says Mr. Custis : —

"After an absence of nearly seven years, it was,
at length, on the return of the combined armies

from Yorktown, permitted to the mother again to
see and embrace her illustrious son. So soon as he
had dismounted, in the midst of a numerous and
brilliant suite, he sent to apprise her of his arrival,
and to know when it would be her pleasure to receive him. No pageantry of war proclaimed his
coming, no trumpets sounded, no banners waved.
Alone and on foot, the Marshal of France, the
general-in-chief of the combined armies of France
and America, the deliverer of his country, the hero
of the age, repaired to pay his humble duty to her
whom he venerated as the author of his being, the
founder of his fortune and his fame. For full well
he knew that the matron would not be moved by
all the pride that glory ever gave, nor by all the
' pomp and circumstance ' of power.

"The lady was alone, her aged hands employed in
the works of domestic industry, when the good news
was announced; and it was further told that the
victor chief was in waiting at the threshold. She
welcomed him with a warm embrace, and by the
well-remembered and endearing name of his childhood; inquiring as to his health, she remarked the
lines which mighty cares and many trials had made
on his manly countenance, spoke much of old times
and old friends, but of his glory — not one word."

But old Fredericksburg tells a story so characteristic that we are fain to accept it. Her neighbors
had gathered at her door to congratulate her; but

x

before they spoke with her, an orderly dashed up, dismounted, touched his three-cornered hat and said, " Madam! his Excellency will be here within

George Washington Parke Custis.

the hour." " *His Excellency!* Tell George I shall be glad to see him," replied the dame; and turning to her wide-eyed ebony maid, she said, " Patsy, I shall need a white apron."

Old Fredericksburg threw its hat in the air and declared that the "Indian Queen" should be swept and garnished, and the Fredericksburg beauties tread a measure with those gay foreigners. This thing of "belonging to the country" was all very well, but George Washington was a Virginian—what was more, he was master-mason in the Fredericksburg Lodge No. 4, and a Fredericksburg boy out and out. "But would Madam Washington come to a ball?" Ay, she would. Her "dancing days were pretty well over," but she would "be glad to contribute to the general happiness."

But here we give place again to Mr. Custis, for he had his story at first hands.

The Chair used by George Washington when Master of Fredericksburg Lodge.

"Meantime, in the village of Fredericksburg, all was joy and revelry; the town was crowded with the officers of the French and American armies, and with gentlemen from all the country around, who hastened to welcome the conquerors of Cornwallis. The citizens made arrangements for a splendid ball, to which the mother of Washington was specially invited. She observed that, although her dancing days were pretty well over, she should feel happy in contributing to the general festivity, and consented to attend.

"The foreign officers were anxious to see the mother of their chief.   They had heard indistinct rumors respecting her remarkable life and character; but, forming their judgments from European examples, they were prepared to expect in the mother that glare and show which would have been attached to the parents of the great in the old world.   How they were surprised when the matron, leaning on the arm of her son, entered the room!   She was arrayed in the very plain, yet becoming, garb worn by the Virginian lady of the olden time.   Her address, always dignified and imposing, was courteous, though reserved.   She received the complimentary attentions, which were profusely paid her, without evincing the slightest elevation; and, at an early hour, wishing the company much enjoyment of their pleasures, observing that it was time for old people to be at home, retired.

"The foreign officers were amazed to behold one so many causes contributed to elevate, preserving the even tenor of her life, while such a blaze of glory shone upon her name and offspring.   The European world furnished no examples of such magnanimity. Names of ancient lore were heard to escape from their lips; and they observed that, 'if such were the matrons of America, it was not wonderful the sons were illustrious.'

"It was on this festive occasion that General Wash-

ington danced a minuet with Mrs. Willis" (one of
the Gregory girls). "It closed his dancing days.
The minuet was much in vogue at that period,
and was peculiarly calculated for the display of
the splendid figure of the chief and his natural
grace and elegance of air and manner. The gallant Frenchmen who were present — of which fine
people it may be said that dancing forms one of the
elements of their existence — so much admired the
American performance as to admit that a Parisian
education could not have improved it. As the evening advanced, the commander-in-chief, yielding to
the gayety of the scene, went down some dozen
couples in the contra-dance, with great spirit and
satisfaction."

But General Washington's dancing days did not
close with the Fredericksburg ball. Mr. Custis did
not know. Two years later Lieutenant McAllister
wrote from Baltimore: "A ball was given to his
most excellent Excellency by the ladies of this
town. A brilliant collection assembled to entertain him, and the illustrious Chief led and mingled
in the joyous dance."

The commanding general had perceived the wisdom of introducing into the camp life some relax-
ation and amusement, as the Arctic explorer arranged
a series of theatricals when starvation threatened his
ice-locked crew. In the year and month in which
Washington wrote his most despairing letter to

George Mason, there were frequent balls in the camp at Middlebrook. "We had a little dance at my quarters," wrote General Greene to Colonel Wadsworth in March, 1779 (the dark hour), "His Excellency and Mrs. Greene danced upwards of three hours without once sitting down."

Bishop Meade, in his intense admiration of Washington and his not less intense abhorrence of dancing, reasons that these reports of the great chief *could* not be true. They were undoubtedly true. Washington, although habitually grave and thoughtful, was of a social disposition, and loved cheerful society. He was fond of the dance, and it was the boast of many Revolutionary dames that he had been their partner in contra-dances, and had led them through the stately figures of the minuet.

Little Maria Mortimer, aged sixteen, was at the Fredericksburg ball. Betty Lewis followed the party later to Mount Vernon. For Maria a great dignity was in store. Her father, Dr. Charles Mortimer, issued invitations at the ball for a great dinner to the distinguished strangers the next day but one, and his wife (Sarah Griffin Fauntleroy), being too ill to preside, that honor fell to the daughter of the house.[1]

The house, an immense pile of English brick, still stands on the lower edge of the town, facing Main Street, with a garden sloping to the river,

[1] "Maternal Ancestry of Washington," by G. W. Ball.

where Dr. Mortimer's own tobacco ships used to run up to discharge their return English cargoes by a channel long since disused and filled up.

The mansion was hastily put *en fête* — which meant swept walks, polished floors, and abundant decoration of flowers and evergreens. The running cedar of Virginia, with its plumy tufts of green, lent itself gracefully to outline doors and windows, encircle family portraits, and hang in festoons from the antlers of the deer in the hall.

The table, as little Maria described it in after years, groaned with every delicacy of land and water, served in massive pewter dishes polished until they shone again.

The chief sat beside the master of the house at the long table, although at his own house his place was always at the side of the table among his guests. Little Maria " with her hair craped high " was taken in by the Marquis Lafayette, or Count d'Estaing, or Count Rochambeau, — they were all present, — and the little lady's heart was in her mouth, she said, although she danced with every one of them at the ball — nay, with Betty Lewis's Uncle George himself!

To this dinner the doctor, of course, invited Mrs. Washington, but equally, of course, she did not come, her appearance at the ball having been an extraordinary effort intended to mark her sense of the importance of the occasion which was intoxicating the whole country with joy.

CHAPTER VIII

LAFAYETTE AND OUR FRENCH ALLIES

IN 1784 the Marquis de Lafayette returned to Virginia "crowned everywhere," wrote Washington to the Marchioness de Lafayette, "with wreaths of love and respect." He made a visit to Mount Vernon, and thence, before he sailed for France, he went to Fredericksburg to pay his homage to the mother of Washington. A great crowd of citizens and old soldiers thronged the town to do him honor. One of the old soldiers from the country had heard much of a new character who had followed the armies, and had lately appeared in Virginia — active, prevalent, and most successful! This rustic determined to see Lafayette, "pick-pocket" or no "pick-pocket." Had he not two hands! One should never let go a firm grasp on the watch in his own pocket. Finally he succeeded, after pressing through the throng, in reaching the general. In his enthusiasm at being greeted so warmly by the great marquis, he seized with both hands Lafayette's friendly grasp, and as he turned away clapped his hand upon his watch-pocket. It was empty!

GENERAL LAFAYETTE.

There is no doubt — not the least — that the honest man never thought his honors too dearly bought.

Escaping from all these good people so keenly and cordially enjoyed by the warm-hearted marquis, he found Betty Washington's son to act as sponsor and guide — lest he should have been forgotten! — to visit the mother of his friend. He wished to pay his parting respects and to ask her blessing.

"Accompanied by her grandson," says Mr. Custis, " he approached the house; when the young gentleman observed, 'There, sir, is my grand-mother.' Lafayette beheld, working in the garden, clad in domestic-made clothes, and her gray head covered in a plain straw hat, the mother of his hero! The lady saluted him kindly, observing, 'Ah, Marquis! you see an old woman; but come, I can make you welcome to my poor dwelling, without the parade of changing my dress.'

" The Marquis spoke of the happy effects of the Revolution, and the goodly prospect which opened upon independent America; stated his speedy departure for his native land; paid the tribute of his heart, his love and admiration of her illustrious son. To the encomiums which he had lavished upon his hero and paternal chief, the matron replied in her accustomed words, ' I am not surprised at what George has done, for he was always a very good boy.'

" In her latter days, the mother often spoke of ' her own good boy,' of the merits of his early life, of his love and dutifulness to herself; but of the deliverer of his country, the chief magistrate of the great republic, she never spoke. Call you this insensibility? or want of ambition? Oh, no! her ambition had been gratified to overflowing. She had taught him to be good; that he became great when the opportunity presented, was a consequence, not a cause."

Would that we could record naught but reward — long life, honor, and happiness — to every one of our brave allies who came to us in our extremity. But, alas! Fortune held in her closed hand these gifts for some — for others disgrace, the dungeon, the guillotine!

Louis XVI was overjoyed at the *éclat* won by the French arms in America. When Rochambeau presented himself at court the young king received him graciously, and said to him, " I have read in the Commentaries of Cæsar that a small army, commanded by a great general, can achieve wonders, and you are a proof of it."

Lafayette threw himself with ardor into the stirring military life of his own country, and came back to us in 1824 to find his path strewn with flowers by Daughters of the American Revolution; and Daughters of the American Revolution but a few months ago crowned his statue with the same laurels with which they crowned the adored Washington!

Great riches and honor were heaped upon the Comte de Vergennes. He was given a position which brought him an income of 60,000 francs. Afterwards the Empress of Russia — as reward — made him Knight of the Order of the Holy Ghost, with 100,000 francs! A serene, very honorable and comfortable old age was Fortune's gift to our friend Vergennes.

And Beaumarchais, who poured money into our empty treasury from his own full horn-of-plenty, — Beaumarchais, the artist, dramatist, politician, merchant, who set all Paris wild with his " Mariage de Figaro," of whose wit and satire and mischievous subtlety our translations give us no idea, — Beaumarchais must needs ruin himself by spending 1,000,000 livres on a gorgeous *édition de luxe* of Voltaire, and yet more than that on French muskets. He died of " no particular disease," say his biographers, " at sixty-nine years." So Fortune for him had a long life and a merry one, and riches of which he made a noble use.

We all know the fate of the pleasure-loving young king, — the husband of the beautiful and accomplished Marie Antoinette! America, perhaps, owes little to him, — but she remembers that little, and can mourn for the bitter hour that ended his misguided life.

But ungrateful, indeed, would she be did she cease to remember Marie Antoinette! Well may we call our beautiful buildings and graceful fashions after her name. Many years after she had bent her lovely head with such courage to the guillotine, Paine wrote, " It is both justice and gratitude to say that it was the queen of France who gave the cause of America a fashion at the French Court." " *Dites-moi*," she had said in parting from Lafayette, " *dites-moi de bonnes nouvelles de nos bons Americans, de nos cher Republicans*," little dreaming, poor lady, that " she was giving the last great impulse to that revolutionary spirit which was so soon to lead her to misery and death."

For one more of the Frenchmen who served us — one who was a loyal friend in the field and a traitor at the fireside — the stern Nemesis holds a strange immortality. The secret manuscript which for one hundred and twenty-five years has passed from hand to hand among Virginia women; which was known to and partially quoted by Bishop Meade; which is known to-day by many who gave, like him, a promise never to print the whole of it, contains the story of a young nobleman's infamy — told that he may be execrated by women, the names implicated kept from publication that the innocent descendants may not suffer. " *Sed quid ego hæc nequicquam ingrata revolvo?* It is vain to lament that corruption which no human power can prevent or repair."

CHAPTER IX

IN CAMP AND AT MOUNT VERNON

PEACE was not declared until March 3, 1783. In the meanwhile the armies must be kept in camp, regularly drilled, and ready at a moment's notice for action. The American army was encamped at Verplanck's Point; that of Count de Rochambeau — alas, for the honor and peace of one household! — at Williamsburg. The brilliant campaign in Virginia attracted immense interest abroad. Every ship brought strangers to visit the camp, — artists, writers, military men. Washington begins to be sensitive about our meagre facilities for entertaining these visitors. "We have nothing to offer," he deplores, "except whisky hot from the still, — and not always that, — and meat with no vegetables," etc. There was always plenty of Virginia hickory nuts! They appeared at every meal. They saved many a day and redeemed many a slender breakfast, dinner, and supper. The commander-in-chief seems to have striven to make them fashionable by devoting himself to their consumption.

M. de Broglie came to Virginia in 1782, bearing letters of introduction to General Washington from

Benjamin Franklin,—letters "rendered doubly agreeable," said the general, " by the pleasure I had in receiving them from the hands of such an amiable and accomplished young gentleman."   M. de Broglie kept a journal which found its way to the columns of the *Courier des États Unis*, and was translated by a Boston literary journal.   The impression made upon this "amiable and accomplished young gentleman " presents an interesting portrait of Washington in the year succeeding the surrender, and also permits our curtain to fall upon a charming picture of the ancestors of the sons and daughters of the American Revolution.

M. de Broglie says: " I found the American Army encamped in a place called Verplanck's Point. There were six thousand men who, for the first time during the war, were well armed, well drilled, well kept, and camped under tents of a regular form.   I passed along its front with pleasure, astonishment and admiration.   All the soldiers appeared to me fine, robust and well chosen.   The sentinels well kept, extremely attentive, and sufficiently well placed under arms, contrasted so completely with the crude idea I had formed of these troops, that I was obliged to repeat to myself several times that I was indeed seeing this army that formerly had no other uniform than a cap upon which was written ' Liberty.'

" I pressed M. de Rochambeau, who received me

with kindness, to add that of making me acquainted
with Washington.   He assented; and the day after
my arrival, he went with me to dine with this famous
man.   I gave him a letter from my father; and,
after a slight ‘ *shake hand*,’ he was kind enough to
say a thousand flatteries and polite things to me.
Here is his portrait, which I have formed from what
I have been able to see of him for myself, and from
what the conversations which I have had with regard to him, have taught me : —

“ The General is about forty-nine years of age;
he is large, finely made, very well proportioned.
His figure is much more pleasing than the picture
represents it.   He was fine looking until within
about three years; and, although those who have
been constantly with him since that time say that
he seems to them to have grown old fast, it is un-
deniable that the General is still fresh, and active
as a young man.

“ His physiognomy is pleasant and open; his
address is cold, though polite; his pensive eye is
more attentive than sparkling; but his countenance
is kind, noble and composed.   He maintains, in
his private deportment, that polite and attentive
manner which does not offend.   He is the enemy
of ostentation and vain-glory.   His manners are
always equable; he has never shown the least temper.   Modest even to humility, he seems not to
estimate himself duly; he receives with good grace

the deference paid to him, but rather shuns than courts it. His society is agreeable and pleasing. Always serious, never constrained; always simple, always free and affable, without being familiar, the respect which he inspires never becomes painful. He talks little in general, and in a very low tone of voice; but he is so attentive to what is said to him, that you are satisfied that he understands you, and are almost willing to dispense with a reply. This conduct has often been of advantage to him in various circumstances; no one has more occasion than he to use circumspection, and to weigh well his words. He unites to an unalterable tranquillity of soul, a fine power of judgment; and one can seldom reproach him for a little slowness in determination, or even in acting, when he has formed his decision. His courage is calm and brilliant. An excellent patriot, a wise, virtuous man — one is tempted to grant him all qualities, even those which circumstances have not permitted him to develop. Never was there a man more fitted to lead the Americans nor one who has evinced in his conduct more consistency, wisdom, constancy and reason.

" Mr. Washington has never received any compensation as General; he has refused such, as not needing it. The expenses of his table are alone made at the expense of the State. He has every day as many as thirty people at dinner, gives good military receptions, and is very attentive to all the officers whom he admits to his table. It is, in general, the moment of the day when he is most gay.

"At dessert, he makes an enormous consumption of nuts, and, when the conversation amuses him, he eats them for two hours, 'drinking healths,' according to the English and American custom, several times. This is called *toasting*. They begin always by drinking to the United States of America; afterwards to the King of France, to the Queen, and success to the arms of the combined army. Then is given, sometimes, what is called a sentiment; for example, 'To our success with our enemies and the ladies!' 'Success in war and love!'

"I have *toasted* several times with General Washington. On one occasion I proposed to him to drink to the Marquis de Lafayette, whom he looked upon as a son. He accepted with a smile of benevolence, and had the politeness to propose to me in return that of my father and wife.

"Mr. Washington appears to me to keep up a perfect bearing towards the officers of his army; he treats them very politely, but they are far from growing familiar with him; they all wear, on the contrary, in presence of this General, an air of respect, confidence and admiration."

For two years after the surrender, General Washington was confined to the routine of camp life.

Y

We read of no visits to Fredericksburg or to Mount Vernon. If he made them, they were brief and uneventful.

His mother lived quietly in her new home, never fulfilling her intention of returning to " Pine Grove" across the river. She was now seventy-eight years old, but remembered by the children of her old neighbors as bright, active, and alert — keenly interested in everything around her. Charming granddaughters were growing up in Betty Lewis's " Kenmore " home. One of these — doubtless our " little Betty," — accompanied General and Mrs. Washington on their joyful return home to Mount Vernon from Annapolis, whither the general had gone to resign his commission. Mr. Lossing has preserved a letter from little Miss Lewis : —

" I must tell you what a charming day I spent at Mt. Vernon with Mama and Sally. The General and Madame came home at Christmas Eve, and such a racket the servants made ! They were glad of their coming. Three handsome young officers came with them. All Christmas afternoon people came to pay their respects and duty. Among these were stately dames and gay young women. The General seemed very happy and Mrs. Washington was up before daybreak making everything as agreeable as possible for everybody. Among the most notable callers was Mr. George Mason of Gunston Hall, who brought a charming granddaughter with him about fourteen years old.   He is said to be one of the greatest statesmen and wisest men in Virginia.   We had heard much of him, and were delighted to look in his face, hear him speak, and take his hand which he offered in a courtly manner.   He has a grand head and clear gray eyes — is straight, but not tall, and has few white hairs, though they say he is about sixty years old."

The little hero-worshipper!   And so reverent to her illustrious uncle and his wife, with no underbred, familiar claiming of kinship with " the General and Madame."

Even before peace was declared, our French allies circulated large sums of gold and silver coin, which put to flight the wretched paper currency of our country, and in an incredibly short time quantities of French and English goods were imported.   "Our people," laments an old writer, " suddenly laid aside their plain, home-manufactured clothing.   Fine ruffles, powdered heads, silks and scarlets decorated the men, while the most costly silks, satins, chintzes, calicoes and muslins decorated our females.   Superb plate, foreign spirits, and wines, sparkled on the sideboards, and as a necessary consequence the people ran in debt, and money was hard to raise."

General Washington's family resumed their old-time habits of living.   They rose early, breakfasted at half-past seven, dined frugally at two, retired early.   "Those who come to see me," said the

general, " will always find a bit of mutton and a glass
of wine. If they expect anything more, they will be
disappointed." Mary Washington and the mistress
of Mount Vernon never laid aside their simple
customs, dress, and occupations. They seemed to
have formed, said Washington Irving, "an inveterate
habit of knitting" in and out of the drawing-room.
Walking about her garden, Mary Washington's
fingers held the flying needles. The results were
sent to somebody less fortunate than herself.
Martha Washington kept up her "inveterate habit"
long after she became the first lady in the land, presenting unfinished gloves of her own knitting to her
friends to "finish and wear for my sake," thus
delicately suggesting a plan by which the gift could
be rendered more valuable, and at the same time
inspiring her gay young visitors with something of
her own spirit of industry.

Inestimable to women is the value of such occupation! For them the curse has been transmuted
into a golden blessing. There could have been no
necessity for Mary and Martha Washington to em-
ploy themselves so diligently in sewing and knitting.
The hands were numerous enough around them
among the negroes and humbler classes for all such
work. But they held an old-fashioned creed: that
the human hand — that wonderful mechanism — was
created for some useful purpose! In their day the
hand had not claimed for its beauty the cunning

skill of the "artist manicure." The instructed
hand made laces, and manipulated the spinet and
harp, but it made garments as well. Let none call
the love of needlework useless — its results not
worth the while! Knitting may not be the highest
use for one's beautiful hands, but it surely ranks
with the highest when it ministers to those who
suffer! And even as an innocent occupation it is
not to be despised. All such work is better than
dull vacuity or lack of interest in domestic life. A
passion for such things is not the worst passion
that can possess a woman's soul. Besides, needlework is an admirable sedative to the nerves. Mary
Washington's knitting helped to relieve her mind of
its tension when circumstances seemed so unfortunate and discouraging. Perhaps the Queen of Scots
sometimes forgot the uncertain tenure by which she
held her beautiful head because she had a passion
for embroidery and was, every day, expecting new
flosses and filoselles from France to finish something very lovely which she had commenced.

But knitting was not with Mary Washington and
her daughters a matter of sentiment or resorted to
as a nerve cure. It was simply the natural expression of pure benevolence. There was no money
to buy — nothing imported to be bought. The
destitution of the soldiers pressed heavily upon the
hearts of these good women. Constantly employed
every moment of their waking hours, they might

hope to achieve something to add to that " cap upon which was written ' Liberty.' " The Phrygian cap might indeed protect the fervid brain of the patriot, but could in no wise comfort his weary feet!

American women have never failed in time of war to give the work of their own hands. With the wife of another Virginia commander, Mary Custis Lee, knitting was as inveterate a habit in the time of America's Civil War as it was with her great-grandmother, Martha Washington, in the war of the American Revolution.

Many were the soldiers who were comforted in body and heartened in spirit by the gifts of these noble women — all the more because they were wrought by their own gentle hands.

CHAPTER X

MRS. ADAMS AT THE COURT OF ST. JAMES

MARY WASHINGTON lived long enough to witness the crowning triumph of the colonies, when the proud country that had sought their subjugation was compelled to receive at its Court their accredited Minister. In 1785 John Adams of Massachusetts was chosen for this delicate position. He had nominated Washington for Commander-in-chief of the Colonial troops, he had belonged to the committee which reported the immortal Declaration of Independence, he had been sent in 1777 as commissioner to the Court of Versailles. Moreover, he was the husband of the accomplished, patriotic Abigail Adams, — "a woman of fine personal appearance, good education and noble powers of mind." A fitting pair this to represent the new land that had just won a place among the nations !

In the drawing-rooms of the late queen — the arbiter of social usage for nearly a century — Majesty stood upon a raised platform surrounded by the lights, larger or lesser, of her court. A few ladies only were admitted at a time. These might not clasp the outstretched hand of Majesty.   On the *back* of their hands her own was laid for an instant, and something like a butterfly touch of the lips was permitted.   Then to the long line of lesser stars were courtesies rendered, and the "presented" lady passed on and out.

John Adams.

Not so did George the Third and his queen receive. Their guests were assembled in the drawing-room, and the king, accompanied by Lord Onslow, passed around first; the queen, as much as two hours later, made her rounds in a similar fashion.

Mrs. Adams wrote to her sister a description of the first drawing-room attended by the first American Minister to the Court of St. James. The company assembled in silence.   The king

went around to every person — finding small talk
enough to speak to them all — "prudently speaking
in a whisper so that only the person next you can
hear what is said." King George, Mrs. Adams
thought, was "a personable man," but she did not
admire his red face and white eyebrows. When he
came to her, and Lord Onslow said, "Mrs. Adams,"
she hastily drew off her right-hand glove; but to
her amazement the king stooped and kissed her
on her left cheek! There was an embarrassed
moment — for Royalty must always begin and end
a conversation. George the Third found only this
to say : —

"Madam, have you taken a walk to-day?"

"No, Sire."

"Why? Don't you love walking?"

Her impulse was to tell him frankly that all the
morning had been given to attiring herself to wait
upon him, but she informed him only that she
was "rather indolent in that respect," upon which
he allowed her the last word, bowed, and passed on.
In about two hours it was Mrs. Adams's turn to be
presented to the queen. "The queen," she writes,
"was evidently embarrassed. I had disagreeable
feelings, too. She, however, said : 'Mrs. Adams,
have you got into your house? Pray, how do you
like the situation of it?'" She, too, yielded the
last word, passing on after an earnest assurance
that the American lady had nothing to complain of.

" She was in purple and silver," said Mrs. Adams
in her letter to her sister. " She is not well-shaped
nor handsome. As to the ladies of the Court,
rank and title may compensate for want of personal
charm, but they are in general very plain, ill-shaped
and ugly — but don't you tell anybody that I said so!"

From the letter of our Minister's wife, we perceive that fashions in dress had not changed materially since the days when Jenny Washington, Betsy
Lee, and Aphia Fauntleroy danced in Westmoreland. The classic David had not yet laid down
his stern laws. The train was still looped over an
ornate petticoat, and all supported by an enormous
hoop; the hair still " craped high," surmounted
with feathers, flowers, lace, and gauze. Mrs.
Adams, when all ready to set forth to the drawing-
room, found time while waiting for her daughter
to describe the presentation gowns to her sister in
Massachusetts : —

" My head is dressed for St. James, and in my
opinion looks very tasty. Whilst my daughter is
undergoing the same operation I set myself down
composedly to write you a few lines. I directed
my manteau-maker to let my dress be elegant, but
plain as I could possibly appear with decency. Accordingly it is white lutestring covered and full-
trimmed with white crape festooned with lilac ribbon
and mock point lace, over a hoop of enormous extent.
There is only a narrow train of about three yards in

length to the gown waist, which is put into a ribbon upon the left side, the Queen only having her train borne. Ruffle cuffs for married ladies, a very dress cap with long lace lappets, two white plumes and a blond-lace handkerchief. This is my rigging. I should have mentioned two pearl pins in my hair, earrings and necklace of the same kind.

"Well, methinks I hear Betsy and Lucy say, 'What is cousin's dress?' White, my dear girls, like your aunt's, only differently trimmed and ornamented, her train being wholly of white crape and trimmed with white ribbon; the petticoat, which is the most showy part of the dress, covered and drawn up in what are called festoons, with light wreaths of beautiful flowers; the sleeves white crape, drawn over the silk with a row of lace around the sleeve near the shoulder, another half-way down the arm, and a third upon the top of the ruffle, a little flower stuck between; a kind of hat cap with three large feathers and a bunch of flowers; a wreath of flowers upon the hair. Thus equipped we go in our own carriage, and Mr. Adams and Colonel Smith in his. But I must quit the pen in order for the ceremony which begins at 2 o'clock."

Mrs. Adams was not one whit "flustered" or nervous on this occasion — unique from the circumstances attending it. The embarrassment was all on the part of Royalty. Very sustaining must be the consciousness of belonging to the victorious party!

CHAPTER XI

WASHINGTON IRVING speaks of the first winter at Mount Vernon as being of such intense cold that " General Washington could not travel through the snows even as far as Fredericksburg to visit his aged mother." General Dabney H. Maury, in his " Recollections of a Virginian," says : " After Washington's military career ended he used to go frequently to Fredericksburg to visit his venerable mother, and his arrival was the occasion of great conviviality and rejoicing. Dinner parties and card parties were then in order, and we find in that wonderful record of his daily receipts and expenditures that on one of these occasions he won thirty guineas at Lop-loo ! Probably it was after this night that he threw the historic dollar across the river, the only instance of extravagance ever charged against him." A dinner-party was usually given to him on his arrival at the old " Indian Queen " tavern. On these visits Washington laid aside his state, and — near his boyhood's home — was a boy again.

Judge Brooke, for many years chief justice of

Virginia, who had served as an officer in the legion
of " Light-horse Harry," used to tell of having frequently met Washington on his visits to Fredericksburg after the Revolutionary War, and how
" hilarious" the general was on those occasions
with " Jack Willis and other friends of his young
days." Judge Brooke remembered one dinner
given to Washington at the " Indian Queen " tavern
at which he was present. " A British officer sang a
comic song. Washington laughed till the tears
rolled down his cheeks, and called upon the singer
to repeat it."

" Light-horse Harry " Lee was always a great
favorite in the Washington family. He was, perhaps, the only person outside of it " never under the
influence " — according to Irving — " of that reverential awe " which Washington is said to have inspired. His summer home " Chatham " adjoined
Mary Washington's Stafford farm ; he was often in
Fredericksburg at the " Indian Queen " banquets.
Nobody could take such liberties with the great
man. The son of his " Lowland Beauty " stepped
right into the place she had left vacant.

The general one day asked " Light-horse Harry "
if he knew where he could get a good pair of carriage horses.

" I have a fine pair, general — but *you* can't get
them."

" Why not ? "

"Because," said the saucy young soldier, "you will never pay more than half price for anything, and I must have full price for my horses."

Silence — broken at last by the bantering laugh of a pet parrot caged near them. The general took the assault upon his dignity in great good part. "Ah, Lee, you are a funny fellow!" said he; "even the birds laugh at you!"

"But," adds Irving, "hearty laughter was rare with Washington. The sudden explosions we read of were the result of some ludicrous surprise."

Still we do read of this rare laughter — this willing yielding to merriment — on the occasions of his visits to his mother.

All of which goes to prove, first, that Washington did not, as has been charged, neglect to visit her during the four intervening years between the declaration of peace and his own appointment to the Presidency, and, secondly, that these were happy visits, notwithstanding his mother's age and infirmities — happy for her, otherwise, they could not have been happy for him.

It is not the purpose of the compiler of this story of Mary Washington and her times to answer all of the witless charges that thoughtless — we will not say malignant — persons have made regarding Washington's relations with his mother; but one of these stories found its way to the columns of a newspaper, and perhaps we may check its echo, now going on

from lip to lip, to the effect that after he became
President, Washington *denied* to his mother a home
in his temporary residence. He entered that residence late in the spring of 1789. His mother died
in August of that year. She was ill when he
parted from her, and he was prostrated for many
weeks with a malignant carbuncle. He was not
recovered when she died; he could not go to her.
It is not possible that she wished to exchange the
repose of her own home and the ministrations of
her loved physician and only daughter for the stirring life of a noisy metropolis.

And as for her noble son — if the splendor of his
record be more than the eyes of his critics can bear,
they are at liberty to veil it for their own comfort
by the mists of their own imaginings. They will
never persuade the world that the purest and best
man this country ever saw could be capable of
neglecting an aged and infirm woman — and that
woman the mother who bore him, and to whom
he owed all that made him greater than his
fellows.

I should doubt the authenticity of any letter,
tending to lower our estimation of Washington's
character. William Smyth of Cambridge University, England, in his " Lectures on History " (Lec-
ture 34, p. 436), warns us that *one* volume of
" Washington's Letters " is spurious and not to
be respected. I have not seen this assertion of

Smyth's repeated, but he could not have made it without authority.

As to the neglect of his mother during the last five years of his life — a charge that has been made more than once — there can be no foundation whatever. He never realized his dream of rest and leisure. The one ice-bound winter succeeding the declaration of peace was his only moment of repose. He found his own affairs much involved — so much so that Congress wished to aid him in restoring them. But he refused to accept any gift or any compensation for his eight years of service. He complained of the enormous burden of the letters he must answer. He found small time for the arboricultural pursuits in which he was so much interested. Hardly had he planted his balsams, ivies, and ornamental trees of various kinds, when trouble in the country claimed his attention. He writes of his longing for privacy and leisure, and remembers that his time to enjoy them must be short. Still he plants " elms, ash, white-thorn, maples, mulberries, horse-chestnuts, willows and lilacs," and writes that his trees grow fast, as if they knew him to be getting old and must make haste if they wish ever to shelter him !

All this was brought to an end by the very serious discords in the country as to the Constitution adopted by the Confederation of States. The story of these discords is a long one, and has been ably told elsewhere. Washington's feelings were intensely excited by the news that the insurgents of Massachusetts had exhibited such violence that the chief magistrate had called out the militia of the state to support the Constitution. "Good God!" he exclaims, "who besides a Tory or a Briton could have predicted this? It was but the other day we were shedding our blood to obtain the constitutions under which we now live, — constitutions of our own choice and making, — and now we are unsheathing the sword to overturn them. If any man had told me this three years since, I should have thought him a bedlamite, a fit subject for a mad house!"

The troubles ended in a call for another convention of which he was, reluctantly, compelled to accept the place of delegate. To serve intelligently he went into a course of study of the history of ancient and modern confederacies, and has left among his papers an abstract of their merits and defects. He must now learn a new trade! He must become a wise and learned statesman.

One can easily see the impossibility of long and frequent visits to his mother at Fredericksburg. The man was bound, hand and foot. He longed for repose, and at first rebelled against further public duty. "Having had some part in bringing the ship into port," he said, "and having been fairly discharged, it is not my business to embark again upon a sea of troubles."

z

The country ordered otherwise. There was a quarrel in the family, and a serious one, and the "Father of his Country" must help to settle it.

Virginia had done what she could. She was rich and powerful, and the weaker states reckoned themselves at a disadvantage beside her. Virginia was the foremost advocate for equality and union, and was willing to make sacrifices to secure it.

She nobly surrendered to the Federal government a great principality. All the country beyond the Ohio, now forming the states of Ohio, Indiana, and Illinois, belonged to Virginia. Says Esten Cooke: "Her right to it rested upon as firm a basis as the right of any other Commonwealth to its own domain, and if there was any question of the Virginia title by charter, she could assert her right by conquest. The region had been wrested from the British by a Virginian commanding Virginia troops; the people had taken 'The oath of allegiance to the Commonwealth of Virginia,' and her title to the entire territory was indisputable.

"These rights she now relinquished, and her action was the result of an enlarged patriotism and devotion to the cause of Union."

Thus she aided in the settlement of the questions before the great Convention of 1788, of which Washington was made President. All the great men of the country were present at this convention, and the result was that the Constitution of the

United States went into operation, and Washington
was elected President by a unanimous vote.

In the face of these vital matters *no* one — certainly not his brave, good, reasonable mother —
could blame him that the hours of the days were
all too short for the great work he had to do.

CHAPTER XII

ONCE more, and once only, do we hear of Mary Washington in connection with her son. We read that her home filled her time and heart; that she, like her son, sowed and planted, arranging her garden as the seasons succeeded each other, delighting in her personal work therein. Who can measure the charm, to a woman, of even a small garden! How often has she not " heard the voice of the Lord walking in the garden in the cool of the day!" She was born in a garden. Her first perception of beauty was awakened by her flowers. With these for companionship, who can be utterly wretched? Not all unhappy was the prisoner, after his " Picciola" had cleft the stone masonry of his dungeon!

We love to think of Mary Washington in the old garden! Nowhere so sweetly, so gently, can a wearied body fulfil its day, until God wills the release of the soul.

On the 14th of April, 1789, Washington received at Mount Vernon official intelligence that he had been chosen President of the United States. He at once prepared to go to New York and enter upon the duties of his office, but before doing so he set out on the evening of the same day, mounted on his horse and attended by his favorite body-servant, Billy Lee, to visit his mother in Fredericksburg. He found her feeble in body but bright-minded and cheerful, and he informed her that he had been elected President, and had come to bid her an affectionate farewell before assuming his office. "So soon," he said, "as the public business which must necessarily be encountered in arranging a new government can be disposed of, I shall hasten to Virginia" — but here she interrupted him and said: "You will see me no more.   Age and disease warn me that I shall not be long in this world.   I trust in God I am somewhat prepared for a better.   But go; fulfil the high destinies which Heaven appears to assign you; go, and may Heaven's and your mother's blessing be with you always."   This was the last meeting between the mother and the son.

But that her heart followed him through the marvellous events of the next few weeks none can doubt.   They helped her to ignore the shadow hanging over her.   She was cheerful, strong, and uncomplaining.

She decided to make two visits, — one to the family of Charles and the other to the widow and orphan children of Samuel Washington.   The families met together to talk gratefully and affectionately of the illustrious one whom the country was loading with honors. He had left Mount Vernon on the 16th of April. An entry in his diary records his feelings. "I bade adieu to Mount Vernon and domestic felicity and with a mind oppressed with more anxious and painful sensations than I can express, set out for New York with the best disposition to render service to my country in obedience to its call, but with less hope of answering its expectations."

To his friend, General Knox, he wrote : " Integrity and firmness are all I can promise. These, be my voyage long or short, shall never forsake me, although I may be deserted by all men ; for of the consolations which are to be derived from these under any circumstances, the world cannot deprive me."

This was the spirit in which he met the extraordinary honors which awaited him. " His progress to the seat of government was a continual ovation. The ringing of bells and roaring of cannonry proclaimed his course through the country. The old and young, women and children, thronged the highways to welcome him." Governors met him at the frontiers of their respective states. Cavalry assembled to escort him. The throngs gathered as he advanced until a mighty host followed him. Arches of flowers and evergreens, and triumphal arches of laurel, spanned the paths he travelled. When he reached the banks of the Delaware he

must have recalled that midnight passage over the
ice-bound river at Christmas, — a representation of
which hangs in almost every humble hostelry in
the country.   How different his feelings then and
now!   Over the stream which flows through
Trenton a bridge was decked with laurel, with the

Washington's Reception at Trenton.

inscription, "The Defenders of the Mothers will be
the Protectors of the Daughters."   The matrons
were there; and the young girls, crowned with garlands, strewed his way with flowers, singing of their
love and gratitude.   No king on his way to coronation ever received such a heartfelt ovation!

And so — on and on — until at Elizabeth Point

he entered the barge with white satin canopy, which was to bring him to New York. Parties of ladies and gentlemen followed the barge singing pæans of welcome. In his diary that night he records, "The display of boats, the songs, the instrumental music, the decorations of the ships, the roar of cannon, the loud acclamations filled my mind with sensations as painful (considering the reverse of this scene which may be the case after all my labors to do good) as they are pleasing."

For, after all, he was a sad man. He had surrendered his soldier's dream of home and peace. He had parted with his aged mother, and knew that he could not minister to her in her last few months of life. He was too great a man to permit such things as these — applause, laurel, songs, salvos of artillery — to fill his heart or even his imagination with pleasure.

She heard it all! Doubtless her mental commentary was her old refrain: "This is too much praise! George has only done his duty."

The world still shares — still marvels at — the worship of Washington then and now. As Lecky says, "He entered the scene as only a conspicuous member of the planter aristocracy, his mind not quick or original, no brilliancy of wit, entirely without the gift of eloquence, with few accomplishments, no language except his own, nothing to dazzle or overpower." Moreover, he had not a university training at home or abroad, and no foreign travel to enlarge his vision. His was the splendid triumph of *character* — character inherited and fostered in the formative years of his life by a faithful mother. No one can read the just eulogy of the accomplished nineteenth-century English writer, without perceiving the close resemblance — in temperament and character — between the two.

"Those who knew him noticed that he had keen sensibilities and strong passions; but his power of self-command never failed him, and no act of his life can be traced to personal caprice, ambition or resentment. In the despondency of long-continued failure, in the elation of sudden success, at times when the soldiers were deserting by hundreds and malignant plots were formed against his reputation, amid the constant quarrels, rivalries and jealousies of his subordinates, in the dark hour of national ingratitude and in the midst of the most intoxicating flattery, he was always the same calm, wise, just and single-minded man, pursuing the cause which he believed to be right without fear or favour or fanaticism."

In short, he triumphed over all through the strength of a character, firm as a rock, which no storm could shake or dislodge. The English writer himself marvels at the unchallenged worship of the world, and he thus explains it. "He was in the highest sense a gentleman and a man of honour.

It was always known by his friends, and it was soon acknowledged by the nation and by the English themselves, that in Washington, America had found a leader who could be induced by no earthly motive to tell a falsehood or to break an engagement or to commit a dishonourable act."

Whatever may be the deep, underlying cause of the idolatry of the American people, it certainly inspires all classes of men. He is the star to which all eyes gratefully turn — the wise and un-lettered, rich and poor. Other heroes are, and deserve to be, admitted into their hearts: but they jealously hold for him the chiefest, holiest place.

"See here, do you expect to get to heaven?" was asked of a peculiarly profane lad — a "hard case" — who indignantly answered: "Course I do! Don't you suppose I want to see General Washington?"

CHAPTER XIII

MARY WASHINGTON made her will only a year before her death, stating therein that she was "in good health." This was one of the years, during which it has been asserted that she was not only neglected by her son but that they were estranged because of her Tory principles! Besides a few small bequests to her daughter and grandchildren, "desiring their acceptance thereof as all the token I now have to give them," she leaves *all* her estate "to my Son General George Washington," also — that crowning pride of the early Englishwoman — her best bed, bedstead, curtains, quilt, and other bed furniture. Long after the Englishwoman had lived in Virginia she held her bed in the highest esteem, and always made special mention of it in her will. She came from the land where, from ancient days, the bed was the most important feature in the whole house — made of feathers and adorned with tapestry or with velvets or with "cloth of gold, or miniver." In the "pane" (the forerunner of our "counterpane" — from *contre-pointe* — adorned with

" drawn thread lattice work ") the ambition of the housewife centred, and was indulged. When Lafayette desired to make a handsome present to Dr. Galt of Williamsburg, who had entertained him, he sent from France a set of velvet bed curtains, dark blue with ornate figuring of gold, quite the handsomest of the textile fabrics exhibited at our Centennial in New York City.

Mary Washington bequeathed the articles in which she had most pride to her "Son General George Washington." She was then, May, 1788, " in good health." It appears, from an old letter, she once fell at her door-step and hurt her arm. Perhaps then she also wounded her breast, in which a cancerous growth appeared not long before her death. In those days the medical and surgical sciences were all wrong, if we may believe them to be now all right. A New York writer had said that more lives had been destroyed in that city by physicians than by all other causes whatever.

Virginians at the school of medicine in Edinburgh had organized themselves, a few years before, into a Virginia Society " for the protection of the profession against quacks and imposters who had degraded the profession by mingling with it the trade of an apothecary or surgeon ! " An eloquent petition is preserved addressed " To the Honourable the Council of Virginia and House of Burgesses," entreating that " laws be passed forbidding the intrusion of pretenders into the domain of the authorized practitioner, thereby dishonouring the profession itself and destroying mankind." We can imagine the enormities committed by the quacks and imposters when we observe the methods of the legitimate practitioner. When a man or woman sickened, the doctors sped the parting guest, — taking from him his very life-blood, by cupping, leeching, bleeding, and reducing his strength by blistering and drenching. Nature was sometimes strong enough to give battle to doctor and disease, and even to win a victory over their combined forces. But in old age Nature prudently retired without a struggle. We hope much for Mary Washington from the gentle ministration of Betty Lewis and the indulgent kindness of good Dr. Charles Mortimer, also Betty Lewis's own testimony, one month before the end, of her patience and resignation. The last word from her lips reveals no earthly wish save the desire to hear from her son's " own hand that he is well." August 25, 1789, she was released from sufferings which had been borne with unfaltering faith and fortitude; and on the 27th of that month she was laid to rest in the spot she had herself chosen as her last resting-place, and over which her monument, erected by the women of America, now stands.

The President did not learn of her death — in

that day of post-riders — until the 1st of September. It was announced to him by his kinsman Colonel Burgess Ball.

On September 13, he wrote to his sister, Mrs. Betty Lewis, as follows : —

" My Dear Sister : Colonel Ball's letter gave me the first account of my Mother's death. Since that I have received Mrs. Carter's [1] letter, written at your request, and previous to both.   I was prepared for the event by advices of her illness coming to your son Robert.

" Awful and affecting as the death of a parent is, there is consolation in knowing that Heaven has spared ours to an age beyond which few attain, and favored her with the full enjoyment of her mental faculties and as much bodily strength as usually falls to the lot of four score.

" When I was last in Fredericksburg I took a final leave of her, never expecting to see her more. . . .

" Your affectionate brother,
" George Washington."

Ten years later he records the death of all of his mother's children.   September 22, 1799, he writes to Colonel Burgess Ball : —

" Dear Sir : Your letter of the 16th inst. has been received informing me of the death of my brother (Charles).

" The death of near relations always produces awful and affecting emotions under whatsoever circumstances it may happen.   That of my brother has been long expected : and his latter days so uncomfortable to himself must have pre-

---

[1] Mrs. Charles Carter, his niece, Betty Lewis's daughter.

pared all around him for the stroke though (*sic*) painful in the effect.

"I was the first, and am, now, the last of my father's children, by the second marriage, who remain.

"When I shall be called upon to follow them is known only to the Giver of Life. When the summons comes I shall endeavor to obey it with a good grace.

"With great esteem and regard I am, Dear Sir, your affectionate serv't,

"Go. Washington."

Less than three months afterwards the summons came. Nothing in his life became him like the leaving it. The generation had passed away! The stars of the western firmament had set. In the same year died Patrick Henry and George Washington!

Mary Washington left a noble band of grandsons who worthily served their country. Bushrod Washington (son of John Augustine Washington), was soon to become justice of the Supreme Court of the United States. When President Washington went to Fort Pitt to visit the troops sent to suppress the Whiskey Insurrection, it is related that as he passed, uncovered, down the line, every man poured forth the homage of his heart in words of devotion and loyalty, and that an escort of cavalry was detailed to conduct him on his homeward way. Dismissing this, after travelling a short distance, he thus addressed the officer in charge, the eldest son of his only sister, Betty Lewis: "George, you are the eldest of five nephews that I have in this army! Let your conduct be an example to them, and do not turn your back until you are ordered."

The five nephews were Major George Lewis, commandant of the cavalry; Major Lawrence Lewis, aide-de-camp to Major General Morgan; Howell Lewis, in Captain Mercer's troop; Samuel Washington, son of Colonel Charles Washington, and Lawrence Washington, son of Colonel Samuel Washington — the two latter light-horsemen in the troop commanded by Captain Lewis, the *first* troop of cavalry to cross the mountains on this expedition. Standing in the field under the new banner of their new government, were six of Mary Washington's descendants. The spirit of the stout-hearted grandmother lived in these men, and inspired them in their prompt response to the call of their country for support of law and order.

CHAPTER XIV

TRIBUTES OF HER COUNTRYMEN

MARY WASHINGTON was laid by reverent hands in the spot chosen by herself near "Kenmore." Tradition declares that General Washington proposed erecting a monument over her ashes, but was restrained by the assurance that the country claimed that privilege.

If this promise was made, it was never redeemed. The American nation, in its reasonable gratitude, dedicated in almost every hamlet some memorial to its great commander. For her it did nothing. No stone or tablet for years marked her resting-place.

Tradition loves to repeat the myth that Congress, which was in session at the time of her death, wore the usual badge of mourning for thirty days, and passed resolutions of respect to her memory and sympathy with the President. No such action was taken by Congress. There is no official record of the fact. Nor does Robert Maclay, who transcribed in his journal every incident of his senatorial life, make any mention whatever of Mary Washington.

We delighted to call her son "a king among men, godlike in his virtues." We knew that he served us for eight years in peril of life and fortune, unsustained by encouragement or the hope of success, leading a forlorn hope against a powerful enemy. We knew that his, more than any score of names, had given us the place we held among the nations of the earth. We knew that he himself said, " All that I am, I owe to my mother."

And yet the country seemed content with toasting his name at its banquets, and left his mother's grave to be marked only by mouldering stones and noisome weeds! The graves of her family were all preserved from decay. Her distinguished son lay, as it was fitting he should lie, in a marble sarcophagus at Mount Vernon. She had chosen for her final pillow, the spot where God had answered her prayers in the gift of wonderful serenity of soul, and in a short while God alone would have known where to find that spot. Brambles and weeds covered it, hiding, for very shame, the witness of man's ingratitude and neglect. Twice, bills were presented to the Congress of the United States, asking for an appropriation for a monument over Mary Washington's grave. By various misfortunes the bills were lost. In 1830 the women of Fredericksburg banded themselves together to rear this monument, and were zealously engaged to that end when they received the following letter from a patriotic man of wealth in New York City: —

"New York, April 11, 1831.

"To the Honorable Thomas Goodwin, *Mayor of the Town of Fredericksburg, Va.*

"Sir : — I have seen with the greatest interest the efforts making by the citizens of Fredericksburg to erect a monument over the remains and to rescue from oblivion the sacred spot where reposes the great American mother, Mary, the mother of Washington. I feel a great interest that the ashes of this good American mother shall remain where they are, and I wish to be allowed the honor of individually erecting the monument, which I assure you, sir, shall be, in style and execution, to please the family of Washington and the citizens of the United States.

"Be pleased, sir, to make this communication known to the Washington family and all interested, and believe me truly,

"Your most ob't s'vt,

"Silas E. Burrows."

The offer was gladly accepted. Work on the monument was at once commenced. The handsome marbles were finished, and the corner-stone laid in the presence of Andrew Jackson, then President of the United States. On this occasion President Jackson said : " Mary Washington acquired and maintained a wonderful ascendency over those around her. This true characteristic of genius attended her through life, and she conferred upon her son that power of self-command which was one of the remarkable traits of her character.

" She conducted herself through this life with

virtue and prudence worthy of the mother of the greatest hero that ever adorned the annals of history. There is no fame in the world more pure than that of the mother of Washington, and no woman, since the mother of Christ, has left a better claim to the affectionate reverence of mankind."

This monument was completed but never erected. The stone-mason and the contractor died before the shaft was placed on the foundation, and, soon after, Mr. Burrows died also. The work ceased, and the unfinished structure stood as the contractor left it, until torn down for the present finished monument. The non-completion of the old monument, therefore, seems to have been providential, and no fault of the projector or contractor. During the Civil War between the North and the South, the guns of the contending armies were fired across the stones, and they became a prey to the vandalism of strangers.

In 1857 Captain George Washington Ball (grandson of the patriot, Colonel Burgess Ball, and his wife — Frances Washington) circulated an appeal throughout the country, asking for donations to complete the monument. For eleven years Captain Ball worked zealously and faithfully. He desired to erect near the monument a noble charity, — an institution of learning for young women, — but it seemed ordained that he should be not immediately successful, and in time he became discouraged. It was a heart-breaking disappointment to "this old man eloquent," — the author of the monograph so freely quoted on these pages.

Finally the women of America reared a shaft over the desecrated spot, and by a hereditary office, held by six hundred of their number, provided a perpetual Guard of Honor over the grave of Mary,

Mary Washington's Monument.

the mother of Washington. The corner-stone of this last monument was laid Oct. 20, 1893. The monument — the first ever reared by women in honor of a woman — is a classic shaft of granite. It was dedicated by President Cleveland on May 10, 1894, in the presence of a large concourse of people.

Fredericksburg made the occasion one of rejoicing and festivity. The day was a glorious one. The sun never looked down upon a brighter scene, — garlands and festoons of flowers, "ripples of ribbons in the air," officers in uniform, maidens in white, music, and song! There was a grand masonic banquet, and a ball.

The procession was headed by a number of beautiful young women habited in black with black hats and sable plumes, handsomely mounted on horseback. The Chief Justice of the United States, the Justices of the Supreme Court, and members of the Cabinet, preceded the companies of infantry, cavalry, and artillery, and again, beside the grave of this modest woman, were repeated words of honor and applause, than which no words in any language could be nobler or better deserved.

These words — from the citizens of her own town, from the senator of her state, from the President of the United States — were for her: not alone as the mother of the adored Washington, but for the true woman "of clear, prompt and decided mind," the woman of courage and integrity, the "Christian woman, devout and worshipful," to whom the "greatest hero that ever adorned the annals of history" ascribed all that had made him great and good.

And very noble was the tribute of Virginia's honored son at the ceremonies attendant upon the

unveiling of the monument reared in her honor
by the women of America. Said Senator Daniel:
"She nursed a hero at her breast. At her knee
she trained to the love and fear of God and to
the kingly virtues, honor, truth and valor, the lion
of the tribe that gave to America liberty and independence. This her title to renown. It is enough.
Eternal dignity and heavenly grace dwell upon the
brow of this blessed mother; nor burnished gold,
nor sculptured stone, nor rhythmic praise could add
one jot or tittle to her chaste glory. Tributes to
the lofty genius, which is the rare gift of nature,
and to the brilliant deeds, which are the rare fruits
of fitting opportunity, fulfil a noble function; but
they often excite extravagant emulations that can
never be satisfied, and individualize models which
few by possibility may copy. This tribute is not to
them. It is to one who possessed only the homely
virtues of her sex; but what is there in human life
that can be more admirable or bring it in closer
proximity to the divine? She was simply a private
citizen. No sovereign's crown rested on her brow.
She did not lead an army, like Joan of Arc, nor
slay a tyrant, like Charlotte Corday. She was not
versed in letters or in arts. She was not an Angel
of Mercy, like Florence Nightingale, nor the con-
sort of a hero, like the wife of Napoleon. She did
not shine amidst the throngs which bow to the
charms of wit, beauty and hospitality; but in any

assembly of the beautiful, the brilliant, the powerful, or the brave of her sex, no form could awaken
a holier sentiment of reverence than she, and that
sentiment is all the deeper because she was the
unassuming wife and mother whose kingdom was
her family, whose world was her home. In the
shadow and in the silence from day to day and
year to year she followed the guiding star of that
truth which tells us that ' to do that which before
us lies in daily life is the prime wisdom.' She was
the good angel of the hearthstone — the special
providence of tender hearts and helpless hands,
content to bear her burdens in the sequestered
vale of life, her thoughts unperverted by false
ambitions, and all unlooking for the great reward
that crowned her love and toil.

" But for the light that streamed from the deeds
of him she bore, we would doubtless have never
heard the name of Mary Washington, and the grass
that grew upon this grave had not been disturbed
by curious footsteps or reverential hands. But it
does not follow that she shines only in the reflection
of her offspring's fame. Her virtues were not created;
they were only discovered by the marvellous career
of her illustrious son. This memorial might indeed
be due to her because of who she was, but it is far
more due to her because of what she was. It is in
her own right, and as the type of her sex, her people
and her race, that she deserves this tribute stone.

" There were ten thousand Mary Washingtons among the mothers of the Revolution, and honoring her we honor the motherhood of heroic days and heroic men. It was in his character, all sufficient in every emergency, that was displayed the overtowering greatness of George Washington, and it is not doubted that this character was toned and shaped by his mother's hand. The principles which he applied to a nation were those simple and elementary truths which she first imprinted upon his mind in the discipline of home.

"Mary Washington was the ' light of the dwelling ' in a plain, rural, colonial home. Her history hovers around it. There she was wife, mother, and widow.

" Home is the pure original fountain from which all patriotism must flow, and the stream can never rise above its source. As the woman is, the man is; as the man and woman are, the home is ; and as the home, so the country. Show me refined, enlightened, virtuous, and industrious homes, and I will show you a good government and a great nation. The nation is the aggregate, the homes are the units; man is the builder, woman is the inspiration. Discuss constitutions, administrations, and policies as we may, the outcome must depend upon the subsoil they spring from. Make the home all right, and the rest must follow. This is woman's mission. Our race, the youngest that has framed a language, moulded a constitution, and made a name, has recognized that mission and held it sacred. Other races roam the earth for pelf and adventure, and condescend to inferior connections. Our race roams the earth only to find the spot on which to build its homes. Indeed it never quits home. It carries home with it. Wife and child, the domestic animals and plants, the household goods go where it goes, over the stormy billows, into the wilderness, and even to the verge of battle. It is a beautiful legend of the Rappahannock that when Spotswood and his companions came sailing hither the air was made vocal by the English swallows that they brought with them. The stars might change, but they would make the skies still resonant with the songs of the olden homes."

And as the ages pass may there be always some to make the skies vocal with the songs of the olden times of the Virginia she loved.

But the "olden homes," alas, are passing away. Their solid masonry long resists the tooth of Time, but the all-destroyer, Fire, levels them at last. The walls fall, the stones are removed, — let us hope for the building of other homes, — finally the drifting earth fills the foundations, and daisies that "look up to God" alone remain to keep vigil.

Pious hands preserve the old historic churches. Old Christ Church in Lancaster, where Mrs. Ball

(the " Widow Johnson ") stood with little Mary's
sponsors in baptism, still exists ; so does Yeocomico
church in Westmoreland, where sweet Mary Ball
prayed to the God who never forsook her; so does
St. George's Church in Fredericksburg, built on the
site of " Old St. George's," where, " devout and

The Avenue of Poplars at Nomini Hall.

worshipful," her venerable form was never a moment too late.

Her last residence in Fredericksburg is tended
by the gentle hands of a society of Virginia women.
The garden she loved is kept " passing sweet with
flowers." Mount Vernon is also thus kept by the
women of the whole country. The ancient home
of " Epping Forest " fell into ruin long, long ago. A

cluster of old trees marks the spot where the mother of Washington was born. Some of the " olden homes " named in these pages are still standing, — " Gunston Hall," the residence of George Mason ; " Stratford," the home of the Lees in Westmoreland ; " Bushfield," the home of Jenny Washington of the dancing-class ; " Mount Airy," where lived the pretty Tayloe girls. These are in good repair, and there are many others whose thresholds were often crossed by Mary Washington in her girlhood, wifehood, and widowhood.

Of " Nomini Hall," where our New Jersey tutor taught and admired the ladies, no trace remains ; except the avenue of poplars which still live and sleep all winter, and in leafing-time nod and whisper to each other of those they once sheltered who are sleeping on forever !

THE WILL OF MARY WASHINGTON, AS REGISTERED IN THE CLERK'S OFFICE AT FREDERICKSBURG, VIRGINIA

" In the name of God! Amen! I, Mary Washington, of Fredericksburg in the County of Spotsylvania, being in good health, but calling to mind the uncertainty of this life, and willing to dispose of what remains of my worldly estate, do make and publish this, my last will, recommending my soul into the hands of my Creator, hoping for a remission of all my sins through the merits and mediation of Jesus Christ, the Saviour of mankind; I dispose of my worldly estate as follows:

" *Imprimis.* I give to my son General George Washington, all my land in Accokeek Run, in the County of Stafford, and also my negro boy George, to him and his heirs forever. Also my best bed, bedstead, and Virginia cloth curtains (the same that stands in my best bedroom), my quilted blue and white quilt and my best dressing-glass.

" *Item.* I give and devise to my son, Charles Washington, my negro man Tom, to him and his assigns forever.

" *Item.* I give and devise to my daughter Bettie Lewis, my phaeton and my bay horse.

" *Item.* I give and devise to my daughter-in-law Hannah Washington, my purple cloth cloak lined with shag.

" *Item.* I give and devise to my grandson, Corbin Washington, my negro wench, old Bet, my riding chair, and two black horses, to him and his assigns forever.

" *Item.* I give and devise to my grandson, Fielding Lewis, my negro man Frederick, to him and his assigns forever, also eight silver tablespoons, half of my crockery-ware, and the blue and white tea china, with book case, oval table, one bedstead, one pair sheets, one pair blankets and white cotton counterpain, two table cloths, six red leather chairs, half my peuter and one half of my kitchen furniture.

" *Item.* I give and devise to my grandson, Lawrence Lewis, my negro wench Lydia, to him and his assigns forever.

" *Item.* I give and devise to my granddaughter, Bettie Curtis, my negro woman, little Bet, and her future increase, to her and her assigns forever. Also my largest looking-glass, my walnut writing desk and drawers, a square dining-table, one bed, bedstead, bolster, one pillow, one blanket and pair sheets, white Virginia cloth counterpains and purple curtains, my red and white tea china, teaspoons, and the other half of my peuter and crockeryware, and the remainder of my iron kitchen furniture.

" *Item.* I give and devise to my grandson, George Washington, my next best glass, one bed, bedstead, bolster, one pillow, one pair sheets, one blanket and counterpain.

" *Item.* I devise all my wearing apparel to be equally divided between my granddaughters, Bettie Curtis, Fannie Ball, and Milly Washington, — but should my daughter, Bettie Lewis, fancy any one two or three articles, she is to have them before a division thereof.

" Lastly, I nominate and appoint my said son, General George Washington, executor of this, my will, and as I owe few or no debts, I direct my executor to give no security or appraise my estate, but desire the same may be allotted to my devisees, with as little trouble and delay as may be, desiring their acceptance thereof as all the token I now have to give them of my love for them.

" In witness thereof, I have hereunto set my hand and seal the 20th day of May, 1788.

" MARY WASHINGTON.

" Witness, JOHN FERNEYHOUGH.

" Signed, sealed and published in the presence of the said Mary Washington and at her desire.

" JNO. MERCER.
" JOSEPH WALKER."

2118164